"Otis Sanford and Dan Conaway? Together in the same book? This may be my favorite Memphis combination since Larry Finch and Ronnie Robinson, since grit met up with grind. Nobody writes about Memphis with more insight and verve than Conaway. Unless it's Sanford. I've been delighting in their columns for years. And now we get both in a single book? That's like combining BBQ and pizza. Great separately. But together? Memphis at its best."

– Geoff Calkins
Columnist, The Daily Memphian

"Memphis is a sweet and soulful place of great beauty and generosity. It also can be a harsh and unforgiving place of great struggle and sorrow. Otis Sanford and Dan Conaway explore those contradictions from different angles with clarity, conviction, and (they are Memphians) distinct personalities."

– David Waters
Distinguished Journalist in Residence and Assistant Director of The Institute for Public Service Reporting at the University of Memphis

"Otis Sanford and Dan Conaway are both great writers. But more than that, they are great storytellers. They tell compelling stories about our Memphis community and the human condition. One writer is focused more on social justice and race, the other on the community and environment that molds us. This will be a fascinating read."

– Terri Freeman
President, National Civil Rights Museum

D1396579

Foreword

When we were launching The Daily Memphian back in fall of 2018, Otis Sanford was one of those voices of calm that helped soothe my anxiety during some of the truly tough moments before and after launch. We made mistakes – and when you do that on a news site, you make those mistakes very publicly.

But Otis would always offer up the kind of low-key, calming advice that resonated with insight and reassurance, coming as it did from his decades of experience in newspapers.

Dan Conaway, on the other hand, just yelled at me.

Dan would yell at me on the phone, by text, in emails and, of course, in person.

"You're doing what??" he would say, incredulous at some sort of idea I mentioned. "Oh, come on, Eric. What are you thinking??"

To be fair, Dan was usually right. Dan not only has a devotion to journalism – and a long family history in newspapers – but his love for this city and his understanding of marketing and branding meant that he could, instantly, see to the heart of what we wanted The Daily Memphian to be.

That love for this city is just as essential, it seems to me, to Otis' work. Even in his columns that are critical of some or another thing that is happening in Memphis, there's never any cynicism. There's skepticism sometimes. Which is healthy. And there's criticism. Which is healthy too.

Criticism and skepticism are, I believe, essential to good journalism.

Dan, as well, is a writer who stays clear of cynicism. And his love for Memphis – for being a Memphian – is always central to what he writes, even when what he writes makes us question the decisions we've sometimes made.

That balance – the notion that we can love this city where we live while still wanting and needing it to improve and change – has always been

In a
colorful place

Seasoned opinion
about Memphis, about home, about life.

A collection of columns by
Dan Conaway and Otis Sanford

ROOSTER
SCRATCH
PRESS

essential to The Daily Memphian. Too often these days, skepticism is used interchangeably with cynicism. The same with criticism, which is so often replaced with ridicule and disdain.

Criticism, at its best, can be hard and even painful to hear. But criticism, at its best, should make you think about who you are and what you've done. And what you'll do. It should make you consider your decisions. It should make you challenge your assumptions and beliefs.

Ridicule and disdain that merely parade as criticism, however, have increasingly become the currency of expression on cable news and, especially, on social media.

But both Otis and Dan know the difference. They can simultaneously celebrate and criticize Memphis. They don't tear this place down. Nor do they turn a blind eye to its – our – failings.

And those interrelated themes – the love of Memphis, the desire to show the city with all its flaws and complications, the necessity of expressing criticism and skepticism (versus disdain and cynicism), and the need to have a news source that is serious, thoughtful and always genuinely of Memphis – were driving forces behind the formation and launch of The Daily Memphian.

To have Otis and Dan included in The Daily Memphian was, from the beginning, incredibly important. I'm honored that both agreed to take the leap and become part of this family.

And I'm grateful that I can call both of these people my friends.

Even though Dan, still, continues to yell at me.

– Eric Barnes
CEO, The Daily Memphian

Otis Sanford at left and Dan Conaway on the right.

Authors

Dan Conaway, a lifelong Memphian, is a communications
strategist, writer, columnist for The Daily Memphian, author of "I'm a
Memphian" and "The Plural of One," and ghost writer of several other
books. He is also, by his own estimation, the writer of "about a gazillion
ads, brochures, TV spots, videos, websites, and the occasional matchbook
cover" as a copywriter, creative director, and owner of two ad agencies.

His experience includes a stint as Ronald McDonald, brand wrangling
of ducks in The Peabody, pandas in the Memphis Zoo, and Grizzlies in the
NBA. Along the way, he's been recognized as the outstanding advertising
alumnus of his university, for lifetime achievement by his peers, for leadership
in his national church, the Boy Scouts, and the Boys & Girls Clubs, and
with more than 400 awards for creativity.

Otis Sanford, a native Mississippian, holds the Hardin
Chair of Excellence in Journalism and Strategic Media at the University
of Memphis, and is the author of "From Boss Crump to King Willie: How
Race Changed Memphis Politics." Sanford also serves as political analyst
and commentator for WATN-TV Local 24 News, writes a weekly political
column for The Daily Memphian online news site and serves as political
analyst for WKNO-FM, the National Public Radio affiliate in Memphis.

Before joining the U of M in 2011, Sanford was editorial page editor and
Viewpoint columnist for The Commercial Appeal, and formerly served as
the paper's managing editor. He has also worked at newspapers in Jackson,
Mississippi, Pittsburgh and Detroit. And he is a 2014 inductee into the
Tennessee Journalism Hall of Fame.

Dan Conaway | Introduction

For the first 40 or so years of my career – God, I'm tired – I wrote in somebody else's voice. I spoke for clients.

The first of those voices was a sausage maker in Knoxville, Tennessee. Their approach on radio had become stale, or more appropriately for sausage, past its sell date. They conducted a contest for new scripts, threw out a few product points they wanted to make, and offered fifty bucks to the winner.

I was a junior in college on my fourth major – journalism – preceded by architecture, art and English. College football fandom, all-night bridge games, keg tapping, and chili cheese dogs were minors. While obviously taking advantage of the concept of university and attending classes in virtually every building on the property, I just as obviously lacked purpose.

And fifty bucks was a fortune in 1969, so, what the hell, I took a shot at sausage.

I won. In fact, they took a couple of my scripts and I got to voice a couple of parts. And I got paid for this.

I had a blast. And I had my final major – advertising – and a lasting career. I was and have been ever since an advertising copywriter, what my two older writer brothers would call an illegitimate writer.

And I've been having a blast ever since.

Reducing complicated products and services to the simplest expressions of what they did and what they meant to people. Exploring human nature, figuring out human motivation, getting inside heads and making them release money. Inspiring action. Causing change. Working with wonderfully creative, gifted people. Competing with people like that.

While I've owned advertising agencies, and owned all the headaches and heartaches ownership brings, the times I sat first in front of a typewriter and later a screen and got it exactly right were worth the hundreds of times, probably thousands of times, I didn't get it right.

Those are the moments I write for, then and now.

More than a decade ago, I started writing in my voice.

When you work for lots of people, representing their interests, and lots of people work for you, and you are responsible for them, your voice can threaten all of that. Now, it's just me and the dogs, and they love everything I write.

Recently, a reader referred to me as "leftist trash." And he wasn't through. After two or three other readers made comments, he was back, this time calling me an "idiot."

Tell me I can't move people.

My columns offer no product features or benefits. They are drawn from the rich and raw natural ingredients of this city, the stuff of a lifetime here and the perspective it brings. They are comprised entirely of the truth as I see it. That's the promise I make to my readers now, and all I ask is that they read and think.

And I'm still having a blast. Come on, I started with sausage and now I'm doing a book with Otis Sanford.

Thanks for reading. Decide for yourself if we got it right

– Dan Conaway

Otis Sanford | # Introduction

Richard Price Darby was a career educator and, most people would say, a good one. He counseled thousands of high school and college students as a teacher and principal in Sardis, Mississippi, and then as a guidance counselor and dean at Northwest Mississippi Community College 12 miles north in Senatobia. He grew up in a world of Southern white privilege, and entered the education field at the height of white defiance to racial integration of public schools in Mississippi. But Mr. Darby – as everyone called him – was a fair and considerate guy. And yet, he nearly torpedoed my journalism career before it really got started.

Mr. Darby was director of guidance when I enrolled at what was then Northwest Junior College in 1971. I was pretty sure what I wanted to study as an entering freshman. But I was told I needed some academic counseling, and Mr. Darby was the man to see. When I told him I intended to major in journalism, he was polite, but dubious. He didn't say it outright, but instantly I sensed what he was thinking. A Black farm boy from tiny Como would never succeed in journalism. It was out of the question.

He scanned my high school records, occasionally nodding at my good grades. I had just graduated from North Panola High School, where he served as principal before integration came. His daughter, Rita Nell, was in my graduating class. Surely that would earn me a little credibility. But I had spent all but my senior year at the all-Black North Panola Vocational High School in Como. That school, Darby must have concluded, was too inferior academically to produce someone angling to be a newspaper reporter.

"I think you're going to have trouble," he told me. "I think you'd be better off with some sort of vocational training." In other words, I needed to focus on a career working with my hands – just not with a pen, a notepad and a typewriter.

"Well, my mother did once say she thought I should get into Industrial Arts," I said respectfully. "That's it," he quickly responded, seeming relieved that he had talked me out of such a lofty career pursuit without insulting me or hurting my feelings. I thanked him and quietly left his office. Later that day, I turned in my official enrollment papers. Where it said major, I wrote in large block letters, "JOURNALISM."

I thought about my counseling session all of five minutes before saying to myself, "I'll show him." I had been in love with newspapers since I was 6 years old. That was the age when my father, Freddie Sanford, gave me my first ever news assignment. He told me to read The Commercial Appeal – which was delivered by mail to our farm six days a week – and tell him what was in it. My dad was a busy carpenter and farmer, plus he was active in church, civic and community affairs around Como. He didn't have time to read the paper thoroughly, particularly the sports section, so he gave the job to me. And I accepted it eagerly.

I ended up telling him far more than he wanted to know about his two favorite baseball teams, the St. Louis Cardinals and Brooklyn-turned-Los Angeles Dodgers. In doing so, I grew to love sports, particularly baseball and basketball. But more than that, I became an avid newspaper reader of not just sports, but the comics obviously, the Mississippi news section, the television and entertainment sections and even the editorials and letters to the editor.

So I decided at about age 10 that I wanted to be a newspaper reporter (I didn't even know what the word journalism meant.) I wrote my first article when I was 12 and in the 7th grade. I wasn't good enough to earn a spot on the 7th-grade "peewee" basketball team, so I decided one day to write a story about one of the team's home games. I submitted it to the high school newspaper and, to my amazement, they published it. After that, I was hooked. And once I entered high school, I enrolled in the journalism class – yes, my all-Black, inferior school had a journalism class – and I eventually became editor of the Eagle Echo.

My senior year in 1970 was also the first year of full forced integration of public schools in Mississippi, 16 years after the U.S. Supreme Court's decision in *Brown v. Board of Education* declared "separate but equal" schools unconstitutional. It also was my first significant experience in any racially integrated setting. I was named co-editor of the Red Raider school paper along with Shelley Stevens, who is white. Shelley and I worked great together, and we remain Facebook friends to this day. But in many ways, it was a difficult, tension-filled year. I just wanted to write for the paper, play basketball, earn college-worthy grades, graduate and move on. My interest in journalism never waned. And I was not about to let Mr. Darby, good intentions and all, steal my dream.

Northwest had a troubled racial history of its own. My older brother Louis, who enrolled there in 1966, still remembers with indignation the racism he experienced on the campus. But the staff of the Ranger Rocket weekly newspaper warmly welcomed me and a fellow high school classmate, John Whiting. I covered the school's football team, wrote entertainment stories and accepted any other assignment I could. It wasn't easy. I had to rewrite many stories to make them clearer and more complete, but I never complained. And I certainly never quit. The Ranger Rocket was consistently the top awarded paper in the state among junior colleges. And it was because we were a dedicated staff and had a fabulous, fun-loving faculty adviser in Robert Edward Oakley, who mentored and taught us well.

From there, it was on to the University of Mississippi in the fall of 1973, with a journalism scholarship to boot that required me to join the staff of the Daily Mississippian student paper. My biggest story was covering an appearance on campus by Tennessee Sen. Howard Baker, who at the time was playing a key role on the Senate Watergate Committee. His campus speech came just a few months after Baker uttered one of the most famous questions ever in politics: "What did the president know, and when did he know it?" My bylined article ran on the front page. That and several other entertainment-related stories helped me earn my first professional reporting job, after graduation in 1975, at The Clarion-Ledger in Jackson.

But my dream job since grade school had always been writing for The Commercial Appeal. On a dare, I had walked into the newspaper offices in May 1973 looking for a summer job, and ended up getting hired as a copyboy. I was essentially running errands for the reporters and editors, but I fell in love with the musty old building that housed the morning Commercial Appeal and the evening Press-Scimitar. When I left the job after three months to attend Ole Miss, I boldly told my bosses that I would be back one day as a reporter. They all nodded encouragement at my words.

After less than two years at The Clarion Ledger, I got the call I wanted – an offer to be a general assignment reporter at The CA. I immediately said yes, and that began a 26-year relationship with what was the most influential news organization in the Mid-South. In my first 10 years at the paper, I went from general assignment to the federal court beat and then to an assistant metro editor job before leaving in 1986 to become assistant city editor for The Pittsburgh Press. That paper folded five years later after a bitter Teamsters union strike, and I moved on to The Detroit Free Press in 1992 as deputy city editor.

But after less than two years in the Motor City, The Commercial Appeal beckoned me back to Memphis as deputy managing editor in 1994. I was now helping to supervise some of the same people for whom I ran errands in the summer of 1973 as a copy boy. In 2003, I was named managing editor, the No. 2 leadership position in the newsroom. But I never lost my desire to write. Throughout my years as a reporter and editor, I had written columns intermittently. I loved the freedom to express my thoughts on public policy issues and share my experiences growing up in segregated Mississippi during the Civil Rights era. In 2007, I gave up the job of managing editor and became editor for opinion and editorials, with complete autonomy to oversee the paper's editorial positions. It was then that I started writing a weekly political column. And I'm still at it today, only now it's for The Daily Memphian online news site.

My eagerness to join longtime friend Dan Conaway in producing this book of columns stems from a desire to share with readers our viewpoints and experiences, as divergent as they may be. Dan's background is starkly different from mine. He's a white guy from the city. I'm a Black guy from the farm. But we have several things in common, the most significant being our love for Memphis – its rich history, colorfulness and rhythm.

My only regret is that The Commercial Appeal and its current owner, the Gannett Company, refused my request to include columns that I wrote for the paper spanning nearly 40 years. So, unfortunately, you won't find in this book the first column I ever wrote for The CA in July 1982. It was a tribute to my first-grade teacher, Mrs. Henri C. Warfield, who turned a terrified kid entering school for the first time into a confident student who loved learning. The column also spoke to the broader point that teachers in segregated schools in Mississippi in the 1950s and '60s were a dedicated group who wanted their students to succeed despite the odds.

Also excluded from this book is my favorite Father's Day column, written in 1996. It was about my dad going more than 100 miles out of his way one wintry Saturday morning to drive me, the 12th man on my grade-school basketball team, to a tournament after I missed the team bus. Once I got there, I didn't even play in any of the team's three games. But my father, who wasn't much of a fan of basketball, did what good dads do – make sacrifices for their children.

And this book does not contain my column from the first inauguration of President Barack Obama on Jan. 20, 2009, when I stood with more than a million other unified souls in frigid temperatures on the Washington Mall to witness the historic swearing-in of America's first Black president.

But this book does contain a collection of columns that reflect life as I see it in my beloved city of Memphis, as well as my roots in Mississippi. These columns pay tribute to trailblazing political figures and address the urgent need to exercise our precious right to vote, to press for accountability from our law enforcement agencies and elected officials, and to treat with fairness those whose voices are ignored in our society.

I have been blessed with a rewarding and enduring career in journalism – one that even Mr. Darby celebrated when I returned to the Northwest campus to speak in the late 1990s. Together, Dan and I hope you will find these columns entertaining, enlightening and thought-provoking. We certainly had a ball writing them.

– Otis Sanford

Contents | Dan Conaway

Contents | Otis Sanford

On Crime and Justice:

On Community:

By DAN CONAWAY

Dedication

To Campbell, Gaines and Mac.

"Writing Memphis" | Author's Note

Writers write for themselves, an intensely personal experience that nobody really wants to watch except for my dogs. It's both joy and torture, between getting it right and pulling teeth, and then sending it out into the world. Then the measure becomes not whether it's loved or hated; it's whether it's read at all.

A few years ago, I was approached by a textbook publisher. It seemed that Dr. Katherine Fredlund, director of First Year Writing at the University of Memphis, was putting together a book about writing about place, and asking students to look out the window for example. She wanted permission to use a number of my columns from my first book, "I'm a Memphian."

"Oh, hell yes," was the first thought, but I wanted to sound professional, so I simply said, "Certainly," hung up, and did a little dance with the dogs.

The textbook is titled "Writing Memphis," and the third edition is about to come out.

Thank you, Dr. Fredlund, not just for choosing me to play a small role in a larger effort, but for seeing Memphis as subject and inspiration, as tragedy and comedy, as a rich resource for a never-ending story, as a teaching moment at any moment in time.

This collection begins with the eight columns she chose, opening with the very first column I wrote for the *Memphis Daily News* in April of 2010.

— — —

All funked up | April 9, 2010

This is my very first column. It's all about what I think Memphis is all about. Let me know what you think. But think first. There's far too little of that going around.

Face it. You're funky.

funky 1 |f ng k|
adjective (funkier, funkiest) informal
1. (of music) having or using a strong dance rhythm, in particular
that of funk: some excellent funky beats. • modern and stylish in an
unconventional or striking way: she likes wearing funky clothes.
2 strongly musty: cooked greens make the kitchen smell really funky.

Rufus Thomas understood. If a chicken could get funky, it would be in Memphis. Just look at the definition. It includes quintessential Memphis words. Rhythm. Beats. Unconventional. Striking. And, yes, greens and kitchen are in there, too.

This part of the world, and Memphis as its capital, gave the rest of the world rhythm and blues, the beat of rock and roll, the king and court of unconventional and striking. And, yes, we gave them greens and cornbread, too, and grits and chitterlings and fried green tomatoes and fried chicken.

We gave them the stuff that sustains life in hard-to-live lives. Soul-stirring music born of abject poverty. Mouthwatering flavor from food easy to come by out in the yard, over in the field. A sense of, "I can make it," "I can change it," "I can create it," because the most ordinary of origins have sent such extra extraordinary gifts to the world from here.

Elvis and Holiday Inns. Self-service groceries and Federal Express. Three 6 Mafia and modern orthopedics. Stax and St. Jude. Isaac, Al and B.B. Clarence, Fred and Kemmons. Billy Dunavant and Billy Kyle. Pit barbecue and Pitt Hyde.

We have over the years in no particular order and without argument been known as the world's foremost city for cotton, hardwood, juke joints, mules, blues, rock and roll, yellow fever, soul, keelboater fights, air freight, trauma nails, and barbecue.

And the assassination of Martin Luther King Jr. All of that, mixed in our rich and dangerously spicy diversity, baked in our sweat-through-everything summers, and left to stand on the kitchen, restaurant and church tables where we all gather, has made us one of the funkiest dishes this country serves. And people from everywhere can't wait for a taste.

We're known the world over for the beat of our mojo, for the depth and breadth of our creativity, the warmth of our hospitality, and as the most giving city of our size anywhere. Yet, if you listen to us, you'd never know it.

We think it's all about crime – or who the mayor is, was, or isn't – or consolidation – or taxes – or what we'll do about my street/neighborhood/school/Bible/gun. Those are real concerns needing real solutions, but people from everywhere have them, and when we bitch mightily as if they were ours uniquely, we can lose sight of what others see in us.

Look at it this way, if everybody sees that funky person you're with as attractive, fun, imaginative, intelligent, capable, different, open and loaded with potential and you don't ... you're the one who's wrong. As John Cleese purportedly said, "If you walk into a room dressed in a suit and everyone else is dressed as a chicken, you're the one who's out of place." Rufus would have understood.

Work on our faults, but build on our strengths.

I'm a Memphian, and I'm funky.

—— —— ——

Worldview | April 23, 2010

We seem to worry a lot about who we aren't, what we aren't and where we aren't. Memphians are always asking, "What in the world will they make of that?" Well, in my experience, we seem to make the world happy. Not a bad thing.

This week begins in Paris.

You may not know them, but they know you.

Paris.

Cabs in Paris are about the size of clown cars, and putting more than three passengers in one has the same effect. So, when the five of us arrived – us, our kids and my mother-in-law – we split up in two cabs. Gaines, 5 at the time, and I had the all-guy cab. The front seat passenger was a dog, part poodle and part Charles de Gaulle, complete with his water bowl in the passenger well. The driver introduced him as "le navigateur." The driver spoke no English. I spoke even less French. Somehow, with Gaines and the dog laughing at both of us, I realized he was asking me where we were from – a place, not a country. He knew we were Americans. Americans stand out in Europe like Hawaiian shirts at a funeral. "Memphis," I said. What happened next was a six-ticket ride. He took a hard right, and a death-defying run around the Arc de Triomphe on the Champs-Elysées. A couple hundred lanes of traffic anarchy. Like NASCAR, except no caution flags and less courtesy. Sweeping into a side street and braking hard enough to turn over Charles de Gaulle's water bowl and my stomach, he stopped in front of a nightclub. Sticking out of the wall was the rear end of a 1959 pink Caddy. "Elvis!" the driver exclaimed.

Amsterdam.

So, we're in line with another Memphis couple at the Anne Frank House. It's going to be a while, so the guys go to get everybody a snack. French fries. Stands sell them everywhere in Amsterdam. With mayonnaise. No, really. But I digress. One particular stand gets our business because the entire thing was painted with the scene from the Sistine Chapel where Michelangelo depicts God giving life to Adam … except, in this case, God is giving Adam an order of French fries. "French fries," I said. "What part of the southern United States are you from?" the vendor asked in perfect English. "Memphis," I drawled. "Friendliest city I know," he said. Seems he takes his family to the United States for two weeks every year, picking a different state for the whole two weeks. Been to Memphis twice. "We had the children with us one night, having a wonderful time walking around when we got a little lost," he related. "We walked several dark blocks when we saw spinning bright lights. Black people, white people dancing and laughing," he said, laughing himself. "They adopted us, gave us huge beers, taught the kids new dances … and called us a cab. Best time we had on that whole trip. Can't remember the name … it's, uh …," he struggled. "Raiford's Hollywood?" I guessed. "Yes, yes," he said, clapping his hands together, "that's it!"

You can't make this stuff up.

I have three packages of Memphis cigarettes from Germany, and a Memphis ashtray I talked a bar owner out of in Munich. I walked by a Volkswagen Memphis model in Salzburg, and I've been to a show in Rome featuring work from a whole design school called Memphis.

In Galatoire's in New Orleans … yes, that's an international city … the waiter engages us in conversation with a heavier European accent than the French fry guy in Holland. "Where are you from?" We tell him. He doesn't tell us about the signature trout or crab dishes, or the wine list, or anything about one of the country's great menus. He simply asks, "So where do you go for your barbecue?"

I'm a Memphian, and I'm world famous.

— — —

Howard and Bill | April 30, 2010

Just as this city is different from any other, each of us is different. If we were all the same, what a great large snore life would be. However, if we fail to respect our differences, or fail to treat each other with simple dignity and common courtesy, what a nightmare awaits us all.

This week you'll meet Howard and Bill.

Two halves make a whole.

In the '60s, Howard Robertson was a Black postal carrier moonlighting as a waiter at the capital of white money dining in Memphis, Justine's, housed in an antebellum mansion. Bill Loeb was a successful white businessman, owner of ubiquitous laundry branches about town, and the brother of Henry Loeb, mayor during the 1968 sanitation strike. Loeb lived in a home literally bordering the Memphis Country Club. Robertson lived in the other Memphis those of us who grew up white then never really acknowledged.

They would meet amid crisp white tablecloths set with crystal and crabmeat, one hosting, the other serving.

One evening at Justine's, Robertson did something that displeased Loeb. In front of his guests and the entire restaurant, Loeb wore him out. Loud and personal. Putting someone "in his place." But that wasn't Robertson's place. He returned the verbal fire, shot for shot, then returned to the kitchen and quit. That took the kind of dignity and courage that comes from deep inside. The kind that says even though this will cause sacrifice for my family, even though that kind of behavior was the norm, I will not take it. Loeb's brother, Henry, would later see that sentiment expressed on posters that said "I am a man."

This is when this becomes a different story. This is when Loeb would show his own dignity and courage. As he talked with his guests, he realized he had been in the wrong. He invited all of them back the following evening, and asked for Robertson. When told he had quit, Loeb asked Justine if she could please try and get him there. It took some doing, but she did, and for the second night in a row, Loeb and Robertson became the center of attention for the restaurant. Except, this night, Loeb apologized. Man to man. They talked. They decided to meet again.

And they kept meeting for the rest of Loeb's life. They watched games together. They talked life. They talked business. When Loeb converted his laundries to very popular barbecue shops, he brought Robertson on as a partner in two of them.

That was then, and that is now.

The sense of two cities in one, a tale like Dickens' "It was the best of times, it was the worst of times," is not only still with us, it divides and defeats us. What Robertson and Loeb did, when it was much more difficult to do, is find the common ground we must all find.

Bill Loeb's children have continued to show leadership in the business, arts and causes of our city. Howard Robertson's son – Howard Jr. – is an involved citizen and business owner, and once told me, "A father is how a son learns to be a man."

Good job, guys, you taught them well, and there's a lesson in it for us.

I'm a Memphian, hopefully, like Howard and Bill.

–– –– ––

One of a kind | June 11, 2010

A number of places have a certain thing about them that is aptly described as unique, but just one or two things in most cases. Duck Hill, Mississippi, for instance, has trees that grow damn near sideways out of that namesake hill. It takes a bunch of things like that before the whole place can be thought of as unique.

Folks, this place is unique.

Really unique is really not. Memphis is.

Nothing is really unique. Unique is unique. If there is more than one of it, it isn't.

Memphis is et up with unique.

The Peabody is unique. Two hammered duck hunters dump their live decoys in the lobby fountain. One is actually the hotel manager, and instead of getting him fired, that drunken prank makes the place world-famous. Almost 80 years later, ducks are still in that fountain by day, live in an air-conditioned penthouse by night, march back and forth twice a day to a packed crowd, and are on TV as much as Daffy and Donald.

Unique.

Graceland is unique. Depending on who you talk to, Elvis has been dead since 1977. Visit Graceland today and tell me you don't think he's still in there somewhere. Somebody has just been napping on that ginormous couch. Those dark TVs are still warm, and somebody's screwing around with a guitar in the Jungle Room. Walk by the kitchen and you can smell peanut butter and banana sandwiches. There's a reason they won't let us go upstairs.

Unique.

Memphis In May is unique. "I've got an idea," someone certifiable said at the first meeting. "Let's have a barbecue cooking contest. Contestants will come from all over the world, bring smokers that look like locomotives, set up booths 30 feet tall, and 100,000-plus will come down to the river to watch them cook food they can't eat."

Unique.

The National Civil Rights Museum is unique. There is one Lorraine Motel, one balcony, one bathroom window through which a modern-day prophet was killed but his dream refused to die. What fed that dream and what feeds it still is on display in one place.

Unique.

St. Jude Children's Research Hospital is unique. What all those unbelievably dedicated people drink over there isn't Kool-Aid, it's great big gulps of hope. What they do every day to give children a chance at life shines a bright light from Memphis the whole world can see.

Unique.

The Rendezvous is unique. It's in a basement. You walk by a dumpster and step over a couple of puddles of God-knows-what to get in. Not only do they charbroil their ribs down there, the restaurant itself has burned twice. The beams are still charred. Everything in this city's collective attic is hanging on the walls or from the ceiling. Their ribs started and continue to fuel a worldwide debate. Wet or dry.

Unique.

Cozy Corner is unique, a barbecue joint famous for … Cornish hens? The National Ornamental Metal Museum is unique, both for what it is and the river view from where it is. Dyer's is unique, deep frying hamburgers in a vat of grease I think Andy Jackson brought with him when he founded the city.

The list goes on and on, and that's the point. Beyond and because of music, and barbecue, and cotton, and race, and hospitality, and river, and creativity, it goes all the way to soul. Uniquely.

I'm a Memphian, and I'm unique.

—— —— ——

Look who's here | June 25, 2010

If you let it, the passing parade that is this city will pass you by. If you pause to take it in, a chimp might sell you a suit.

"38 regular," I told the chimp.

Take a minute and look around. You may see a story. And it may last a lifetime.

Before he was Prince Mongo, he was Robert Hodges. Oh, he was clearly from a place far, far away, but he had not yet assumed the title. When I first became aware of him, the heir apparent to the house of hinky used to ride around town on a motorcycle in a leather jacket and goggles. Sitting behind him was a chimp ... in matching leather jacket and goggles. It was the late '60s, and sightings of the weird and wonderful, both natural and chemically-induced, were commonplace, but this caught your attention.

Hodges owned a men's store in those days ... no, really ... called Dalian et Rae. I went in there one day to look around and saw no one, no one human at least. The chimp appeared from behind a clothes rack, in a nice little jacket and pants, and held up his hand. At this point, you have to make a decision – either go for the whole experience or turn around and walk out. Either way, you've got a story, but what makes Memphis Memphis is that the stories can always get better.

I took his hand.

He walked me to the men's suits, and stepped back as if to say, "You look like a 38 regular." That's where he stopped, and that ... a couple thousand super-sized fries ago ... was my size. He smiled, and, buddy, chimps can smile. I was about to ask him, I swear, what he had in a double-breasted blazer, when I heard a voice. No, not the chimp, but a guy who worked there who had been in the storeroom. I never saw the chimp again but his bananas owner went on to cosmic infamy.

The truth of what you can see every day in Memphis is better than the fiction other cities have to come up with to make them interesting.

Like that day in 1965 when a 16-year-old in his momma's convertible pulled up to the light at Union and Cooper. A Harley pulled up next to him, and, with a big smile, Elvis said to the kid, "Nice car." I might still be sitting at that light if the guy behind me hadn't laid on the horn.

Or the time I ran into Isaac Hayes in a break room and we spent an hour talking about bathroom renovation and fireplaces.

Or when I was screwing around with a wedge in my parents' front yard when Cary Middlecoff walked by, and spent 30 minutes showing me how to hit down on the ball.

I have hundreds more, and whether you realize it or not, so do you. Start looking around for your stories. They're everywhere in this town because giants ... giant heroes, giant goats, giant characters ... have walked and continue to walk among us.

I'm a Memphian, and I have a story.

—— —— ——

Two ways to look at it | April 8, 2011

Most cities are looking for something to hang a civic hat on – a single thing that can define and attract and separate.

Might be they're the birthplace of something or someone significant enough to brand a whole city. Or perhaps they're known as the center or capital of some enterprise, the place where something is made or from or named after.

If they're really lucky, really rare as cities go, they'll have more than one such thing and a few, incredibly few, might have such things from both the right and left brain, both cool and profitable.

Of course, they'd have to realize it.

It all depends on your point of view.

Coming from Arkansas, it looks like Oz.

It appears suddenly, just past that truck in front of you, between that truck and the one next to you, glimpsed between rearview mirror checks of that truck behind you. You've somehow survived the concrete gauntlet of West Memphis and the semi cowboys whipping their rigs into a frenzy, driving them to market across the modern-day trails of I-40 and I-55.

There in front of you is a city on a hill. It's an urban island; surrounded by the agrarian sea of cotton, soybeans and rice you've just navigated. You'll reach it by crossing a bridge of lights and a river so great that a great nation uses it to define its east and west. You see the city spread out across the horizon, and to my taste, a feast for both eyes and spirit.

Okay, that's a truckload of metaphors, but I think the view is pretty trucking impressive.

You're looking at a place where new ideas come out of nowhere and go everywhere, where cultures, races, circumstances and history all come together and give rise to new ways to see, hear and heal. From here – from a brand-new waterfront town and a 30-story stainless steel pyramid on one side to an old city makeover and fledgling arts district on the other – you can't see the problems, but you can still see the possibilities.

Coming from Mississippi, it looks like a Star Wars set.

It appears to the right, just past that truck in front of you, between that truck and the one next to you, glimpsed between rearview mirror checks of that truck behind you. You've somehow survived the challenge of the Lamar corridor where Mississippi turns into Tennessee and farm turns into industry as suddenly and chaotically as a five-truck pileup.

There beside you at Shelby Drive is the old Tennessee Yard, the new Memphis Intermodal Facility. BNSF dropped a $200 million upgrade here and rolled in those ginormous cranes that look like Empire war engines and can lift the national debt. The wheels are bigger than my house. They pick up 40-foot containers from railcars and put them on trucks and vice versa, and they do that 600,000 times a year with capacity to do it a million times a year.

You're looking at a place where things come from everywhere and go everywhere else, where river, rail, air, road and geography all come together. From here – from the permanent ruts in the road made by the world's heavy loads – you can see what made Memphis storage closet and delivery service to the known universe.

Two views, one of a city of imagination, an incubator where new things are born and grow strong in the Delta heat, and another of a city of purpose, a critical transfer point where whatever's wanted comes to be sorted and sent.

One city.

I'm a Memphian, and our original music includes the sounds of boats, trains, trucks and planes.

— — —

Can I get an amen? | April 29, 2011

Regardless of how the playoffs turn out, Memphis has won.

Glory be.

As the Duke divinity graduate rises and throws up a prayer, an entire city rises with him. All know his name, as he was chosen by them in the beginning and then banished to the wilderness. Well, to Houston anyway. Now he returns. Now he holds their hope. A moment later and 10 years coming, we are delivered of our distress in high-def, screaming for joy in front of our TVs. Heaven help us, Shane Battier has ripped a three pointer and the Memphis Grizzlies have won their very first playoff game. Bless their hearts, the San Antonio Spurs have just heard the first lesson in their own house.

Transcendent.

The sinner stands at the center of attention – his only option is himself – and releases it. As it rises, all in the building rise with it. His bruised and purple past are in it, all the ugliness and thuginess in its arc, but when it comes down it is the act of a changed man who pays other people's utility bills, whose talent has electrified us and whose heart has captured ours. All in this congregation are on their feet, joy has erupted, people are dancing in the aisles and, I'm pretty sure, speaking in tongues. All hell has broken loose, Zach Randolph has ripped a three pointer and the Memphis Grizzlies have won their very first playoff game at home. Bless their hearts, but here endeth the second lesson for the West's No. 1 seed.

Redemptive.

God isn't on the Grizzlies bench any more than on the Spurs'. Despite all the thanks that come his way in post-game interviews, Jesus has never worn one team's sweatshirt or the other, and has caused no blown layups or bricked free throws. Muhammad has never screamed at or questioned the parentage of any referees. Hinduism would not support my belief that Manu Ginobili will come back as a flopping carp. Buddha would not find anything said by either analysts or fans – or Phil Jackson for that matter – to be particularly enlightening.

However, for me anyway, the presence of something larger than our understanding, deeper than our knowing, beyond our explanation can be felt just as much or more in big water, big skies and big weather – and in moments great and small with each other – than in spaces prescribed for it.

Comfort, structure and form can be found in liturgy, and in a jump shot. Joy can be found in a favorite hymn, in a smile or touch, and in the crazed grins of 19,000 people waving towels.

If churches are the most exclusive and segregated places in Memphis on a Sunday morning, FedExForum is the most inclusive and integrated place in Memphis on a Saturday night. Every income, political stripe, racial profile, religious belief, class distinction, address and opinion stand side-by-side united in a celebration of renewed faith in and of a city.

Rejoice and be glad in it.

I'm a Memphian, and I believe.

—— —— ——

Building models | May 27, 2011

Most of the solutions we're being offered for our various and sundry urban problems seem to have several things in common:

The loudest come from white people over 50 and usually start with, "And I'll tell you another damn thing...."

They are simplistic so as not to strain simple minds.

They are not merely dogmatic, but red-in-the-face, a-little-spit-at-the corner-of-your-mouth dogmatic.

They are based on some time in the past, generally a hybrid of King Arthur's Camelot, Robert Young's "Father Knows Best," and your choice of John Wayne movies.

They are most often voiced with the greatest volume by those with the least knowledge of the subject at hand and the least experience in dealing with or managing it.

So let's get started with this week's column, and I'll tell you another damn thing....

A 99.6% success rate

We've seen the letters to the editor, heard the guy two stools down, the geniuses spitting into talk show microphones: "It's not the teachers, it's the parents."

If I'm 17 in South Memphis right now, we don't have time to teach or reach my parents to teach or reach me. I have little brothers and sisters I'm responsible for, they're hungry, I'm mad. And I just put a gun in my pocket and walked out the door.

When there's one exhausted parent or no parent at home, where would you have me go? When home is no place I can safely come home to, when the corner is my mentor, the street my support, what would you do with me? When there are thousands of me one meltdown away from you, can you actually pretend that we have nothing to do with each other?

I'm next door. What happens to me tonight when I walk out that door happens to you as a city tomorrow. The flat-earth Tennessee Legislature – declaring war on teachers and marching education backwards in lockstep – doesn't get it. People who talk just in terms of what used to be or in terms of 20 years from now – or just talk – don't get it either. We need to stop these teen pregnancies, graduate these kids, save this generation so it can save the next.

We need to stop that kid at that door and open another one right now.

There are people who get it. Alisha Kiner, principal at Booker T. Washington High School, gets it, and the tough love she gives out keeps kids from giving in. Digger Phelps, legendary coach and motivator, gets it, recently telling an audience of prominent Memphis business people to get off their assets and get into a mentoring program. President Obama gets it, coming here for the BTW commencement in recognition of what that amazing inner-city class did, raising their grades, raising their graduation rate more than 20%, raising the hope of a city, and symbolically through his appearance, the hope of a nation for inner-city schools.

There are programs that get it. The Boys & Girls Club, building model citizens from the very raw product of urban reality, gets it.

Half of BTW's graduating class went to the Porter Boys & Girls Club across the street instead of staying on the street. For mentoring and guidance. For role models, reinforcement, and a sense of self-worth. For what can happen when parents can't be there but others are willing and able to step in and stand up.

The graduation rate for Memphis City Schools is in the low 60s. Last year, the Boys & Girls Clubs had a graduation rate of 97.6% among the seniors in their six clubs. This year, with three times as many seniors, the graduation rate was 99.6%.

Our kids can do anything, but not if we do nothing.

I'm a Memphian, and our kids can inspire presidents.

–– –– ––

Driving while stupid | January 24, 2014

If you're reading this or anything on a phone or a tablet, or sending anything on one while driving – congratulations – you're one of us.

If you think the people behind and around you in traffic either ought to know what you're about to do or don't deserve to know – welcome to our club.

If you know you can step off the curb and beat those oncoming cars to the other side, or better yet, get halfway across and keep everybody guessing your next move while you balance on the dividing line, or better still, just amble on out there and make everybody stop because you can – you're among friends.

You're an idiot.

Driving us crazy.

I write about things Memphis, and there's nothing more Memphis than the idiots on our roads. Our driving is like our unpredictable, even dangerous creativity, our shtick of doing old things in new ways and scaring people to death while we're at it.

My father-in-law once backed his car a quarter mile down the interstate shoulder against traffic to get back to the exit ramp he missed. My mother-in-law used to keep time to the car radio by tapping on the gas pedal, shaking down the road like Elvis on Ed Sullivan.

These are the people who taught my wife how to drive.

Long before cellphones or texting there was the distracting world inside my mother's head. In there, the colors in the trees or the shapes in the clouds were far more interesting than the road in front of her. That's how she drove into a ditch off Kirby with me riding shotgun. We were fine. The car not so much.

She was taking me out for a driving lesson at the time.

Friend Allan had parked his car on the side of the Mallory exit ramp – stupid in and of itself – while he harvested errant golf balls from the interstate side of the Riverside golf course fence when a semi blew by and took that ramp far too fast. Barely missing his car, the rig started lurching sideways like a dinosaur in a death throe, crashed on its side and slid to a stop with a final smoking metal screech. Allan ran to help and just as he got there, the driver stood up through the driver door window and exclaimed to no one in particular, "Shit! Second one this month."

We all have these stories.

We all know that mere rain kills cars in Memphis, let alone snow, leaving them dark and abandoned on wet streets. We all know that lane lines are just suggestions, and moving in and out of them is to be done either very quickly or ever so slowly with little regard as to who's already in them and never, ever, giving the move away with a turn signal.

Evidently, virtually everybody in Memphis was frightened by a turn signal as a baby and avoids them at all costs.

We all know that our pedestrians and our drivers are at war.

Today or tomorrow, you'll probably almost hit somebody crossing the street just about anywhere, except, of course, in a crosswalk. In Memphis, jaywalking isn't a crime – it's a birthright.

On the other hand, our drivers consider crosswalks to be lines marking the center of the first car at a light or cross street. In Memphis, pedestrians don't have the right of way – they need to get the hell out of your way.

Observing the rules of driving – the real ones, not ours – would be, well, pedestrian. Whatever else you may want to call it, our driving, like our city, is never pedestrian.

I'm a Memphian, and y'all be careful out there.

—— —— ——

Fascination | February 7, 2014

The smallest and most ordinary of things become larger and most urgent.

Look! My boots are purple. Look! Look! My pants are pink. Isn't that fascinating?

The way she sees things from the very beginning will color her vision to the very end.

What kind of city would you like to see?

Urped my oats.

"I urped my oats," the 2-year-old announced from the backseat. "Urped her oats? Did she throw up back there?" her grandfather questioned. "Yes, baby," her grandmother said to her, "you do have purple boots."

Last week, her grandparents took 2-year-old Campbell to see her first movie on a big screen.

"My plank sink," came the next announcement. "My plank sink," her grandfather repeated. "Wait, maybe that was stink – we better check that diaper." "Yes, sweetheart," her grandmother said to her, "your pants are pink."

She was very excited and chattered all the way there.

"Be moisee, be moisee," Campbell exclaimed. "Moisee," Granddan wondered, "Maybe that's mouse?" "Beats me," said Doee, this time also stumped, "Maybe she's been listening to French tapes." "Be MOISEE!" Campbell repeated loud and clear, because, inside her head it was perfectly clear to her. "It's big movie, you idiots, big movie!"

And when the movie started we were all speaking her language. Mesmerized by the allover size of it, the everywhere sound of it. The blanket of the big dark space covering so many. The big-as-a-house images on the big bright screen reflected in so many little bright eyes. The comfort of a lap to sit in, a neck to hug when it gets scary, a laugh to share when it's funny, a gasp to gasp and a song to sing all together now. And all with popcorn.

We're talking fascination, the language of first-time, wide-eyed wonder that comes so naturally to her and is so tragically lost to so many of us. Once as fluent in fascination as she, we now struggle to find as much of it in a day, even a week, as she finds in every hour, even every minute.

When we argue about whether or not we should feed a hungry child today at school, or a hungry mind in pre-K, or a hungry heart in a lonely childhood, fascination dies early and we starve our own tomorrow. When we fail to see the difference early childhood makes in the kind of adults we become, our lack of vision has failed a generation if not several.

Campbell will always be loved and supported, but, at 2, she doesn't know that. She's just fascinated, and the delight of that shines in her eyes. Even at 2, there are far too many in a city as giving as this who are already aware of a lesser, darker reality, the light in their eyes already dimming.

"Seize biscuit," she laughed on the way home, pointing out the window and rocking her car seat. "Seize biscuit! Seize biscuit." Nora and I were clueless what that meant, but we were laughing, too.

You can see yourself – what you once were, what you hoped for – in the eyes of a child. It's up to all of us to make sure what we see there, in all those eyes, is fascination, not desolation.

I'm a Memphian, and I have to run. I have to go seize the biscuit.

—— —— ——

Preaching to meddling | February 21, 2014

Like the Bible, people selectively cherry-pick our Constitution to justify selective behavior.

Being no exception myself, and being relevant to both documents, the cherry I'm picking today is our founders' wisdom in prohibiting the imposition of religion – anyone's religion – on everyone's laws.

I pick the very American notion of inclusion over exclusion, open over closed, self-determination instead of institutional control.

I pick the freedom of choosing my own beliefs and freedom from yours, and respecting that right for both of us and the law for all of us.

So did the founders.

Our new Pharisees.

Pharisee |`far`sē|
noun • a member of an ancient religious sect, distinguished by strict observance of traditional and written law, commonly held to have pretensions to superior sanctity.

From the church of Nashville:

If you believe that religion should dictate law, then stand and repeat after me.

It is only necessary for me to believe in something in order to deny you anything.

If I believe that only those people who believe what I do should have a hamburger, I will not serve others a hamburger. Or anything else.

If I believe that only those people who believe what I do should have a couch, I will not sell others a couch. Or anything else.

If I believe that only those people who believe what I do are people, I will not treat others like people. But something else.

If I believe that only those people who believe what I do can be loved, I will not allow others to be loved. Only to be hated.

If I believe that a horn grows out of a horse's head and makes that horse a unicorn, then I will deny the civil rights of anyone who doesn't believe that and make myself a horse's ass. And I will make that law.

Amen.

• *a self-righteous person; a hypocrite.*

Note, brothers and sisters of the legislative gavel, since the Pharisees and Jesus were Jewish, they'll differ with you on points of religion. Jesus, I believe, is going to differ with you on virtually every point.

I also believe when legislators impose religion on law, they mean their religion. They would be shocked if a Hindu denied them their steak or an Orthodox Jew or Seventh-day Adventist their barbecue, enraged if a Buddhist would deny their carry permit or the Amish their SUV, stunned if an atheist told them who they could marry, and – most of all – inconsolable if so-called Christian law would be replaced with Sharia law.

And since I believe that, I deny you the basis in law or in common sense to dictate anything to the citizens of Tennessee based on your, or anyone's, religion. But I really don't have to; I have a Constitution that already does.

So just stop for God's sake.

Stop paying attention to the pandering of small people to small minds for their own political gain.

Stop giving credence to incredible sanctimony, credibility to incredible hypocrisy.

Stop being silent when mean-spirited, self-serving legislation screams for condemnation, and make sure that the authors of such legislation are remembered for it and can't slink away from the ugliness of it.

Legislators regularly propose bills that are probably unconstitutional and definitely unconscionable and then tried to hide when things go sideways. While my religion requires that we forgive them, our conscience requires that we never forget what they did.

So it is written.

In my book, Jesus is about love and others before self. I'll leave it to you what most laws offered in God's name are really about.

I'm a Memphian, and that's what I believe.

—— —— ——

Ceiling reflections | February 28, 2014

Imagine all of us around one great big family dinner table. Imagine how many weird uncles, fidgety kids, colicky babies, warring siblings, bored teenagers, nosy in-laws, overbearing parents, clueless cousins, picky eaters, and troubled relationships and lives who would all be fighting over the mashed potatoes.

Imagine how loud it would be, and how far it could be heard, if they all laughed at the same time.

Family time.

"You're no happier than your most unhappy child," a wise friend said.

I remembered those words as I stared at the breadbox on the ceiling. I'll explain. Back when we were living in the Georgian Woods with about 27 cents, we didn't buy anything we didn't need and couldn't justify. Nora needed a breadbox, so she used the occasion of my birthday to give me … a breadbox.

Since then, any gift that either of us gives with other than selfless intent is a breadbox. Got one for my birthday last year – a fancy little clock radio that projects a digital image of the time on the ceiling because Nora couldn't see the former – and perfectly fine, I might add – clock radio.

3:06 AM, declared the breadbox.

The time families reflect on and are reminded of all those times on the continuum of problem to crisis, and also on the continuum of smile to pure joy.

Should we go in there or let him cry? Why haven't I heard her cry? The first step and first fall. The first tooth and the first day of everything. The little boy and girl just there behind that twinkle in the eyes of that grown man and woman. From worrying about what to do to worrying about doing too much. From wondering who will they become to the wonder of all they've become. From so very frightened to so very proud. And back.

3:31 AM
A city is like a family, sharing in the victories and in the defeats.

The glow on the Mississippi as the sun sets and the mist on the Wolf as it rises, urban forests in Overton Park and Shelby Farms and one of the nation's most majestic canopies above it all – all ours – as are the potholes, the pension shortfall and the loss of public trust. The promise of every commencement on every campus, every achievement on every stage is ours, as is the broken promise of every hungry child being raised by a grandmother, every woman working three jobs, every man looking for just one. Every celebration, every positive note and new move in our creative and collective song and dance are all ours – as is every needle in an East Memphis teenager's arm, every gun in a Midtown teenager's hand, every stare of the homeless at the underside of an overpass as I stare at the ceiling.

3:52 AM
Life is just another word for experience and family often frames that experience, both good and bad, made more of one than the other by how the experience is shared. We can't run from our shared problems, because that doesn't solve them and they will overtake us.

You know the old saying; if family knocks you've got to let them in.

4:11 AM
"You, too?" said the voice next to me in bed. "Yeah," I said, as I put my hand over hers and, together, we got through the night.

I'm a Memphian, and we are blood kin.

—— —— ——

The Heartbreak Hotel | May 2, 2014

Thirty years ago in The Heartbreak Hotel – in an area just then minted The Edge – mornings were quiet. The sun bounced off the backside of the Memphis skyline, trash in the weedy lots barely stirred, ghosts of past success slept in the abandoned spaces, people moved through on their way to greener grass.

Some mornings, I'd climb out the window of my office onto the flat roof of the empty building next door, dragging a chair and a cup of coffee with me, and steep myself in that one so-Memphis thing the neighborhood was so full of, that elusive thing we can all see all around us but can't quite seem to reach.

Potential.

But here's the thing – Memphis is also full of people who never stop reaching, and that puts anything within our grasp.

On the edge of things.

"They're calling this area The Edge, and it's about to explode," Ben said.

We were looking up at The Heartbreak Hotel, a stack of bricks where traveling salesmen about a century ago would rest their sample cases for the night, rising three tired stories above the all-but-forgotten intersection of Monroe and Marshall – pretty much like Elvis sang – down at the end of Lonely Street.

"Maybe I'll turn it into condos," he said, "start with my office down here, put a swimming pool in the courtyard. Worst case, I'll end up in an office with a swimming pool."

That's the way Ben Reisman looked at things, with pragmatic imagination, seeing reality and what's possible at the same time. He'd bought the place for a song after the owners got in a fight and closed their restaurant there. They'd called it The Heartbreak Hotel, painted a picture of the King on the side of the building, and used the tail end and trunk of a 1957 Cadillac for a salad bar.

It was 1985. I was starting a creative service for radio stations and I needed an office with a creative personality, and I needed it cheap. Ben carved out a corner for me on the second floor with a couple of bay windows over the street, and I stayed for five years.

He never did put in that pool, and everything above the ground floor remained empty except for my office, but the building was full of personality. An architect, an interior designer, a fashion accessories boutique, a developer, a contractor, a home health care consultant, a couple of lawyers, several dogs, and a receptionist who would bite your head off.

Sun Studio was a short block away. They shot the movie "Great Balls of Fire" right in front of us. Weekly, buses full of tourists would stop right below my window and, as we stared at each other, I'm sure the guide told them this was THE Heartbreak Hotel.

I look up at that window, the space behind it long dark, every time I pull into Tracy's across the street so Sam and his guys can work on my car, and sometimes I think of Ben.

After we'd left The Heartbreak, Ben and his wife, Laurel, fell in love with a little girl and sued the state for the right to adopt her and won. Before, the Reismans, a white couple, couldn't adopt a mixed-raced child in Tennessee.

Then they sued again on behalf of all children and won again, changing adoption policy in Tennessee regardless of racial classification.

Ben died in 2000, and his lawyer in those cases, Hayden Lait, was quoted in Ben's obituary, "He just had that innate sense of what is right."

The Edge didn't explode back then, or even heat up, but it's certainly getting hot 30 years later, and it looks as if Ben was right after all. After all, he did change things.

I'm a Memphian, and we're in a better place because of Ben.

— — —

I was a teenage werewolf | May 16, 2014

Many of you don't remember Michael Landon. That's okay. That's because he was from before your time, or because you can't remember much of anything, and you're amazed at what shows up, uninvited, in your memory.

I can relate.

Before he was Little Joe on "Bonanza" and in little houses on prairies – before he was much of anything – Michael Landon was a teenage werewolf.

Again, I can relate.

Memories of parking. And full moons.

Last week, if I remember correctly, I mentioned CRS – that remarkable condition that blocks the knowledge of what one had for breakfast but allows a clear and concise image of something that happened in, say, 1966.

This week, I find myself recalling one of those lost arts that there's simply no application for any longer, one that I was, modesty aside, damn good at, like smoking – all those hours popping my jaw to blow perfect smoke rings wasted, the ability to light a cigarette on a golf course in a 50 mph windstorm wanting a purpose.

But this time the memory was parking.

Not the kind where you stop your car in a brightly-lit space and get out of it to accomplish something, but the kind where you stop your car in a dark place and stay in it to accomplish something. Those that came before had bench seats, a wide and level playing field. My generation was the first to face the challenge of bucket seats in full-size cars and the obstacle of center console gear shifts, the combination requiring Cirque du Soleil acrobatics by those involved, moves that would require hospitalization if attempted today.

This particular memory was prompted by a drive through my old East Memphis neighborhood and by a certain cove – full of houses today but home to only a few when I parked there on a certain night in 1966 under a full moon.

My date and I were talking, just talking, and somehow the subject of werewolves came up – maybe the moon – and she confided that she was particularly frightened of that prospect. Being the sensitive guy I am, I immediately started acting like a werewolf, including jumping out of the car and running around in a crouching and, evidently, convincing snarl.

She locked the doors. And screamed. And again.

One of those houses in that lonely cove heard and called the cops. In no time at all, bouncing flashlights with a cop behind every one of them were rushing towards us across a vacant field. In no time at all, I was face down on the car's hood with my hands behind me, trying to explain my excellent werewolf imitation, made more difficult because my date was still screaming, now scared by all those guys with guns.

In a couple of minutes – felt like a week – she calmed down, unlocked the doors and corroborated my story. We never went parking again, but we're still friends, which would not be the case if I shared her name.

All the cops but one started walking away. He took me aside, gave me a practiced withering glare, and said, "Son, don't fool with things you don't understand." He reached down to his gun belt, pulled a silver bullet from one of the loops and showed it to me, then turned and joined the retreating flashlights without another word.

I'm a Memphian, and many of my Memphis memories are solid gold. One is pure silver.

–– –– ––

Light and dark | July 4, 2014

Clear images and understanding are impossible in the dark, and too much light is just as blinding. While TV news and the 24/7/ad nauseam news cycle would have us see the world through a screen darkly, those who would have us see the bright light of their view would gleefully burn the unenlightened.

How we see the whole of our lives is wholly up to us.

When stories are told in the dark, leave a light on.

As I watch what leads the local TV news – basically a visual evening recap of whatever that day's monitoring of police scanners and chasing sirens can produce – and what passes for TV reporting – basically an evening twist to whatever might be salacious or sensational in that morning's paper – I wonder if all of our better angels have left town.

The 30-minute horror show we're being shown daily is no more indicative of the whole of who and what we are than a 30-minute Chamber of Commerce PowerPoint presentation, no more reflective of what you're dealing with in your kitchen than what Kelly English is dealing with in his at Restaurant Iris. We are all of us somewhere in between.

It's just intellectually lazy. Truth and balance are tough. Fear and pandering are easy.

In 1987, 14 years before 9/11, my family was returning from a trip to France from Paris Orly airport. We pulled our 15 pieces of luggage through doors guarded by two guys with Uzi's, the submachine gun of choice those days, and proceeded to a huge waiting room accommodating 10 or more lesser known airlines, hundreds of people, and several more guys with Uzi's.

It was going to be a while so my wife, mother-in-law, 12-year-old daughter and 5-year-old son decamped in search of food and I kept watch atop mount luggage. While they were gone, a patrol spotted and approached an unaccompanied carry-on bag in the vast room. Whistles blew. Officials scurried. Announcements were made in several languages. We were all to depart the building immediately with our luggage.

Over the years telling this story, I'm often asked, "How did you move 15 pieces of luggage?"

When a guy with an Uzi says move the luggage, you find a way.

With all of us outside on the tarmac, they put a huge can over that little bag and blew it up.

I then dragged, kicked and muscled our bags back into a surreal smoky room, smelling like Baileys Irish Cream and cordite, filled with tiny pieces of floating fabric and paper. That had been the contents of the ill-fated bag – a bottle bought custom-free, somebody's underwear and somebody's trip photos.

Presently, my family returned after a heart-stopping adventure of their own recapturing the 5-year-old who had escaped to explore the vast Orly terminal solo. A man with a chest-long beard in some sort of military outfit turned a cardboard sign around that read "Air Malta" revealing our charter "Tower Air" on the other side, and we were off.

More than just remember, I could mark and measure our trip by that experience. Or by Paris, the Loire Valley, or by seeing my mother-in-law see Europe. Or by my daughter's wide eyes or by an old dog named Ursula rolling around on a 13th-century chateau floor with my son.

I remember, mark and measure by it all. If we live in fear embracing only the dark, light is lost and terror wins.

I'm a Memphian, and part of the whole story.

—— —— ——

Raise a glass | September 26, 2014

Legal lion Lewie Donelson, 92 or 93 at the time, was sitting next to me at the Wiles-Smith counter looking at the condensation on his malt and the yellow-brown perfection of his grilled cheese and tomato sandwich. "Kind of sad," he said, "I can't have bacon on this anymore."

None of us can, Lewie, but we have the memories.

Raise a glass. Institutions are passing.

What's your pleasure?

Maybe a chocolate malt or a single malt. Maybe a vanilla soda or a Scotch and soda. Maybe a root beer or a draft beer. But these guys wouldn't ask that question because they already knew your drink.

What's your name?

Across generations. The very old and the very new. Maiden and married. Regular and irregular. They wouldn't ask that question either, because they already knew who and how you are.

Charlie Smith and Lafayette Draper have passed into legend and this city should mourn.

Charlie – pharmacist, soda jerk and Midtown fixture – is still very much with us, but he's closing his Wiles-Smith Drug Store. Lafayette – bartender, friend to a city and namesake to music halls and watering holes – has gone on to a place where he'll be the one served.

Charlie can be as prickly as the stuffed porcupine that sat atop the shelves in his store and is as conservative as the hard-right humor of the cartoons taped above his cash register. But his large heart is in the right place, a place that's been something special since 1944, something that Charlie made since he stepped behind the counter in 1962.

"Charlie!" exclaimed the man in the bathrobe with the intravenous drip bag in his hand, "can you do something with these damn tubes?" It was the middle of lunch hour at Wiles-Smith, counter full, when Ernie walked in with his problem. Recuperating from open heart surgery at home, he'd pulled his tubes loose so he did what Central Gardens has been doing for decades: he came to Charlie for comfort, medical or malted. As a bonus, he opened his bathrobe and showed all the diners his truly spectacular, bright red scar.

Just another day at Wiles-Smith. And those days are gone.

"Winter," said the bartender in a deep baritone, "so it's Scotch, right?" It was a rhetorical question. Lafayette not only knew my name, he knew I drank Scotch in the cold months and gin and tonic in the hot ones. Even though it could be months or even years between the times I saw Lafayette behind the bar all over town, he greeted me with my name and my drink as if I'd just been there minutes before, laughing about something with him as always. I'm not special, but Lafayette made the truly special, the wannabe special, and the very ordinary feel very special indeed – straight up or on the rocks.

Just another drink with Lafayette. And that bar is closed.

As I've said before, I believe the past and the present should be used to inform the future, but the past is not a destination and the present is past tomorrow. However, impressive things and people that won't come our way again should be remembered – not necessarily by statues or plaques, but by the stories passed along.

And chocolate malts and single malts served with character can become legend.

I'm a Memphian, and here's to Charlie and Lafayette.

— — —

Different windows, same views | October 17, 2014

Wherever you are, I guess it's all in how you look at it. And in what you fail to see.

This morning. This town.

This morning, I woke up in a challenged neighborhood.

You know the challenges well.

The population is declining and aging – talking about the good old days, bemoaning the present, fearful of the future. The city – built on a booming business now faded and all but gone – is trying to reinvent itself. Young people aren't returning. One major employer dominates and other jobs are mostly in government or in lower-paying positions in service or tourism. People outside the city point to it as the source of the area's problems.

"Abandoned neighborhoods and crime," says the right. "Far too much controlled by far too few," says the left. "Far too many up to no good," say both.

All of that was in the ebb and flow of the conversations I was floating through at last night's cocktail party. One local woman, a Ph.D. in anthropology, was putting things in historical perspective. Another woman, an engineer and Russian, and another engineer, a man from Wales, were comparing their commutes and jobs. A delightful Earth mother from across the road brought a basket of tomatoes from her garden, her carrots were in the carrot cake. The retired teachers brought a savory sausage dish served with warm charm on the side. Everybody brought a sense of humor, something common in this diverse group.

While this sounds like down South in Memphis, this was a different neighborhood, different voices.

This was my brother and sister-in-law's house outside of Gloversville, New York, down in the southern part of Adirondack Park, the largest park, state-level protected area, and National Historic Landmark in the contiguous United States. Instead of cotton, Gloversville's faded business is the eponymous leather tanning of 150 years ago. Instead of FedEx, the area's major employer, and the employer of that Russian engineer, is GE. And if you don't know anything about Gloversville, that's okay, they don't know much about you either. The aforementioned Ph.D. asked me if Memphis – headquarters of the aforementioned FedEx – had an airport.

This morning, I awoke to the wondrous racket of 16 or 17 wild turkeys outside my window, and the roar of a stream dropping 15 or 20 feet over two falls into a rocky pool. Upstream, beaver are out in the water building a dam on the Earth mother's property and she's out there building one right beside them. In a couple of months, it will all be under a couple of feet of snow and the neighbors will be coming to cocktail parties on cross-country skis.

What was outside my window was what I wanted to talk about, but that's their everyday view. They wanted to talk about local problems and challenges. They wanted me to talk about the Mississippi River, grits, the blues, and why brother Frank no longer sounds like I do.

People share problems in common. When they look out the window they tend to see those problems, failing to see their own mountains or rivers or wonders, looking for something else.

I'm a Memphian, and I keep my eye out for the unique.

—— —— ——

May we remember | October 31, 2014

Last week, Ben Bradlee died. If you don't know who that is, you are far from fully informed about one of the biggest stories of the 20th century.

Last week, I visited with Lyman Aldrich. If you don't know who that is, you are far from fully informed about the biggest party in Memphis.

Last week, I was reminded of a story that changed a country, and one that changed a city.

May we note lest we forget.

The day after Benjamin Crowninshield Bradlee died last week, I told my audience that I was going to open my remarks with a question, and I knew I was going to be depressed by the answer.

"How many of you know who Ben Bradlee was?"

There were about 150 people in front of me and five hands went up. Five people out of 150 had heard of the legendary executive editor of The Washington Post, the man in charge of Bob Woodward, Carl Bernstein and the newsroom that broke the Watergate story, the bulldog that barked the truth to power and, as much as anyone, caused the only resignation of a sitting president in our history.

Five out of 150. And that's not the most depressing part. The 150 were in a mass communications class at the University of Memphis, the majority journalism majors.

This is not an indictment of them for failure to be informed, this is an indictment of us for failure to inform.

This is about forgetting, something I get better at every year, and about reminding the present of things past pertinent to who and where we are now. It's about stories that still need to be told.

Nationally. Here.

Which brings me to Memphis in May – helluva segue don't you think?

The day after I spoke to that class, I ran into Lyman Aldrich at RiverArtsFest. How many hands up for Lyman?

In 1976, Lyman was a young banker working Downtown, and Downtown was dying from the malaise that began with the assassination of Martin Luther King Jr. The Chamber was bankrupt, South Main was boarded up, Beale Street was quiet and dark, and so was the spirit of the city.

So, Lyman threw a party with a few friends – Rodney Baber, Harold Shaw, Mose Yvonne Hooks, Tif Bingham, Martha Ellen Maxwell, George Brown, Robin Davis, Jeanne Arthur, Philip Strubing, Richard Bethea, Wise Smith and Tom Batchelor among them. That diverse group took a dormant idea from the struggling Chamber and turned it into the reality of the Memphis in May International Festival. They lit the fire under the barbecue cook-off, turned on the amps for the music festival, tuned up the Sunset Symphony, focused the eyes of entire countries on Memphis and returned the entire city to its riverfront and its soul.

They gave us our pride back and shared it with everybody.

So, if you happen to see Lyman or any of the volunteers from those first years, tell them thanks. They're not responsible for Memphis in May today, or the RiverArtsFest, or the many celebrations we share so often, but without those folks, none of those things would have happened, and none of us would be celebrating what would have happened to Downtown.

As for Bradlee, he's not responsible for what passes for journalism today, but without him, we wouldn't know what we know, and truth would have been given a pass.

I'm a Memphian, and truth and parties are worth remembering.

— — —

Anonymous friends | November 7, 2014

People in Memphis talk to each other everywhere, strangers perhaps in the sense that they don't know each other personally, but open to each other in the sense that they share this place and this day.

That makes this a warm place to be despite the cold and indifferent wind that blows our way from those who would ignore the very many for the benefit of the very few.

We should talk about that.

Honest exchanges.

Parked at the curb, he honked his horn when I walked by, earbuds firmly in place, somewhere in the middle of Morning Edition.

"Where's your wife?" he asked through the open door of the city bus he was driving. "Stress fracture," I answered, "I'm on my own." "Hope she gets better soon," he said, "and tell her I'm retiring November 21st." "I'll do that," I said, leaning in to shake his hand, "and good luck." I stepped back, and he pulled away with another toot of the horn and a wave. He's been waving at us like that for years since his bus is generally passing when we walk out of our driveway each morning, as familiar, he to us and us to him, as one morning is to another, a dependable sign that this day is up and on schedule.

And we don't know his name.

Her shoes were three or four colors, every one of them bright, and the effect served to brighten the dark blue of the Kroger uniform above them. "Nice kicks," I said. "Three bucks at the thrift shop," she beamed as she pointed me to an open self-service checkout station, "and you know I'm all over those sunglasses." A couple of weeks before, I left those sunglasses behind and was about to pull out of the parking lot when she ran up beside me and handed them to me. I see her all the time, and the guy that talks football and shares jokes with me, and the woman who wonders how I find anything but cheerfully serves as guide anyway.

And I don't know their names.

He goes through the mail every day at the UPS Store looking for checks for me. Okay, he sorts everybody's mail that has a box, but we have a system. I walk in the door, catch his eye among all the people and boxes and tape and bubble wrap, and hold a thumb up. If I get a thumb up back, I have mail – two thumbs up and a smile, I have a check. In fact, if there's no check, and he spots me on the phone in the car or in the rain, he'll come to the door and give me the sign not to bother.

And I don't know his name.

These are just a few of the people who share my everyday journey – a very Memphis journey, probably like yours, every day marked by simply genuine and quietly selfless one-on-one exchanges between people who don't really know each other at all. In fact, they're more genuine and far more selfless than the public exchanges between the people supposedly representing our best interest.

And we know their names.

Be honest. At this point – after this or any mud-covered, truth-stomped election – who would you rather run into today – that bus driver, the woman at Kroger, the guy at UPS or any special interest or agenda you know by name?

I'm a Memphian, and that's a name I take personally.

—— —— ——

Who? | January 16, 2015

Two couples of a certain age – let's say mine – are cooking out. The guys are by the grill, their wives across the patio.

One guy says, "We went to a great new place for dinner last night. Just terrific. Loved the food, good service, cool atmosphere. Price was really reasonable."

"Oh," says the other, "what was the name of it?"

"Uh...um," struggles the first, "okay, okay ... red flower, thorns ..."

"Rose?" guesses the other.

"Yeah, yeah, that's it," says the first, and turns to yell across the patio.

"Hey, Rose! What was the name of that place we went to last night?"

And so it goes.

Known but nameless.

Who the hell are you?

I'm not mad at you, I'm mad because I don't know who you are and I should. No clue. Known you since the Earth was cooling and I couldn't come up with your name under Dick Cheney's enhanced interrogation, not if I had to listen to Barry Manilow sing or Rush Limbaugh talk until I came up with it. You look so familiar we might be brothers ... but I know my brothers. Their names are ... give me a sec. I don't have any sisters. I think.

Did we work together, go to school together, get arrested together? Were we ever, well, together? Did I ever give you a pin, a ring, a good time or a hard time? Did you give any of them back? Do I owe you money or you me?

Am I the godparent of one of your children or you mine? Who's your daddy?

All of the above?

This week, every week, somebody behind me somewhere will tap me on the shoulder just as I hear the dreaded, "Hey, Dan." I know as well as I know my own name (Dan, right?) that I won't know theirs when I turn, that whatever goodwill might have built up over decades will be at risk in the nanosecond it takes them to figure out I got nothing....

"Hi," I say, looking into nameless eyes, "(pick one) buddy, pal, bubba ... lady, girl, darlin'... how you doin'?" So pathetically busted.

When I was growing up, I remember my mother turning to call someone and having to go through the entire litany of everyone in the house, including dogs and the odd hamster, before she got to the right name.

I'm so there, Mom.

Growing up in Memphis, you have a zillion associations and more cousins more times removed than clothes at a jiggle joint. My wife Nora used to help me with all those names and connections, but now we stare at each other at a party, a business function or a family gathering, eyes hungry for a hint.

Both starved for recognition.

I used to think that everyone past a certain age – maybe 15 – should be required to wear a nametag, introduce themselves when they see you, and be arrested for stealth name calling if they sneak up behind you. But now we have technology. We can do something much better. We can do an app.

The Who-The-Hell-Are-You App.

When you walk into a room, your smartass phone – in the guise of a call or text, readout on your watch, discreet earpiece, one-way scroll inside your glasses – will tell you if you know anyone in that room and why, who their people are, nickname if any, and if you should run.

If people you're supposed to know blindside you by calling your name from behind, they'll receive an effective bolt of Bluetooth – ask your dog about invisible fences.

I'm a Memphian, and I've got a guy working on this. Can't remember his name.

—— —— ——

Lifelong fan | February 6, 2015

So many people spend so much time worrying about what they think they once had, or might have had, or what they think they're going to lose, that they fail to realize that today – right now – is going to be what the old farts 40 years from now are going to be longing for.

Enjoy the moment. No telling how long it'll last.

You gotta love 'em.

When some fall in love, falling headlong and defenseless, even despite subsequent events and the weight of time and change, never mind the disappointment and the heartbreak – never mind life – the love remains because that fall and the feel of it last a lifetime.

Being a Cubs fan is like that.

"Son," the Knoxville cop said, shining his flashlight in the eyes of the passenger in the car he'd just pulled over, "are you a Cubs fan, or do you just like that hat?" The passenger in the Cubs hat was my son, Gaines, and the driver was his friend, Rob. Both were a little to a lot worse for wear, both back in Knoxville for a reunion weekend with buddies a few years after college. It was 3 in the morning.

"When I was 8," Gaines answered, a bit thick-tongued but meeting the flashlight head-on, "my father took me to Wrigley Field. We sat down the first base line, opposite right field. We had hot dogs. Andre Dawson was right in front of us. He came to bat four times in that game and hit four home runs. I thought he was God." He leaned into the final pitch, "Hell yes, I'm a Cubs fan."

After a long moment, the cop lowered the flashlight. "Y'all be careful," he said, and returned to his cruiser – a chance meeting in the night of two people jilted by the same lover, long-suffering, but still in love.

The Cubs date from 1870, the oldest continuously operating professional sports franchise in the country, and they're loyal and true, the only original National League charter team to still be in their original city. Ernie Banks – Mr. Cub - the Hall of Fame shortstop who slid in safe for the last time two weeks ago – played his entire mid-century career at Wrigley, and he'll be remembered as the best player to never play in the post season. You see, the Cubs haven't won a World Series since 1908, a pennant since 1945.

Being a Memphian is like that.

We bitch. We moan. We have a double-header of an inferiority complex. Hating Nashville for their bluster, Atlanta for their success, trying to be somebody we're not. Like the fans at Wrigley Field, we're so caught up in our miseries of the moment that we no longer feel the love of the place, the warmth of our shared experience. We don't see the impossible green of the grass anymore, the charm of the ivy on the outfield wall, the magic of all those people on rooftops across the street watching the moment.

But we should. We should see our city like we were 8, noting the home runs we're hitting of late and expecting still more from our lineup, seeing the promise of undeveloped talent.

We should be like Ernie, who used to say after any game in his city, win or lose, "Let's play two."

I'm a Memphian, in fact, hell yes, I'm a Memphian.

(Yeah, yeah ... I know. Since this writing the Cubs won the World Series in 2016. Maybe they read this column. I'm going with that. Meantime, keep swinging.)

-- -- --

Listen for home | June 12, 2015

Down here, talking to each other, both invited and uninvited, is more than expected; it's required.

Down here, talking and food are more than linked; like inhaling and exhaling, one follows the other and both are necessary for life.

Down here, talking and laughing are more than common; their absence means someone's died. Wait, we talk and laugh at funerals, too.

Up there, they may wonder how we deal with such things as heat, poverty, trailers that go airborne and legislatures that go backwards.

Well, we talk about them. A lot. And we laugh. A lot. Crying just messes up your grits.

Up there, they need to loosen up.

When you're home. You can hear it.

I was recently reminded of a story I heard from an actor friend years ago when he was in town for a commercial I was making. His name was Robert Lansing – if you're old enough, you'll remember him from TV's "12 O'Clock High."

While making a movie in Georgia, he and a production assistant hit it off. She was as Southern as biscuits and he was as New York as the Carnegie Deli, but she softened his edges, made him remember his childhood in Arkansas. She had a movie in New York in a few weeks – she'd never been there – and he had nothing pressing so they rented a car and meandered up the coast.

After an easy-going thousand miles of grins and grits, they pulled into the city … and a cab cut him off. He got out. The cabbie got out. The box got blocked. The single-finger batons and symphony of horns all rose. He and the cabbie exchanged words, one word employed as noun, verb, adjective and adverb, accented by chest bumps. Vented, both returned to their cars. He noticed that she was all the way over against the passenger door, looking at him like somebody staring at a sweet hound dog just gone rabid.

"Hey," he said, "I'm home."

I remembered that story while visiting our daughter and son-in-law in Lancaster, Pennsylvania – think Harrison Ford going Amish plain in "Witness."

The Amish farms and stone houses, teams of horses plowing fields, buggy spaces reserved at Target and Walmart, rolling hills and flowing streams – all charming. The people, not so much.

The interesting restaurants and long-established markets, the small towns and shops – all big on history. The people in them, just big.

Around here, you can't have anything against big folk, and I don't condemn time spent over Dutch ovens any more than over a mess of ribs, but we serve big personalities on the side. Eating like that, you have to talk about it or it would be against the law.

The other night, I had dinner at the Shady Maple Smorgasbord in Blue Ball, Pennsylvania – no, I didn't make that up and it is, in fact, just down the road from Intercourse, Pennsylvania. Nobody up there thinks that's funny. See what I mean?

The place is a football stadium of food with 1,100 people in there throwing down, nobody saying anything. I've been in noisier libraries. Surveying two acres of stuff covered with several colors of gravy, I couldn't get a word out of the guy next to me about the wonder of it all. I did, however, get a pretty good stare.

A few days later I'm almost back and topping off my tank just outside Memphis when the guy on the other side of the pump starts a conversation about this and that – two old men, one Black and one white, talking about kids, grandkids, dogs, trips and rain, about nothing and everything.

It's not the place, people; it's the people in the place.

I'm a Memphian, and, hey, I'm home.

—— —— ——

Granddad, Hambone and the KKK – a family feud | July 20, 2015

If the Klan doesn't like you, pat yourself on the back.

Before their last sheety little show here a couple of years ago, an Exalted Cyclops of the KKK – must be just one hole in his hood – was quoted on Channel 5 and in The Huffington Post, "Y'all are going to see the largest rally Memphis, Tennessee, has ever seen. It's not going to be twenty or thirty – it's going to be thousands of Klansmen from the whole United States."

Or not. What I said then on that non-occasion, I want to say again.

Whenever the Grand Cretins start blowing smoke, there's not much fire. Something always seems to keep the hood count down. Can't find a clean sheet. The Rottweiler's sick. Nobody to cook the meth. The truck throwed a rod. Something.

But here's the thing. If changing a park's name is enough to get their sheets all twisted and promising a grand racist rally, that's proof the name should be changed. If the Klan is marching against you, you're moving in the right direction. Conversely, if you're for what the Klan's for, you're way out of step.

My grandfather, J.P. Alley, was the editorial cartoonist for The Commercial Appeal and part of the editorial team that won the Pulitzer Prize for the paper in 1923 fighting the Ku Klux Klan.

Moving in the right direction against people worth fighting whose beliefs are worth nothing.

Conversely, the same man created "Hambone's Meditations" in 1916, a cartoon caricature of a black man who delivered his down-home observations in deep dialect. Oblivious of those demeaned and stereotyped, Hambone was endearing to readers, syndicated in hundreds of papers, and quoted daily over thousands of cups of morning coffee in places that would have refused to serve that coffee to Hambone. In its heyday, "Hambone's Meditations" appeared on the front page of The Commercial Appeal's first or second section. My grandfather drew and wrote it until his death in 1934, and my grandmother wrote it and my uncles drew it until it was finally cancelled decades later. That year was 1968, and Martin Luther King may well have seen it in the local paper that last morning.

Way out of step, accepted even adored by Jim Crow, part of our history best left in our past, and a lesson for us today.

My contemporary understanding of how hurtful Hambone was to so many, how illustrative that cartoon was of institutionalized racism, makes me no less proud of my grandfather's immense talent, sharp pen and even sharper wit. He was an accomplished man of his time and never intended Hambone to hurt but simply to amuse, but that time has past and the hurt was real.

Imagine if Hambone was in the paper today. Or on a horse in the Medical Center.

Hurt and hate and attention feed the Klan, so let's stop serving it up. Wherever and whenever those clowns show up with their hooded circus, just ignore them and they'll starve.

I'm a Memphian, and I'm proud that the KKK doesn't like us.

—— —— ——

The original pop-up | February 19, 2016

The 40 Days of Calvary Waffle Shop – aka, Lent – have begun, and it's time once again for an appropriate reading – aka, a Lenten sacrifice you have to make. Over the years, I have provided a recipe for tomato aspic, asked you to try fish pudding on faith, and brought you down front for chicken hash. This year, Boston Cream Pie. But the Waffle Shop version is about as Boston as Beale Street, and if made properly, you shouldn't drive anywhere after having some. (See the "bourbon to taste" part referenced below.)

Boston Cream Pie
Custard

3½ cups milk	¾ cup sugar
5 T flour	3 egg yolks
1 whole egg	tiny (scientific term) pinch of salt

dash (kind of like tiny) of vanilla

bourbon (or sherry, or rum) to taste (go on, give it a shot)

Put milk in a double boiler over medium to high heat. While milk heats, prepare other ingredients. In a large bowl, combine sugar, flour and salt. Add slightly beaten eggs and blend very well. When the milk has formed a skin and bubbles around the edge, pour egg-flour mixture into it and begin stirring with a whisk to keep it smooth, and continue until it thickens. Strain into a container and add vanilla and bourbon/sherry/rum, stirring to blend. Cover with plastic wrap and then the container lid.

Crunch

Equal parts sugar and pecans

Caramelize sugar in heavy skillet on low heat. Mix in equal amount of pecans. Place on greased cookie sheet and let cool. When cool, break into small pieces and grind in a meat grinder (you do have one, don't you?). Don't use a food processor (heaven forbid). This must be done (this is my favorite part of the recipe) on a dry, sunny day.

Spoon custard over slices of sponge cake. Top with whipped cream and crunch.

Pop-up waffles

Pop-up concepts are hot.

Popping up in spaces – Broad, the Edge, the Brewery, the Fire Station – reclaimed and repurposed to show what's possible, the original character of the space adding flavor, the here-today-gone-tomorrow aspect adding spice, the unusual nature of the things served – things not seen every day and everywhere – adding adventure. Millennial curiosity addressed, the need for gratification met, the existential question asked and answered.

What the hell is tomato aspic anyway?

The Calvary Waffle Shop, the original pop-up restaurant in Memphis, has been popping up for more than 90 years for 40-day runs in the basement of the city's oldest public building, Calvary Episcopal Church.

People magically appear down here once a year to make mayonnaise – just mayonnaise, just so – for decades. They stand at a waffle iron making waffles – just waffles, just so – for decades. Mildred Wiggs White did that for 70 years. They put a waffle on her casket. The other day, Steve White – my friend and her son – was serving sausage in front of a plaque honoring his mother's awesome waffleness.

Good stories pop up down here and come back year after year.

This isn't just food, this is Memphis ritual, the flavor of who we are served up one plate, one story at a time, one storied speaker at a time in the church above, for a short time in early spring. It's open only during Lent, and I give up the stuff served here 325 days a year to get to these 40.

Join in the ritual.

On Tuesday it's gumbo, turnip greens, shrimp mousse, pork belly, cornbread and Tennessee bourbon pie. On Wednesday, it's fish pudding and strawberry shaum torte. Fish pudding again on Friday and chocolate bourbon cake. On Thursday, shrimp mousse is back, and corned beef and cabbage and fudge pie. Any day, it's chicken salad and chicken hash, spaghetti and rye bread, peppermint ice cream and chocolate sauce, and the booze-soaked richness of Boston cream pie, the eggy excess of homemade mayonnaise, and the wiggly wonder of tomato aspic.

And waffles and sausage all the time.

Up in the church, noted speakers from across our city and land mount the pulpit for the Calvary Lenten Preaching Series. Down in the basement, the comforting liturgy flows from the kitchen and is richly shared at table. Would-be kings, queens and heirs apparent to our commerce, politics and jurisprudence sit elbow-to-elbow with our hoi polloi, with our characters, legends and pretenders, all in common praise of greased, salted, sugared and floured conversation.

From that pulpit, I once heard famed preacher John Stone Jenkins dealing with one of those existential questions. As to whether or not God answers prayers, "Well, of course God answers prayers," he said, "but very often the answer is no."

Well, until March 18, the answer is, yes, the Waffle Shop is open.

I'm a Memphian, and if you see Millennials at your table acting like they discovered the place, humor them. After all, they are the future.

— — —

High water marks | May 13, 2016

May is a good time in Memphis. Literally.

To those who wonder why we throw such a big party when we face such big problems as a city, why we celebrate so hard when life is so hard for so many of us, I can only offer – because that's what we do.

We live life here realistically, and enjoying each other's company, sharing smiles and songs and food and drink in twos, and threes and thousands is really as good as it gets.

Lord knows, the creek does rise.

The last time I was on a cook team, the Mississippi was lapping at the top of Tom Lee Park and I'd been lapping at a number of things for a couple of days myself.

On May 15, 1983, the river crested at 39.2' on the Memphis gauge, the river and I way above flood stage on anybody's gauge. Very early that morning, I opened my eyes and found myself alone. And on top of the bridge of a towboat, not on the bridge but on the roof, the only thing apparently holding me there was one arm wrapped around an antenna, 10 feet above one steel deck, 20 feet above another, 30 feet above the rising river.

And with absolutely no clue how I got there.

That's when I made one of those deals, "Lord, get me down, and I swear I'll never be on another cooking team." Although I'm not sure the Lord was concerned with one idiot among thousands that night, even one so spectacularly idiotic, I will say this. I'm still here, and I kept my end of the deal. That was my last night as an official participant in the Memphis In May World Championship Barbecue Cooking Contest.

To protect the guilty – no one on that team was innocent – and because there may still be outstanding warrants, I won't name the team, but we did have an impressive run. In my three years, the team won showmanship twice and placed once in shoulders, no small feat for people all but unconscious during the entire competition.

Lord knows, it was and is a party.

On May 10, 2011, the river hit 47.8', the second highest on record. National networks reported that the river was (pick one) 4 or 3.4 or 5 or 3 miles wide at Memphis and that it was normally a half-mile or about a mile and that hundreds or thousands or whole neighborhoods or square miles were evacuated or leaving or fleeing for safety or watching their dreams sink or their lives go under.

Or whatever.

While the nation stared at a raging river behind the reporters scaring the grits out of their viewers, Memphians, including lots of kids and dogs, partied in front of those reporters at the water's edge. Rather than be intimidated by the rising water, the whitecaps seemingly at eye level, people did what people around here do: they helped each other rise above it and turned the whole thing into a larger event than it was before, shared in the power of the moment.

Lord knows, we need our parties.

That capricious river out there is why we're here, its mix of everything and the power of its highs and lows the best metaphor for our challenges and opportunities, its banks the best location for Memphis In May – a month-long celebration right smack dab in the middle of flood season.
In Memphis, we face whatever comes, and dance whenever we can.

I'm a Memphian, and we go with the flow.

— — —

Bridging imagination and reality | September 23, 2016

In 2011, I heard about a new bridge, a new use of an old bridge, actually, and I thought it was a great idea, so I wrote about it. Bridges are great metaphors, after all – connections, divisions, all that. Ideas are great thought starters, after all – inspiration, vision, all that.

This bridge would require a lot of money, private and public, and a lot of engineering. Before that, it would require a lot of cooperation between several city and county governments, a couple of states, federal agencies – and worse – railroads.

So it wasn't really going to happen, but the idea was fun.

Then a funny thing happened.

Getting a big idea across.

Next month, a big idea becomes Big River Crossing, an inspirational bridge between imagination and reality.

Bridges are hard.

I came to that realization a lifetime ago in engineering science lab. In front of me was a pile of balsa wood, Popsicle sticks, string, rubber bands and a slide rule. The assignment – design and build a bridge. At that moment – while I was trying to figure out whether the number on my slide rule was 10,000, 100,000 or 10 million, while those around me began to conquer canyons with their Popsicle sticks – at that moment I knew I would not be an architect.

Bridges are magic.

They connect, enable, overcome, elevate. They make big things possible when they weren't before. They make it reachable for the many rather than the few, doable, accessible. I can continue on a path, finish a journey.

I can get there from here. And I can get back.

They inspire, too. The bolts in their bones that master the mysterious forces of nature, the breadth of their spans that takes our breath away, the height of their towers and the might of their cables that suggest the work of giants rather than mere mortals. The very fact that they exist is a symbol of human accomplishment, testimony to the human spirit.

Come on. Tell me you don't get a little rise every time you drive across a bridge high above the most powerful river in America, our powerful symbol of home.

Imagine walking or running or biking across. Imagine a view of our skyline like no other, pausing over the churning current for the long view past the Hernando DeSoto Bridge to the north and around the big bend to the south. A soaring city on a bluff over here, the oxbows and wildlife over there, and the reason we're here at all flowing far below.

The boundless imagination of Charles McVean and visionary, patient and determined partners public and private have made that view a reality against all odds.

They have resurrected the northernmost roadway of the Harahan Bridge, built in 1916 and shut down in 1949, and converted it to pedestrian use – the longest pedestrian crossing of the Mississippi under the sun, beautifully LED-lit by night, an accomplishment and view stunning enough to give us pause along the way. The reality of the Big River Crossing and the Greenline and all the work along the Wolf means that somebody in Collierville can soon – sooner than anyone thought possible – take a bike or a hike on a dedicated trail all the way to Arkansas.

Big water, big bridges, big skylines and big vistas experienced up close and personal can provide new perspective for big problems. Sharing a trail can give new meaning to sharing views.

Providing all of that on a people scale is a trail marker for a big-time city.

I'm a Memphian, and we've taken a big step.

—— —— ——

One of us | November 18, 2016

We all have a good side and a bad side.

You know, like when you drive by a wreck on the interstate and the good side knows you shouldn't slow down and stare at the carnage, but the bad side makes you do it anyway and backs up traffic for miles.

Well, the bad side just got elected president, and the next four years are going to be just like that.

Implicitly and explicitly, one of us.

I've been reading about implicit bias lately. It's complicated but I like the way the National Center for State Courts describes it. In part:

"Unlike explicit bias (which reflects the attitudes or beliefs that one endorses at a conscious level), implicit bias is the bias in judgment and/or behavior that results from subtle cognitive processes (e.g., implicit attitudes and implicit stereotypes) that often operate at a level below conscious awareness and without intentional control."

In other words, implicit bias is inside of all of us, and explicit bias is what we choose to show.

If you tell me you've never told and/or listened to and/or laughed at a racist or sexist or homophobic joke, I know that's not true, but don't worry. You've been given permission to laugh openly at the expense of someone's soul.

If you tell me you've never assigned, not even a little bit, certain behaviors to entire races, religions, beliefs and countries based on your observations while driving, standing in a grocery line, at work, I know that's not true, but relax. You've been given permission to viciously stereotype anything and everybody anywhere.

If you tell me you've never said anything out loud, not knowing that you would be heard, that revealed something private and hurtful, I know that's not true, but don't be embarrassed. You've been given permission to say any damn thing you want publicly, no matter what it is, no matter who it hurts.

I'm reminded of something the late Redd Foxx said in response to a question about why he used so many foul words in his standup routine. Redd replied if people claim that they never say those words, he'll take them outside and slam their thumbs in his Cadillac door and see what they say.

Last week, the election slammed my thumb in that Cadillac door, and I said all those words.

While we've all done the things above to some regrettable degree, implicitly exposing a darker nature, a nature controlled in the light by civilized behavior, compassion, understanding and maturity – by progress – we've now been given permission to do those things openly with no regret.

Those darker things have now been made explicitly presidential.

So angry about being ignored and marginalized, about a changing world, white males mobilized with such force – many voting for the first time in years – that they ironically voted for change and elected a president that is disliked if not despised by 60-plus percent of America.

So thrilled when he shouted into a microphone the things they wanted to hear but wouldn't dare say outside their circle of support, they not only licensed those things, they celebrated them.

Donald Trump is one of us, but the part of us he appealed to – pandered to, in fact – isn't the part that inspires great things; it's the part that rips us apart.

Now that the worst in us has been released and enabled, pray it can be calmed and controlled.

I'm a Memphian, implicitly and explicitly.

— — — — — —

Thanksgiving. For real. | November 25, 2016

Differences make us who we are, and making room for all of them made us America.

Be thankful for that, and be suspicious of anyone or anything that would make us all the same.

No religious test. No absolute ruler. No citizen above any other. No right denied.

That's American exceptionalism, and it remains an experiment.

Norman's Normal.

You've probably seen "Freedom From Want," Norman Rockwell's iconic Thanksgiving painting.

You know, Grandmother with the turkey so lovingly prepared. Grandfather preparing to lovingly carve it and serve it to the loving bunch assembled. Aunts, uncles, in-laws, kids and siblings, all smiling, all whiter than the white meat in that turkey, the view of the outside world obscured by white curtains.

That was presented as the normal Thanksgiving table of my youth, the table so many of my generation want to set again, the bounty again promised, the control again assured.

Except that nothing was normal when it was painted, and I'm convinced, this year more than ever, that normal is a mythical condition sought in times of trouble, offered by those who would profit from such myths.

Life just isn't normal.

Rockwell painted it in 1942, the world at war. He photographed people at different places for reference and painted them around a mythical table. When it was published as the cover of The Saturday Evening Post in 1943, I wasn't at our table yet. My brothers and mother were, but my father was fighting in the Pacific, and the country was far from free from want.

Thanksgivings at my house were a bit different. The only thing my stone-deaf step-grandfather carved was a tip off a cigar while yelling at my grandmother to get him this or that. My mother and my aunt didn't care much for each other, competitors all of their lives for this or that. One uncle favored rare moments of silence to drop bombshell family secrets about this or that. One older brother was a sullen teenager – aren't they all – brooding about this or that, and the oldest brother was an aspiring writer concerned with deeper meaning about this and that. Another uncle and my father drank a lot of this or that during the proceedings.

And there were guest stars, like a great-uncle who once cold-cocked an uncooperative mule with his bare fist or a cousin who went to the University of the Seven Seas.

As the youngest, nobody was paying much attention to me, attention being very hard to get, so I just watched the show and made sure I got some of the potatoes.

If normal is raised forks and voices, spilled food and confession, too much salt and denial, opinion and people as varied as dishes, and laughter as common as bacon grease and genes, then I guess Thanksgivings were normal.

In my experience, what passes for normal isn't nearly as interesting as that table.

Rockwell painted his scene to give a nation hope, but all the hope we need may be around our actual Thanksgiving tables, because those are real people. No matter how different you may be, you're sharing that table with each other.

No matter how different we may be, we share a country, and we should be thankful.

If we remember that, we can be hopeful.

I'm a Memphian, and, thankfully, I'm not normal.

—— —— ——

Naked truth | January 6, 2017

David Williams, Leadership Memphis President/CEO, recently asked past participants to share their experiences in the program – what was memorable to them, even transformative – what was meaningful to them, even redemptive.

I thought about a story I've told before about skinny-dipping. Then I thought of another about people from housing projects and suburban neighborhoods, very different people from very different places.

Then I realized that all of that is the same story about the same place.

David shared it in the recent Leadership Memphis newsletter, and I'm sharing it here to begin a new year in a very real city.

Naked, and up to something.

Of the occasions I've been skinny-dipping, only one had any class to it. I reprise that story as a reminder that this city truly values reality over pretense, and that is the measure of our worth.

My 1982 Leadership Memphis class held their closing retreat at Pickwick. After I shared a friend's story about a previous retreat ending in late night skinny-dipping, the entire class headed for the dock to continue the tradition. Leaving our clothes in a quick pile, two of us – she will remain nameless – were in the lake immediately.

As it turns out, the other 48 remained ashore; content to have us represent the class and, judging from their laughter, quite happy about it. We swam to a lonelier, darker dock and eased out of the water with a wide-eyed fisherman's help – his jacket, and those wide eyes, went to her and all I got was an oily tarp.

While leading by example doesn't necessarily cause everyone to follow, I was elected alumni president and we both went on the board. After all, we had nothing to hide.

The point – beyond jumping naked into lakes – is the freedom, awareness and empowerment that come from loss of pretense, from knowing exactly who and what you're dealing with, and knowing they know that about you, too.

That Leadership Memphis class began clothed in their respective colors and attitudes, dressed to the nines in custom-fit roles and tailored assumptions. By the closing retreat, all of that had changed because our view had changed, all of us able to see past the surface trappings.

A couple of folks in that class come to mind, on the surface as superficially different as our predetermined boundaries. One was a neighborhood organizer, a struggling African American mother living in the projects trying to make sense out of that life, to make something more. She was Black, loud and proud. Really. One was a bright white suburbanite all the way up to his starched white shirt and at least as stiff, president of his neighborhood association, politically connected, astute. He was right. Very.

When the class got started these two had already marked each other for a tussle or two over the coming months and, sure enough, when the class ended, they had broken out into a knockdown, drag-out, no-holds-barred … hug.

She had something she needed to propose to City Council, something to get passed, but she didn't have a clue how to proceed. He took it on, not taking it over, but taking both of them somewhere together. With him, she got it written, proposed and passed. With her, he found a larger Memphis, larger reasons to be involved.

At the end of that Leadership Memphis class, all of us could see the whole city, warts and all, and we could see us in it together. By then, while just two jumped in the lake, all of us were metaphorically skinny-dipping.

I'm a Memphian, and you haven't seen Memphis until you've seen it all.

— — —

The us of us | February 10, 2017

When President Trump or his surrogates say that his actions are what Americans want, that is only partially true.

The majority of Americans voting did not vote for Trump. In record time and a record low for a new president, a poll released last week (CNN/ORC) shows that 53% of Americans already disapprove of his performance so far.

What is wholly true is that while a president is empowered to speak for America, this president does not speak for a majority of Americans or for what America stands for around the world.

Recognizing that could change and define his presidency. Denying it defines delusion.

I am us.

I am Muslim.

I am a COGIC Hindu Jewish WASP Jehovah's Witness. I am a Roman Catholic Buddhist Satanist Seventh-day Adventist and Latter-day Saint. I am an Atheist Agnostic Humanist Evangelist. I am a Sunni Shia Christian Rastafarian Taoist Sikh. I am a Foot-Washing, Holy-Rolling Jain Spiritualist and whatever Lord Voldemort is – and I am not.

I believe that Karma is a bitch, and I believe in God and Jesus Christ, Muhammad, Yahweh and Ra, Voodoo, Vodou, Vodun and Vudu, and the Holy Spirit, the Great Spirit, Wakan Tanka and Gitche Manitou, and whatever it is that Joel Osteen believes in – and I do not.

I am and believe any and all and none of those things, and that is my right.

I am a latte-sipping, pro-choice, Times-reading, bleeding-heart, civil-rights-whining, know-it-all, gun-toting, Bible-quoting, beer-guzzling, tin-hat-wearing liberal conservative, elitist blue collar redneck suit, and climate-denying, pro-life, social activist skinhead, millennial boomer, pothead professional teetotaler, wrestling fan and champion of women's rights and the far right left.

I am complicated.

I am African-American African Aussie Latino Hispanic Anglo Native-American Scots-Irish Asian, and French Italian Peruvian on my mother's side. I am Middle-Eastern Eurasian Eskimo Russian Scandinavian Lithuanian Swiss Welch Haitian, and Basque German Portuguese on my father's side.

I am human.

I live in the Rust Belt, the Bible Belt and the Grits Belt – and I take a belt now and again. I live on that coast and the other one, and on the shores of the Gulf and all the Great Lakes, and the ones not so great and all the rivers large and small, and in the swamp and in the valley, and on the mountain and this side of the wall. I live in the flyover, the done over, and the all but done. I live up there, down there, over there and out there, in town and in the country, in peace and in conflict, in certainty and in doubt, in wealth and in poverty – and less and less in between.

I am local.

I am a married heterosexual homophobic homosexual single tranny granny. I am a straight queer macho butch bisexual male biker in touch with my feminine side. I am a gender neutral transgender lesbian logger in a gay mood. I am a perfect gentleman and a real lady and a guy's guy on a girl's night out.

I am who I am, and my right to be is guaranteed.

I am equal to everyone by law. I am subject to no religious test by law. I am, whether just born here or just sworn in five minutes ago or tracing to the Mayflower, just as much a citizen as any other citizen by law. I am, whether in a tower or a cellar, boardroom or bordello, answerable to the law.

I am an American.

And because of all of that – all – I am a beacon to the world. When any of that – any – is denied, the light dims.

I'm a Memphian, and an American.

—— —— ——

Of camels and Spoon | May 26, 2017

So we were having a family dinner a while back, a visiting brother and sister-in-law, all our kids, all their dogs and ours. Somebody dropped a piece of steak and meat-lust chaos ensued. My wife Nora was the first to dive under the table to separate the warring dogs and emerged with a bleeding ticket to the emergency room.

I don't believe for a second that Spoon was the culprit. I believe, like Nora, she was just trying to restore order, not add to the chaos. While technically a dog, Spoon was above that sort of thing.

She was above it all.

Spoon. 2002-2017.

We took a left off of I-55 somewhere around Coldwater and drove about 10 miles through farms to our destination. There was a wooden sign with hand-painted numbers by the gravel drive. There was a Shetland pony in the yard. And emus.

And a camel.

Outside the house, seven or eight feral children were playing around a broken-down truck and chasing ducks, geese and each other. Inside, the living room was dominated by two enclosures – a large cage with two wide-eyed, loud and unhappy lemurs in it, and a big playpen holding three wheaten Scottish terrier puppies. A wiggly male. A sleeping female.

And one female apart, considering us quietly, regally, and above all of the above.

From that beginning, we knew this relationship was not going to be ordinary. She was the third Scottie we'd had, so we named her Spoon, the Scots' original name for the three-wood in the game they invented. She was the only dog we've ever had that actually watched television, barking at the dogs she saw, and at the horses – she hated horses – and at the animated bee in the Nasonex commercials.

True to her name, she was the only dog – or person for that matter – that would snuggle next to me and watch golf for an entire afternoon.

While our other Scottie, Putter, would wander the house, Spoon would lie at my feet while I worked. Of course, she loved everything I wrote.

When she was the honorary office manager of Conaway Brown, she was steadfast comfort and a reliable smile among the wild ups and downs of life in an ad agency – beloved of all of us, of our clients and suppliers, of everyone actually, with the possible exception of the carriage horses by The Peabody she barked at as she passed on her way home.

When she got liver cancer a couple of years ago, we made her a promise; she would not suffer. We kept it. Last week, wrapped in a blanket in my arms, her head in Nora's hands, Spoon died.

Quietly, regally, and – as Nora posted on Facebook – above it all.

There are markers in our lives, as unexpected as a camel in a front yard, as indelible as the memories they write, as deep as the love they give and get.

John Brooks, a golfing buddy, gets it. John's in his 70s, and he recently told me he wouldn't get another dog until he was 82. "I've done the math, and I figure that dog will outlive me," he said. "Dan," he added, his hand on my shoulder, "I can't put another one down."

She had a favorite chew toy, a raccoon, and the raccoon and I are sharing a drink as I write this, and Putter is wandering the house looking for Spoon. You can stop, sweetheart, we're never going to find another one quite like her.

I'm a Memphian, and Spoon is gone. In her memory, the family asks that you bark at a horse.

—— —— ——

My American story | June 23, 2017

Spit in a tube, send it off, and the next thing you know you're a Viking. Best of all, your status as an American remains unchanged.

Don't call me Cherokee, just call me Lief.

As a kid, I was told I was part Native American on my mother's side – probably Cherokee, they said, maybe Chickasaw. My mother, my aunt and my uncles weren't sure which and how much,

and my grandmother wasn't talking, but one look at any of them, or at me or my children with our profiles of various 1950s Pontiac hood ornaments, leaves little doubt and more is more likely than less.

That was before Native American ancestry was all the rage, before we talked much about what we've done to our native people, before we became obsessed about being from here, and before we forgot that everybody but Native Americans came from somewhere else.

I've always thought it was cool – using it to claim a spot here from the get-go, to explain why I never liked Columbus, why I thought Tonto in buckskins was always cooler than the guy in the mask and leotards, to explain why my brother and I can't grow beards and our mustaches are pitiful, etc.

But now I know why our other brother is blond and why my son can grow a beard over a weekend.

We're no more Native American than the Queen of England.

My wife gave me an Ancestry DNA kit for Christmas and, being a popular gift, it took months to process. Great Britain, 26%. Ireland, 21%. Europe West, 19%. Iberian Peninsula, 11%. And Scandinavia, 20%. Native American? Not even an arrowhead's worth.

Scandinavia, 20%? I'm boring Brexit white. I'm Viking white. Clorox white.

After I sent the family an email telling them that while a piece of the oil or casino money was out, a discount at Ikea was suddenly possible, my son's response was the best:

"My whole life is a lie."

Instead of feeling sorry for myself at the loss of American original status, I've decided to take advantage of our current alternative-facts environment. To wit:

20% Scandinavian could be Norwegian, which could connect me to Leif Erikson, who was the first European to actually set foot in North America 500 years before Chris, who has his own U.S. stamp, who Congress recognized in 1964 by declaring October 9 as Leif Erikson Day, which is one day before my birthday, which is close enough, ergo....

I'm related to Leif Erikson. Status restored. Eat your hearts out.

Or maybe not, and maybe we can stop using where we were from millennia or centuries or generations ago to determine what kind of Americans we are today. Maybe we can remember that the person who took the oath in broken English this morning in a courtroom is every bit as much of an American as any of us. Maybe we can remember that welcoming the world to our shores was the original American exceptionalism, and that diversity is our DNA.

If we can remember that, we can see just how forgettable our actions as a nation have recently become.

I'm a Memphian, and an American, and don't you forget it.

—— —— ——

Not ours, not theirs | July 7, 2017

As a bona fide Memphis homer, I'm reluctant to talk about anybody else's hometown, but New York just might be America's. After all, there are more of us of every variety in closer proximity there than anywhere else on our shores, so it's a good place to take a pulse.

And they know a con when they see one.

Not the apple of The Apple's eye.

The only other person on the subway platform that night years ago was in a hood-up hoodie and seemed to be about 8 feet tall, and seemed to get taller as he walked toward me. Even sober, I wouldn't be able to do anything about whatever he had in mind, and I was far from sober after a three-hour meal in Tribeca. I was done.

"You look lost, man, where you headed?"

I mumbled something about Brooklyn and Grand Army Plaza, possibly my last words. He then led me up the stairs and pointed to another station two blocks away, told me the train to take, and disappeared back down the stairs, taking another New York stereotype with him.

We think we know about New York – rude, crass, dangerous after dark, cold and impersonal in daylight – teeming streets far below, literally and figuratively, the balconies of those who would control them all, protected by doormen and tax codes and all that money can buy.

We know the stereotypes, but we don't know the city.

In my visits there over the years, I've been impressed and intimidated, awed and anxious as I walked the streets, stunned by the size of buildings and bills, the size of life there.

A few weeks ago, I was charmed.

People smiled and spoke – like they do in Memphis but this was Manhattan – as I strolled for blocks through a Saturday street fair – like Cooper-Young but this was Park Avenue closed to traffic. Bartenders started conversations. Hotel clerks remembered names. People in stores said excuse me when they bumped into you.

With all we've been through as a country lately, we don't have any more time for stereotypes, deciding about everybody and everything based on preconceived, shallow generalizations.

The Democrats lost because they took a huge part of America for granted, and the Republicans won by playing those same Americans like a fiddle. The whole country was had as sure as a game of three-card monte in Manhattan or a $3 bill in Memphis.

We need to get to know, really know, each other again.

Which takes me back to New York, the city the rest of the world thinks of as quintessential America – about 9 million of every kind of everybody from everywhere. There's a statue in the harbor about that. I don't care who you are or what you do or what you're into, all of that is within walking distance, and will walk by you while you're having breakfast. The waiter who served me mine was from North Carolina and wanted to debate barbecue.

Citywide, New York voters rejected Donald Trump eight to one – his neighbors in Manhattan about 10 to one.

They really, really know him.

He will eventually pass into history like a national kidney stone, but if we don't learn to listen to each other again, to respect facts and seek common ground, the pain we're feeling now will only grow.

I'm a Memphian, and if we can't talk – fuhgeddaboudit.

—— —— ——

Watches tell time, and stories | August 11, 2017

I've seen watches like it.

Individuals and families have donated them to the National WWII Museum in New Orleans. Who wore them where and when is identified on cards, both on the European and Pacific Theater sides of the museum. You wonder about those who wore them, who they were, what happened to them.

I've seen watches like it, but this is the only one exactly like this.

It's about time.

It's an old 700 series Rolex watch – stainless steel with a small, military-style black face, hands and numbers that once glowed in the dark, a simple, stainless-steel band and a small brass rivet for a fastener – nothing special by Rolex standards.

It's the most special watch in the world to me.

On one side of the band, this is engraved: Lt. Frank E. Conaway, CEC USNR, 282195 O T-7/43. On the other: Good Luck, Co. B, 123-USNCB.

Much of that is military identification – name, rank, serial number, acronyms for Civil Engineering Corps, United States Naval Reserve, Company B, 123rd United States Navy Construction Battalion (The Seabees). The O is blood type, and my favorite notation, the one people can't figure out when I show it to them is, T-7/43 – the date of Dad's last tetanus shot at the time, July 1943.

This was my father's watch. On his wrist on Peleliu and Guam, and across the Pacific Theater.

On his wrist across my life, and on mine since he died in 1987.

His men gave him the watch. While he slept, they copied the information from his dog tags – even that tetanus shot – and engraved all of it on the watch band, a band they made after also measuring his wrist while he slept and bending the band just so to fit. Family legend has the stainless steel coming from a shot-down Zero, but the fact that his men gave him the watch and made that band requires no further legend.

Over the years, it's run fast and slow, and a lot of not at all. Rolex dealers have looked at it and seen only an old watch, and an opportunity to sell me a new one. Watch repair people have seen only an old watch, and an opportunity to sell parts and charge a lot of money only to tell me there's no guarantee it will run well or for long.

Colin Britton looked at it and saw a special kind of time, time marked in history, time shared across generations, meaningful time, time worth saving. Colin owns Memphis Mean Time – a vintage sort of craftsman, artisan really, in a vintage sort of bungalow on Cooper, who repairs and sells vintage timepieces.

He took Dad's watch and kept it for over a year. I visited regularly and got updates on parts from here and there, found in cyberspace and tried, machined and drilled and tried, sent to Amish specialists and returned, rebuilt and weighted and waited upon and reweighted and adjusted.

I was charged for some of that, but that stopped long ago because Colin became invested in the solution, and what it meant to a guy who kept showing up like someone visiting a family member in ICU.

Lt. Conaway, the men of Company B, and I would like to thank Colin Britton for understanding what's really worth your time in a time of instant gratification.

I'm a Memphian, and the watch is back on my wrist.

—— —— ——

A matter worth raising | August 25, 2017/July 31, 2020

After the sad and revealing events in Charlottesville, I wrote a column in 2017 about symbols. The events of 2020 bore repeating it.

We may actually be on the verge of burying the war no one should mourn. We, the South, may be finally admitting that the primary cause of that war was slavery, and that the loss of that cause should be celebrated rather than honored, that there should be no monuments to any responsible for the rebellion and its unequalled carnage.

One of those, an iconic one of those, understood.

When asked to attend an event at Gettysburg, "for the purpose of marking upon the ground by enduring memorials of granite" the battle, Robert E. Lee declined the invitation in a letter dated Aug. 5, 1869. He ended with, "I think it wiser, moreover, not to keep open the sores of war but to follow the examples of those nations who endeavored to obliterate the marks of civil strife, to commit to oblivion the feelings engendered."

I couldn't agree more, General.

Some 30 years ago, Nora approached the concierge desk at the General Walker Hotel in Obersalzberg, Germany, just below Hitler's infamous retreat, the Eagle's Nest, and just above the town of Berchtesgaden. We'd heard that there was a museum in the hotel's basement. The man behind the desk was behind a newspaper when Nora asked, "Excuse me, could you tell me how we get to the Hitler museum?" He snapped the paper down and in a tone the Fuhrer himself would have been proud of and loudly enough to turn heads in the lobby, he sneered:

"There is NO Hitler museum in all of Germany!"

He then dismissed her by dramatically snapping the paper back up in front of his face.

That response has been our go-to for emphatic denials ever since.

His righteous indignation might have been because he'd been asked that question far too many times, or perhaps the idea of such a museum is embarrassing because of what it means to his country, or maybe just hearing that name even though his hotel exists because of it just ruined another beautiful morning. For so many reasons, Germany doesn't want to dedicate anything to Hitler.

They're not denying history. They're just not publicly reminding themselves of their national disgrace, or turning it into some sort of glory, choosing instead to move on.

Before you say there he goes again, another reference to Hitler to make a point, another gratuitous tie to racism and war and murder on a horrific scale, waving a symbol of all of that in our faces… like the swastikas and Rebel flags waving in the ill wind of Charlottesville, like any symbol that stands for the superiority of race or religion or creed unto the death of others, like any monument that would glorify a crushing defeat of such ignoble causes.

Imagine a statue of Hitler in a city where the majority of the residents are Jewish, or on public property in any city.

Imagine a statue of Rommel in North Africa because he was a great general, ignoring what he fought for and that he thankfully lost. Imagine a statue of Reichsmarschall Goering at Dunkirk or Omaha Beach in honor of all the brave Germans who died in the war, or one of Emperor Hirohito on any number of beaches in the Pacific.

Imagine a statue to Benedict Arnold at West Point, honoring his plan to surrender it to the British.

Imagine public statues anywhere here to the heads of governments and their generals who fought a war against the United States at the price of a generation of their young men to preserve the right to buy and sell human beings.

Just imagine.

Symbols matter. Just ask any of those flag-waving, tiki-torched cretins in Charlottesville.

Ask the men who raised a flag on Iwo Jima and decide – once and for all – which flag to stand for, which flag to follow.

I'm a Memphian, and it's time to look up to something that looks down on no one.

—— —— ——

Hey, hope, how are you? | October 6, 2017

Health care isn't politics. It's not close votes or cold numbers or hot heads or independent scoring. Health care is someone in a bed, dependent on tubes and screens and strangers and mysteries and miracles.

Health care is reason for hope. Health care is survival. Or not.

"Hey, Dan."

I was attempting to visit a friend in extended care at Regional One. That's in the Turner Tower. "The what?" the parking lot attendant replied, and then added, "Got to be one of those."

"The those" were all the backs of all the buildings we were staring at, an architectural metaphor both for the disparate mess our health care system has become and for the navigation of same.

I followed someone in scrubs through a door and asked someone else in scrubs where Turner Tower was. She was kind enough to take me on a "short cut" through all sorts of swinging doors and down long hallways between buildings and by lots of people in nametags to an unmarked service elevator.

When the elevator doors opened, I walked around a corner and into Tem Mitchell's room.

Tem has been an art director and production manager in a couple of my ad agencies, and a steady friend and reliable smile across my unsteady career. When a bookkeeper's malfeasance cost me the last of those agencies, Tem cried when I made the announcement – not for the loss of his job but for pain he saw in my eyes and in the slump of my shoulders.

On a Saturday two months ago, he was playing with his grandkids on a Horseshoe Lake dock. A couple of days later he was in the emergency room, and then ICU, conscious but barely, confused and in pain, and then in some sort of tortured, suspended state. His facial expressions were a map of a mind receiving awful signals and unable to verbally express them, his responses and movements were primal, and then they were almost nothing.

They didn't know what it was – some sort of encephalitis – and then came the diagnosis – West Nile Virus – for which there is no cure. Can mosquitoes ever leave us the hell alone? Gini and the family watched, waited and talked to him all the time with no response. Reality became a visitor as well. Living wills became a subject. Recovery became a hope, and then a distant hope.

He was moved to extended care.

Then I heard he was better. Said something. Told Gini he loved her, knew names of family members, the name of his cat.

"Hey, Dan," Tem said when I walked into the room.

I cried. Not in the room, I was laughing in the room, but out in the hall as I retraced my steps. Scrubs No. 2 walked by again. "Are you all right?"

"Oh, yeah," I said, "I'm fine."

Tem's long and tortuous journey is what health care is really about, not that scary clown circus performing as Congress, not the indifference to millions upon millions who would never have an opportunity for recovery, who would die from a mosquito bite for want of insurance.

No family should have to go through what Tem's family has, but every family should have every chance to hear someone they love say "hey" again.

I'm a Memphian, and hey, Tem.

— — —

Thanks for the light | November 10, 2017

This week, I'm saying thanks for one of this city's true originals as its time is passing. I'm also asking for us to realize that this is a beginning as much as an ending.

Thank you, old friend.

Thanksgiving is coming up, so I'd like to give some to an old friend.

Like many old friends, this one has been there my whole life and has meant more to me than I've said. More talented is this old friend, but sharing of that talent and inspirational in the sharing, and patient in the teaching of those less talented.

Like many old friends, this one has made an indelible mark on this city and that too has gone if not unnoticed, largely unsaid or not said enough. This friend's time is all but past, but the love I have for the passion I saw in this friend and the product of that passion, and the transformative, timeless nature of it remain, will always remain, will always surprise, will always challenge, will always comfort.

This friend has left me breathless since I was a boy and lit something in me that burns still, a creative spark that lights my way.

So, thank you, old friend.

For the smell of linseed oil and wet clay and creation. For pieces of wood and stone and glass and paper and metal and form and promise. For the journey of light across a day and into shadow and through a mind and over paper and canvas. For tubes oozing color with colorful names, and palettes of it, and pencils and ink of it, and pastels of it, and thick oils and acrylics and ghostly watercolors and imagination.

For all of that on drop cloths and in dust from chisels and blades and bleeding out in buckets of brushes. For all of that through tall windows in soaring spaces. For all of that in a forest older than any in the city in a building newer in every way than any I'd ever seen in a time that would help define how I see everything.

And thanks for doing that for my momma who would introduce us. And for my kids who I would introduce to you. And for my city who you would introduce to all of that over generations. Some would earn degrees. Some would become famous. Some would return and teach. Some would just come Saturday mornings. All would gain.

Art is never fully supported in the way that it supports, never fully understood in the way that it understands, but its value is beyond measure and its absence is a particular kind of emptiness, a darker darkness.

Thank you, Memphis College of Art. Thank you for the light.

Perhaps we won't know how cool it is to have a college of art at your city's heart until it's gone, how blank a civic wall can be without its own creations displayed. Perhaps we won't know what architect Roy Harrover gave us in the building itself until it stands empty, the light catching only dust.

Perhaps, but we can create something else here – something painted anew on this canvas – pentimento of an old friend.

I'm a Memphian, and let's begin again.

—— —— ——

This is not a squirrel. | February 16, 2018

Shiny objects, loud noises, sudden movements. And lies.

Distractions and those who would distract turn our attention away from things that truly matter.

Distraction.

Spoon hated squirrels.

Every so often, I would yell "SQUIRREL!", and Spoon would charge the window from wherever she was in full and frantic bark mode, whatever she was doing forgotten in the urgency of the moment. Sometimes there actually was a squirrel, but most of the time I did it for the reaction.

Before I can join Spoon in the afterlife, I'm pretty sure I'll have to atone for that.

A friend and fraternity brother called the other day to talk about the state of this and that. He spent a number of terms in Congress in the House, and after retiring he now splits his time between home and Washington where he does some consulting.

Before leaving office, he rose pretty high in NATO civilian ranks and sat in the meetings when pretty heavy things were on the table. How high and how heavy and his name aren't the subject of this column, because that would just be a distraction. Distraction is the subject of this column. Suffice it to say he's a credible source.

He told me a story. In 2010 – 2010, people – he sat in a NATO intelligence briefing about Russia's plans and priorities. He told me it boiled down to three:

1. Disrupt the European Union and "weaken long-standing western alliances."

2. Undermine bedrock American institutions and beliefs, "specifically the free press and an independent judiciary."

3. Employ cyberattacks to aid in all of that, and to target the electoral

process in western democracies. "When they started in on this one, I had no idea what they were talking about. We all know now."

Well, it's Russia-3, us-0.

When we jerked to the window to look at email squirrels in the basement in a private server, Russia was in our social media like hashtags in Twitter. When we were being told past president squirrels were spying on current presidential candidates, Russia was up in our private business like Julian Assange in a WikiLeaks staff meeting. When deplorable squirrels and small-hand insults were breaking out on every side here, Brexit was actually breaking away in Europe and Russian hackers were breaking in everywhere.

When we were told by every U.S. intelligence agency what Russia was up to, we were then told that it's just fake news about squirrels in the attic.

When there's more evidence of Russian involvement in our election than Russian dressing on a Reuben, we're asked to swallow a tin-foil-hat memo claiming that it's all deep-state squirrels in the FBI and Justice Department.

This is Russia. You remember Russia, right?

As in James Bond and Lotte Lenya and that poison blade in the boot thing. As in Khrushchev, Kennedy and missiles in Cuba. As in Putin in the KGB, in Ukraine, and evidently in your inbox.

This isn't about squirrels. This is about a hungry Russian bear. He's really out there and he's not playing.

I'm a Memphian, and this is a threat to all of us.

—— —— ——

Let's see what you got | June 1, 2018

If we see some of us in what we're watching, some real effort in the endeavor, some real joy in success and real pain in failure, some sharing of all of that with those around us, then we'll get in the game for as long as it lasts.

If we see pretense, we'll walk.

The real game

I've handled two kinds of Canadian Grizzlies.

The first furry transplants played football in the World Football League, changing one of their two names from Northmen to Southmen when they arrived here from Toronto, and keeping their Grizzlies name/mascot/logo, too. I inherited all that as their ad agency.

In a deal that shocked the NFL, the Grizzlies brought Miami Dolphin stars Larry Csonka, Jim Kiick and Paul Warfield to town. The morning after they arrived in 1975 – and stayed out all night partying – I had them, the walking dead, on the Liberty Bowl field to shoot TV spots.

Warfield never said a word, but ran the patterns requested and caught the passes, and wrapped himself in a wet towel. Kiick threw up. Twice. I'll never forget what Csonka said to my cameraman and me:

"You get one more take. If you ask for another one, I'm going to shove that camera up…."

I'm guessing you can finish that phrase. I'm also guessing you already know we only needed one more take.

Memphis loved them.

The second batch of bears played, and still do, in the NBA. When they arrived from Vancouver with a bad team, bad colors and an even worse logo, they decided, what the hell, we'll keep the bad name, too. I inherited all that as their ad agency.

Their president of business operations, Andy Dolich, got Memphis faster and better than anyone I've ever worked with from out of town – and he was from way out of town, a native New Yorker and adoptee of the San Francisco's Bay Area. He knew you had to get involved, you had to relate, and you had to make the whole thing a whole lot of fun. In the first three seasons of bad basketball in a dead building, we built a fan base.

Right before his first season in 2001, the National Player of the Year out of Duke and Grizzly signee, Shane Battier, was jogging by my office as I sat out front eating a sandwich. I'll never forget what he said when he stopped and shook my hand:

"Is that barbecue?"

Memphis loved him.

In Memphis, it's not larger than life that attracts; it's life. People and moments, shared spaces and places that are part and parcel of where you live and what you do, and dealing with all of it.

Our music is about that. Our celebrations and our tragedies are about that.

It's not slick; it's real. It's about us, about things you can't make up.

So now comes a new pro soccer team to share the field with the Redbirds. Some wonder if they'll make it, others moaning that they're not "big league," but that doesn't matter.

We'll go, we'll drink a beer, and if we have a good time – we'll come back.

I'm a Memphian, and if you give us the best you got, that's what matters.

— — —

Lessons from Ronald McDonald | July 6, 2018

You're about to find out that I was Ronald McDonald once. Paid 25 bucks an hour. In 1972 that was serious money. If you don't believe me, I've still got the suit. Keep that to yourself. McDonald's doesn't know.

A lot of what I know about marketing and messaging, McDonald's taught me, and now it runs in the family.

Circles and arches

Our son, Gaines, called the other night and we talked a bit about business, his now and mine once.

My mind wandered to a convertible in a Christmas parade in Jonesboro, or maybe Jackson, Tennessee, or it could have been Tupelo. Wherever it was, Ronald McDonald jumped off the back of the convertible, ran along the edge of the crowd shaking hands with kids and doing the Funky Chicken with any volunteers he could find.

That particular Ronald McDonald attended the very first Ronald McDonald School in 1972 at McDonald's brand new headquarters in Oak Brook, Illinois. The second day, everyone was paired with someone for the makeup training … think pancake and half a jar of cold cream. For several hours, each Ronald-in-training sat six inches across from another Ronald and critiqued the red and white face in front of him.

I was that particular Ronald McDonald, and the face across from me was Ray Kroc's … as in founder. He was in his early 70s at the time, but he attended every session because he wanted to see how it was done, and could be done better.

Two all beef patties …

A couple of years later, a McDonald's owner/operator in Birmingham sent me some Big Mac product footage and told me to listen to the jingle embedded. He thought there might be a promotion in there somewhere, and he knew my ad agency was looking for something for this market.

special sauce …

With a big chunky tape recorder, we went all over the city of Memphis getting people to say those now familiar words in four seconds or less – from cops at the jail, to potheads in Court Square, to the trading floor of E.F. Hutton – as in – "if E.F. Hutton says …"

lettuce, cheese, pickles, onions …

The first 60-second radio commercial that Allan Tynes and I put together at WREC in the basement of The Peabody had 32 edits in it, done with a razor blade and splicing tape. You know the rest. The idea went national, first on radio and then TV.

and a sesame seed bun.

My career began with McDonald's, and I worked on the account for about 12 years. While I learned a lot about hamburgers, fries and a Coke, I really learned about product mix and preparation, food and paper cost, customer preferences by product and time of day – and that each of those customers was the boss, that each restaurant was the measure of the company worldwide, each French fry the marker. And I learned how the makeup looked on each Ronald McDonald.

Now I've come full circle, because Gaines has been a regional marketing manager for corporate McDonald's for a couple of years, and then moved into regional operations.

I'm hearing lessons learned in a phone conversation with the next generation.

So, I want to thank McDonald's for several things: jumpstarting my career, for Gaines' career at this stage, and for the Egg McMuffin.

I'm a Memphian, and that's a damn fine sandwich.

—— —— ——

Memphis to the bone | August 2, 2018

Here through it all, from a booming post-war Downtown to a virtual ghost town to today's revival, you could always get a cold beer and local flavor in Charlie Vergos' basement.

The next generation runs the show now, a hit for 70 years – updated, yes, but still Charlie's original script. There are waiters who have been there 40-plus years, a father and son collectively serving 60-plus years. My son worked the bar years ago. There are pictures hanging crooked on the wall that haven't been straightened in my lifetime, and people I've known that long are in there every time I go.

It feels like family in that basement, and the family is doing fine.

"We're not blowin' smoke, we're makin' it."

There was a Downtown bar my brother, Frank, and his crowd used to visit during college in the middle '50s. The place was in a basement, dark and funky, but the beer was cold and cheap, and the food was simple and satisfying.

"They served one thing," Frank remembered, "a ham and cheese sandwich, a huge thing the owner would build from the chunks of ham and cheddar he hacked off and slapped between pieces of rye. There might have been pickles, yeah, pickle spears. You took it the way you got it. You didn't mess with this guy. I once saw him come out of the back room with a keg of beer under each arm – two kegs at once, Danny. There were no fights down there. Nobody got out of line."

The ham got its character from a coal chute converted into a smoker, and the place got its character from its owner. Original. Straightforward. Real. So Memphis you can smell it and see it in the wood and brick, in the color and cookers, in the blackened ceiling beams from former fires, in the city's eclectic pulled from the corners of our attics to cover the walls, in the meat served, in the meat of the place itself – like its city, a place you can't make up, you can't fake.

You can't fake Charlie Vergos. You can't fake the Rendezvous.

Charlie's gone but Charlie's here in the smoke. The ham sandwich is still here, but the ribs Charlie invented under that coal chute and added to the menu made the place work, and Charlie's stubborn refusal to do anything any way but his made it iconic. You could get beer – I think just Michelob draft, a soft drink – I think just one brand. Don't ask for coffee or iced tea, or salad or dessert. If you had a pitcher with something in it and ribs left to eat, you could stay. Otherwise, we got people waiting.

"Not since Adam has a rib been this famous."

When my friend John Vergos convinced his father to let him reopen the shipping business 20 years ago, he asked my agency to help. My business presents more opportunity than most to have a certifiable blast, and writing for the Rendezvous was way up there.

"Your basic Rendezvous basement: off an alley, behind a parking garage, full of three generations of family junk, and the most tasteful place in the world to eat ribs since 1948."

The Rendezvous just turned 70 and the party was a couple of weeks ago. John, Nick and Tina – generations of the Vergos family were there, regular folks, the famous and those who would be were there, our memories were there.

Be assured, even though John has eased wine onto the menu and slipped in his momma's Greek salad, Charlie is still there. John's been careful. You don't mess with Charlie.

The Rendezvous is the stuff of Memphis.

I'm a Memphian, and happy birthday to one of our own.

—— —— ——

Just imagine | November 16, 2018

Incoming Gov. Bill Lee is said to be what's known in these parts as "an upstanding Christian." He's also said to be against accepting aid long offered to the least of us.

Like all of us, he has some work to do.

I'm feeling better, thanks.

It all started more than two years ago with a little yip in my giddy-up and proceeded up and down both legs in pain levels measured from 1 to 10 – 1 being that yip and 10 being OMG if I move at all I'll never stop screaming – settling on a constant 4 to 6.

There's a precious little chart in examining rooms with those pain levels illustrated by smiley and frowny faces. Every time I see one of those, I go up a level.

A year and a half or so of this odyssey was with the bone folks, including tubing in an MRI, two nerve blocks and a bunch of physical therapy, and then I moved on to the spine folks, a much noisier MRI, two more nerve blocks, and, finally last week, spine surgery.

Just imagine.

I started writing this a couple of weeks ago sitting in yet another doctor's waiting room to get yet more blood tests preceding surgery. Right after pouring out 12 vials of blood for those last week. Right after filling out yet another ream of badly-copied forms, a couple hundred "yes" and "no" checks about the myriad options of general human malaise.

Right after doing all of that for the doctor who sent me here, right after doing all of that for the doctor who sent me there the week before that. Long after doing all of that over and over for the doctor who started all of this. These people really have to start talking to each other.

Counting the 18 vials on this visit and the three I chipped in right before surgery, I'm 33 vials in. I've been tested more than the entire Russian Olympic team, but that's a low bar.

Just imagine. Just imagine if I didn't have insurance.

You think I've been complaining up to now. Not at all. Following last week and with all that time in waiting rooms to think about it, I'm immensely thankful for the care I've been given, and incredibly aware of the privilege inherent in that care because of the insurance I have. All those tests. All those tours of beautiful tree-lined medical campuses in East Memphis, Germantown and Collierville. The instructions to surgery included, and I'm not making this up, "after valet parking under the awning, turn right inside past the Starbucks to ambulatory surgery."

Just imagine, if I hadn't been able to pay for insurance all these years so I could live long enough to get Medicare.

Just imagine if I was working two jobs with that kind of pain still underinsured or without insurance at all, still under the poverty level, but not far enough under to get Medicaid.

Just imagine living in our state, where 300,000 or so of our fellow working citizens are still denied Medicaid so somebody can make some kind of sad, sadistic political point, so we can be among national leaders in rural hospital closures and increased pain for our poor, so our federal tax dollars can provide that kind of life-saving help to 36 other states but not our own.

Of course, we have an opioid crisis in Tennessee, because even if our uninsured can get to an ER, they're going to be given pain pills and sent home because that ER is overwhelmed, or they're going to get some anyway they can to make it all go away. Of course, we're unhealthy and fat, because we're not only denied preventive care but any care at all.

Just imagine that. In 2018. In Tennessee.

I'm a Memphian and I'm feeling better, thanks. My state, not so much.

— — —

Remember | June 13, 2019

When I first wrote about my brother's Alzheimer's and my memories of him, Harry Freeman, a very thoughtful friend, sent me a Nellie Fox baseball card. My first glove was a Nellie Fox model, given to me by my father and brother, Frank Sr. and Frank Jr., when they taught me to play baseball.

I wrote about that memory, and as I write this, I'm looking at that card and remembering.

Stream of consciousness

A couple of weeks ago, we made our way down the steep hill behind my brother's house in the southern Adirondacks, winding our way through the many trees guided by the roaring sound of the stream below, water over falls, gathering as we did at a pool at the bottom.

On what would have been his 83rd birthday, my brother Frank's family spread his ashes across the fall above that pool.

On his 82nd birthday, he and I shared birthday cake on the screened porch above the stream, and we shared stories and laughter that could have been shared on the porch at 491 S. Highland where we grew up. He was clear and focused – his hands gracefully sculpting the story as he told it, casting words as he did the line from his fly rod thousands of times on hundreds of rivers and streams.

He was enjoying himself – his laugh, sudden and big, rewarding me for something I said. The moment erased decades and the weight of their passage. He was my big brother and I was a little boy, and he was all mine on that porch – a rare moment in both of our lives.

The next day, he wouldn't remember any of it.

When Frank was diagnosed with Alzheimer's a few years ago, I wrote about remembering him, and I'm remembering again today. He was 13 years older, the blond guy in the living room reading books and blowing smoke rings, off to college when I was 5, married and off to the Iowa Writers'

Workshop when I was 12.

The summer when I was 6, I was playing with a stick in front of the house, pretending it was a Musketeer's sword. I waved it at some young man passing and he yanked it away, broke it, and pushed me onto the sidewalk. Frank saw that from the porch, caught up with the guy two doors down, and knocked him through a hedge.

Frank wouldn't remember that, but I do.

The summer when I was 7, I came home in tears because everybody knew how to play baseball and I didn't. Dad and Frank knew this was a crisis and spent the rest of that day and most of the next out in the yard with me throwing, catching, swinging, running and then rubbing my brand-new glove down (Nellie Fox model) with neat's-foot oil, sticking my brand-new ball in it (Rawlings), and tying it up with string.

Frank Sr. and Frank Jr. wouldn't remember that, but I do.

Alzheimer's insidiously took our father, and I think our mother, too, the constant pressure of caring for him causing the aneurysms that eventually took her. Frank's Alzheimer's was a quieter monster than the one Dad lived with but still hell's own invention. The strength of my sister-in-law, Terry, and the devotion of their friends were powerful weapons and the medications to keep the monster at bay weren't there for Dad 30 years ago. But still.

In the last years before he died last November, Frank lived in the moment. When the moment had no pain, and there was laughter in it, sharing in it, clarity and light in it, it was truly fine. When the pain and the anger came, there was blessed irony in the knowledge that they too will be forgotten.

I still haven't spoken to my other brother, Jim, or my children about hereditary implications of Alzheimer's, or being tested, or other things in the closet or under the bed and maybe we'll get to that, and I don't know what's coming, but I do know this.

It is up to us to make sure that those we love are reminded of that love and remembered.

It is up to us to make the most of our moments because they are fleeting.

I'm a Memphian, and my big brother is remembered.

—— —— ——

A mixed drink in Memphis | July 5, 2019

I joined a friend for a drink at the brand-new diner/bar at the brand-new Hotel Indigo the other afternoon, at once retro and completely fresh. Late afternoon sun streamed through the big windows and bounced off the slick and shiny surfaces of the reimagined space, bringing that space back to life again, and taking the corner in a new direction. Once an innovation – an old-school highway Holiday Inn complete with rooms opening onto outside walkways over a courtyard pool, stacked on top of a parking garage in an urban setting – the concept first became tired, and then abandoned, and then forgotten in a forgotten block, and now remembered in ways cool enough for this and the next generation.

And on another corner of the same block is the Sterick Building, once the tallest building in the South, once full of the promise of a region, now and long empty of any promise at all.

Different corners, same block, same city.

When I left the Indigo and walked west on Court, I was struck by the sight of the Hebe Fountain in Court Square, framed by trees in a bright halo of light. The same late afternoon sun that had bathed our table and lit the contents of our glasses roared through the water pouring over the top of the fountain, backlighting the whole of the flow, and at the same time, illuminating a thousand individual drops dancing through the fall.

And yet only one side of the fountain worked, the working shining side seemingly laughing at the hapless other, one celebrating, the other left to watch.

Different sides, same thing, same city.

I spent a recent morning in Crosstown Concourse writing, seven floors up in a sun-filled atrium, the sounds of bustle rising from the lobby below as the diverse purposes of this place go about their business in creative concert. Up here, a young man three chairs down the balcony was working in his journal, a young woman over there in her sketch book, and another behind me beneath a window had drifted off, both she and her laptop sleeping for the moment. A peaceful moment. A hopeful moment.

And there I was in this giant testimony to vision and innovation because I had no power in my office at home for the second day and I needed a place to plug in and work, my City Council unwilling to invest in utility upgrades and infrastructure. And there I was writing the column that ran last week about senseless loss and deadly violence that so challenges our spirit and troubles our soul.

Different experiences, same people, same city.

All of that is Memphis, and none of that is all we are. The Hotel Indigo is one example among many lately of the promise so many see in us that we don't see ourselves, and the willingness outside investors have to bet on us. While the Sterick Building stands as one reminder among still too many of what doing nothing looks like, Crosstown Concourse stands as a reborn fortress of Memphis imagination, and it's far from alone. We all share the pain of crime and violence, poverty and neglect. To get better, to be better, we must also share the nascent prosperity that seems headed our way.

And as for the Hebe Fountain and the larger metaphor, while only half of it works, I'm hopeful that the whole of it is now drawing our daily attention.

I'm a Memphian, and here's to tomorrow.

(It should be noted that the landscape – the mix if you will – is changing yet again as the pandemic has its way with us, with the world. We will survive.)

—— —— ——

Memphis still amazes. It just amazed me. | August 16, 2019

Toledo, Ohio, visited Memphis the other day and I went along.

They began at the Tennessee State Welcome Center just off Riverside. You know, that place you've never been that you pass by on the way to Bass Pro. You know, the former Pyramid.

They mingled with three other tour groups, four buses full, and two bearded bikers in leather and bandanas on tricked-out Harleys. The tour groups were from all over the country. The bikers were from Switzerland.

They wandered around the bustle-filled, babble-filled building, spending time with the big statue of B.B. King, posing for pictures in front of the big statue of Elvis, taking in the imposing view of the bridge and the Wolf River harbor, hitting the restrooms and grabbing brochures, and then back on buses and gone, the building empty again, waiting again like a beginning you've looked forward to, like a smile about to happen.

Just another 20 minutes in the Tennessee State Welcome Center Downtown.

My friend Lynn had the microphone on the bus. He tells Toledo about Memphis in more of a casual conversation than a presentation. He doesn't read anything; he doesn't pitch anything. He just tells them a story about a city.

About this building or that place outside the bus windows and their role in history. About things that changed the world. About the first Piggly Wiggly at Main and Jefferson and the invention of self-service shopping. About an apartment in government assisted housing where a kid from Tupelo lived in high school. A kid named Elvis whose music changed the world. About a river that made us a city and put railroads and highways here, about a company that made our airport the second largest cargo airport in the world. A company called Federal Express whose system of delivery has changed the world. A shot fired from a rooming house bathroom window toward a motel balcony. A shot that killed a modern-day prophet and changed the world.

The first stop was St. Jude Children's Research Hospital, you know, that huge coral-colored complex that's getting even huger, full of huge and even huger hope for children and their families. A place that changed and is changing the world. Toledo actually gasped when they saw it. They couldn't wait to see the Danny Thomas Pavilion, his gravesite, and the exhibits about St. Jude's history. They knew all about St. Jude.

You see, a Roman Catholic kid born Amos Muzyad Yaqoob Kairouz grew up in Toledo. You know him as Danny Thomas. As the story goes, when he was down and out as a young man with a young family, he prayed to St. Jude Thaddeus, patron saint of hopeless causes, for help with his career, promising to build a shrine to the saint upon his success. He founded St. Jude Children's Research Hospital in 1962.

One of the key figures in founding the hospital with Thomas and placing it in Memphis was our own Dr. Lemuel Diggs. In 1963, Dr. Diggs saved my life. He was called in when I lay in a hospital bed for weeks with my platelets and my parents' hope falling by the day and nothing working. Whatever he did, I went home because of it. Something that changed my world.

And I learned about Dr. Diggs' involvement with the founding and work of St. Jude in the middle of writing this column when I Googled Danny Thomas.

The last stop for the bus was the requisite visit to The Peabody, a nod to the ducks, and up to the roof to see their digs. A woman stood next to me as we looked over the edge and rooftops to the river. "Beautiful," she said. "Just beautiful."

I agree.

Even with all of our problems – and we have our share – even with our colossal civic inferiority complex – and it's a beaut – this city's capacity to surprise and amaze in meaningful ways is still a source of amazement for me.

If you think our ability to change the world with things we do here is behind us, just ask the people at St. Jude about what they do every day, or FedEx what's taking off, or Indigo Ag what's being planted, or the National Civil Rights Museum what's moving forward from that balcony.

If you think what Memphis has done and can do doesn't matter out there, just ask the people on a tour bus from Toledo.

I'm a Memphian, and just ask me.

—— —— ——

The extraordinary ordinary | September 6, 2019

We walked along the edge of the water, my son and I, talking about this and that, beers in hand. We had to actually dodge dozens of bald eagles who were also walking along the shore, casually scavenging, and not paying much attention to us. Once in a while, one would pause to stare at us as we passed. And, my friends, an eagle can stare.

Across the water, I could see three layers of snow-covered peaks. My son noted that I had stopped talking, rare for me, and that my jaw was hanging open in the moment.

"Yeah," he said, "Pretty much mountains, pretty much everywhere."

We were in Gustavus, Alaska, and Gaines had already been there for three months when Nora and I visited.

After graduating college, he was working the summer at Glacier Bay Lodge in Glacier Bay National Park, and what we were looking at was his ordinary, everyday experience.

We were there for just four of those ordinary days.

I saw the aforementioned eagles on shore, and I fed sea bass from my hand to eagles in the air from the transom of a small boat in the Icy Strait.

I saw countless king crabs with 4-foot wingspans off the dock one morning, and at least 30 30-ton humpback whales leap out of the water just off our port and starboard rails one afternoon.

I saw huge glaciers calving huge sheets of impossibly brilliant blue ice formed from snow that fell during our Revolutionary War, and a whole rocky island covered with thousands of puffins.

What we didn't see during a full day on the water in sight of shore was a single sign of human habitation or endeavor other than two kayakers we picked up from an island.

I saw a big bull moose watch us pass from the edge of the road on the way from the airport to the lodge, and I saw a 140-pound halibut on the end of my line that felt like I'd just hauled up a barn door from the bottom.

What we didn't see was an 8-foot grizzly stand up on his hind legs and look through the window of our room at the lodge, but the people on the lodge deck did.

The modest lodge is the only hotel in the park, and the park is more than 3 million acres in southeast Alaska, 2.8 million acres of it official U.S. Wilderness with 700 miles of shoreline. That's about the size of Connecticut. Put another way, you could carve Yellowstone out of it and still have more than a million acres left.

The only road into the park was the shortest federal highway in the country then and probably now, less than 10 miles from the tiny town of Gustavus to the lodge, and you can only get to Gustavus by air or boat.

The Gustavus airport was the smallest in the country to allow Boeing 737's to land, one flight a day in the summer when we visited and always in daylight. There were no lights: Our flight landed, taxied to the end of the single runway with the nose almost touching primeval forest, turned around like a big truck in a cul-de-sac, and returned to the ersatz terminal.

There were two small buildings. One was for the single jet and staffed by one bored ticket agent and one bored TSA agent with one scanner. The other was for the many small planes and staffed by one sturdy woman with a sturdy pigtail who made the coffee, baked the muffins, tended the small bar, took the tickets for small prop plane passenger flights, loaded and unloaded the luggage, and kept the locals company on the front porch where they sat and watched takeoffs and landings.

Pretty much unique, pretty much everything.

That trip was 16 years ago, and I'm still reminded of it often, and I'm often surprised by what reminds me.

This morning, I saw three finches scrambling for position on the bird feeder outside my screened porch. A few days ago, I saw our daughter hold her new nephew for the first time on his father Gaines' birthday, and I saw his family and ours around the table at Pete & Sam's.

I'm a Memphian, and the sights in Gustavus, and on my screened porch, and at Pete & Sam's, are extraordinary.

— — —

4,000, 801, 70, 24 and counting | September 20, 2019

Recognition is every bit as much a part of a bicentennial as celebration, the whole of history much more informative and instructive than the picking and choosing of the parts we like, honesty more genuinely healing than fantasy.

It's time to revisit a past column, because it's well past time to be honest about our numbers and their toll.

As people are being shot while shopping and praying and driving because of where they might or might not be from, or because of what they might or might not believe, or just because of what they look like, it serves us well to remember that we have plenty of history of homegrown terrorism.

We didn't import it from Syria or Mexico or the vilified country or religion of the month – not even from somewhere else in this country. It's from right here, directed at fellow citizens, and as Southern as grits and as local as barbecue, and a lot more recent than we'd like to think.

About 4,000 people were lynched in the South between the Civil War and the civil rights movement, about 800 more than previously thought due to the research of the Equal Justice Initiative. The 'about' part is significant since those kinds of statistics are more carefully hidden than proudly claimed.

They were brutally murdered – many times before cheering crowds and reported in local newspapers – in 801 Southern counties, 70 of those counties in Tennessee. And of those, Shelby County was first with 18 lynchings, according to the Tennessee Encyclopedia of History and Culture. That sad number is at least 24 according to research by the Lynching Sites Project of Memphis and others.

I first wrote about this two years ago after reading two things that caused me to take a wide-eyed look at myself and where I live, and to see the danger in denial and the hope in honesty.

One was a book, "Just Mercy," by a Montgomery, Alabama, civil rights lawyer and founder of the Equal Justice Initiative, Bryan Stevenson. The other was an article by Jeffrey Toobin in The New Yorker about Stevenson and his work. Stevenson was honored by the National Civil Rights Museum in 2016 with the Freedom Award.

Since then, Stevenson and the EJI have opened the Memorial to Peace and Justice in Montgomery, a memorial to the 4,000 who died so horribly and have been so forgotten.

Central to its design are 801 columns – one each for the lynching counties, each colored by soil from that county – that visitors see as they approach, and then note that each is hanging. There are 801 duplicate columns as well, and Stevenson's vision is an invitation to each of the counties to come and claim their column and then display it at home.

Since then right here at home, the Lynching Sites Project of Memphis has launched a Duplicate Monuments Task Force to do just that, coordinating all the various entities that must come together to make it happen. They also continue their work to place monuments at the actual lynching sites in the county.

I'm repeating my earlier recommendation about where our duplicate column should go, on a perfect corner to remember what Billie Holiday called "Strange Fruit" in her haunting song, and perhaps be haunted no more.

I visited that corner when a group of people as diverse as the city gathered there in 2015 for an "Interfaith Prayer Service for Truth," asking that our whole history be told, that we share the pain of our past and the responsibility for our present and future so that healing can begin. They read the names of victims of lynching in Shelby County, and asked that they not simply be remembered but the sites marked, the truth noted. We all sang "Amazing Grace," the redemptive hymn written by a slave ship captain turned Episcopal priest.

I visited the corner again in 2018 when a marker went up telling the whole history of what was once there: a slave market owned by Nathan Bedford Forrest. The new marker was sponsored by Calvary Episcopal Church, Rhodes College and the National Park Service. The old state marker at the site simply notes that his home was there, and that "his business enterprises made him wealthy."

The corner once had a statue of Columbus, since moved, but the platform remains, and waits. Directly across the street is the site of justice in Shelby County, the D'Army Bailey Courthouse.

Only the whole of history can warn us of what we're truly capable of and truly inspire us to be better.

If we have the courage to, as Stevenson says, "confront the truth of our past" and simultaneously our present, we should applaud when our column stands at the corner of Adams and B.B. King, when the infamy of being first in lynchings in Tennessee can rest in peace.

I'm a Memphian, in whole and in part.

—— —— ——

A note on my birthday | October 18, 2019

We sat on the edge of the loading dock behind the main library and went through the pages of the book together. Pausing to figure out what we were looking at, where it was, what's there now.

He was African American and younger than me, probably about 40 but that's decades younger than me, so I remembered many of the places pictured and he didn't, and I had what old men like me love; an audience that was interested in what I remembered, the pictures and places coming back to life for both of us in a shared moment.

The small book was "Memphis Movie Theatres" by Vincent Astor. It was on top of a big box of books I was donating to the library. He worked at the library and was taking a break out back when I pulled up. I won't tell you his name because I guarantee he was out there with me longer than that break was supposed to last.

I was going to take the book back home because it was inscribed and I hadn't intended for it to go in the box, but now I knew the book was staying with him. He saw magic there. Places he'd never seen in a place he'd lived all of his life.

As we talked and looked and laughed, I realized that he not only didn't know about the old movie palaces and neighborhood theaters, he didn't know about what's there now. He didn't seem familiar with the current Memphis, much less the old one.

But it wasn't that at all.

He didn't know about my Memphis, my reference points old and new, and I didn't know about his, his city compass mostly south to north, mine east to west.

Different worlds in the same world. Different cities in the same city.

Last week I had a birthday – a big one – and birthdays can cause reflection. What's changed and what hasn't. The technology I've seen and yet paper towel dispensers still don't work. Becoming a food city and yet decent onion rings are harder to come by. Coming so far and yet trying so hard to go back.

Progress and no progress.

And last week I got a note from my friend, Howard Robertson – I'm calling it a birthday card.

He was remembering when he was 21 and trying to figure out what to do and his father arranged for him to get a tour of an advertising agency. I was the older, experienced guy assigned to give him that tour. I was 23. In the note, Howard said that tour and my enthusiasm convinced him that world was where he belonged.

The real reason for the note was to give me the news that his son, Ryan, has just been named one of the "Top 40 Under 40" nationally by Ad Age – if not the bible of advertising, certainly the hymnal – and Howard was trying to say I had something to do with getting the family going in advertising.

Buddy, you and Beverly and a community – and Ryan – did this. What I think you're saying is thanks for being there from the beginning and for knowing how hard, and hopeful, and fun it's been. Right back at you, and give Ryan a hug for me.

Howard and I have always had our differences – he's taller, but I'm cuter – he's African American, I'm Viking white – but we've always been able to bring differences together for more effective communication in the projects we've shared in the city we love since that agency tour in 1973.

There's a guy on a loading dock, on a lot of them, and people on corners, thousands of them, who are a nudge, a notion, an opportunity and a belief in themselves away from changing everything.

The progress we want doesn't depend on knowing our place; it depends on sharing it.

I'm a Memphian, and my city and I are having big birthdays this year, and we're both far from through.

—— —— ——

They took his balls; we'd like them back | November 1, 2019

As I write this, Michael Dickerson (extra points if you know who that is) is nodding at me. So are Pau Gasol and Shane Battier. And Lorenzen Wright and Jason Williams and Stromile Swift. And, of course, Elvis is right in the middle in his Grizzlies jersey, No. 01. They are all enshrined in a case on my desk, a full set of the original Grizzly bobbleheads and one of my proudest possessions.

The bobbleheads were the idea of my friend, Andy Dolich, the first president of business operations for the Memphis Grizzlies, and the full set was a gift to me during season one.

He sent me an email the other day. This was the subject line: "I've lost my balls."

You've got to open that.

When the Grizzlies came to town almost 20 years ago, all the major ad agencies in town went after them and threw heart and soul into the effort. Come on. This was the NBA and a literal game changer for Memphis. When we made the final two, I was as proud of my bunch as I'd ever been.

We went to the Grizzlies office for that presentation and watched the other finalist leave after making their pitch, looking happy, shaking various hands. Then somebody came out from somewhere and told us that management had been called into an emergency meeting and a conference call with ownership and we'd have to reschedule.

In other words, don't call us, we'll call you. I watched the air go out of my people like footballs in the Patriots locker room. After all the days and nights of work, all the strategy, all the creative energy, all the left and right brain strain – we were done.

So, I called the office, shut down the agency, and had everybody reconvene for the balance of the day and into the evening in a bar. This loss deserved a wake. Some of those folks still remind me of what I said to close the party down as I stared at the bill, turned to the full room and shouted:

"What the f—k is a Grey Goose and who had seven of them?"

I was wrong; it was a party not a wake. The Grizzlies did call back after all, and they came to our place for the final pitch. We were awarded the account. That's when I met Andy Dolich, and the next three years working for and with him were a blast.

We took a bad team in a dead building and asked the city to come watch them lose, to watch Pau pout and Jason throw no-look passes behind his back into the third row, to watch Shane be classy, Ren be lovable, and Stro do whatever it was that Stro did, and to fall in love. We tried everything – "Tix For Tats" comes to mind, a ticket giveaway tied to spectacular tattoo displays, Allen Iverson, and the 76ers game – and it was all wacky and wild and almost surreal.

Andy got Memphis faster and better than any client I've ever had from somewhere else, understanding our pain and our joy, our stubbornness and genuineness, our sense of humor, and our enormous, breakable hearts.

I remember what he said when he hired me: "I took a call today from some random guy who told me, 'You got to keep the emphis on Memphis.' That's what we're going to do."

I also remember when, under ownership pressure, he fired me three years later, "I've got bad news and good news. Bad news is, you're fired. Good news is, I'm buying lunch." He later asked and took my advice about who to hire and they have the business still.

Andy came to Memphis along a path from his hometown of Brooklyn and on to management positions across minor and major league sports of virtually every description except Roller Derby, and I'm not sure about that one.

He not only knew from promotion, he loved promotion. Like most clients in my experience, he wanted to write headlines. Like very few in my experience, he could.

Which brings me to the one about his balls that he wrote for that subject line.

When they were building FedExForum, they had to put up protective bollards of some kind around the plaza… you know, something heavy and concrete to keep cars from driving into the plaza or crazies getting too close with vans, etc. Andy came up with not only the idea of balls, but also of painted balls. Great big basketballs and baseballs. Tennis balls and billiard balls. Golf balls and soccer balls. Beachballs and volleyballs.

And so it goes. And so it went all around the plaza.

Now back in his beloved and adopted home of the San Francisco Bay area, imagine his surprise when a friend sent a photo of the big, boring, gray balls of concrete that sit there now like so many ceremonial cannonballs around a battlefield and just as somber.

"I called," he said in his email. "They told me the painter died."

Really? God forbid something should happen to whoever cleans the bathrooms in FedExForum. Evidently their team depth is lacking in certain positions.

Later exploration reveals that they've painted them gray in anticipation of selling them to sponsors. As I mentioned, Andy loves promotion but there's a limit to what he's willing to put a logo on.

It took a unique set of balls to open and run an NBA franchise in a small market. Let's get them back.

I'm a Memphian, and I have an Andy Dolich bobblehead, too.

Christmas was a piece of cake | January 10, 2020

Anyone who has ever used the expression "a piece of cake" in describing a task as easy has never made a cake from scratch.

Our Syracuse snowbound daughter and adventurous cook, Hallie, still looks south for inspiration from time-to-time and this caught her attention in Southern Living: "Cool peppermint-vanilla cake and fluffy pink buttercream make a merry combination. Finish with whimsical dollops of mint frosting."

She called her mother.

Nora and Hallie wait for the holiday season in anticipation of advent: the arrival of peppermint ice cream in grocery stores. Spring follows winter in the sure sign of peppermint ice cream covered in fudge sauce at Calvary's Waffle Shop. A bag of York's peppermint patties hides somewhere in the refrigerator year-round as sure as any medicine is kept for emergencies.

Of course, they decided to make this cake when Hallie came home for Christmas.

As I write this, I'm emerging gingerly from three weeks of bronchitis – three weeks of fever, a racking, bone-shaking cough, loss of strength and appetite, and a weight loss approaching 30 pounds. Mornings have been so clouded by codeine the dogs were regularly checking me for a pulse and in the evenings, I didn't even want Scotch, people.

But I didn't have to make a cake from scratch on Christmas Eve. In my condition, I was relieved from duty and watched the process from the couch.

You see, conditions aside, our 40-plus-year tradition of hosting a Christmas Eve dinner for our family and the family of the people who were our neighbors for 25 years, and their extended family and ours, wasn't taking a break.

That cake, and even I, would have to rise to the occasion.

Math, exact measurements and temperatures are required in making a cake from scratch. There's no app to handle it. Your phone can't stir or pour or taste. Your tablet can't find that rack you haven't seen since the kids were little, or the pans, or the cake stand. A linear process of steps must be honored, and steps within steps. This is one followed by two, analog not digital, and if you mess up one, two doesn't matter. In fact, if you mess up two, one doesn't matter, not to mention what happens if you mess up twelve.

I watched the two of them wrestle this creation out of midair.

Panic and laughter. Order from chaos. Praying over the blender. Breaking the hand mixer. Where the hell are the toothpicks to check the cake? Trying to be relevant, I supply a decorative toothpick – complete with the confetti top for martinis – from my bar. The pink peppermint buttercream goes in between. The frosting covers. The crushed peppermint candy decorates the frosting. Swirls of frosting from a snipped corner of a zip lock plastic bag on top.

Damn, it's a cake.

Mother and daughter dance a dance of millennia, from the baking beginnings of the ancient Egyptians, to the Vikings who gave us the word 'cake,' to our kitchen. Sure, we have blenders and mixers and sophisticated ovens, but this is not about that. This is about respect for time-honored process in a short-cut world, about pride in completion, about creating something for others, about each other. As chef Hallie said, "Baking is hard."

This is about doing what you need to do. Every step.

I described the cake to a friend in Austin as a peppermint carpet bomb. He said that was the name of a hot new band in Austin.

I'm a Memphian, and cakes from scratch are an inspiration.

— — —

Wolfschmidt and a lifetime | February 21, 2020

Today is kind of a valentine a week late, sort of.

My second date with Nora Ballenger was a college rush party in the summer of 1967 at the top of the King Cotton Hotel, where the Raymond James/TBD building stands today.

The King Cotton was in deep decline, and there could no better evidence than renting out their grand ballroom to frats – both high school and college. Accompanying us was a bottle of Wolfschmidt Vodka – I think a fifth or maybe a barrel, and just typing the name makes me throw up a little bit in my mouth.

Nora drank Tab. I drank the Wolfschmidt. All of it.

In the course of the evening, I proposed a bet, claiming that I could get all the way from the windows over the city to the elevator without touching the floor. I had many takers and all bets were covered when I launched, leaping from table to table, disrupting each and every occupant and whatever they were drinking, all the way to the very last table before the elevator lobby.

Waiting there were the two guys I enlisted to catch me and carry me the final 50 feet. I won. They got a split.

Nora drove my mother's car home, pulling over to the curb every few blocks so I could lean out and say goodbye to a bit more of the Wolfschmidt, and whatever I'd eaten since April. I had to spend a couple of hours in detox in Nora's parents' driveway before even attempting the drive to my parents.

She went out with me again. No, seriously. And just a minute ago she asked me if I'd taken my cough medicine.

The fact that I'm still here – post Wolfschmidt and post a thousand stupidities – is by the grace of God, and by the grace of God, Nora. Very different people, we have yined and yanged our way through a lifetime, side by side, up and down, and have become both. Finishing each other's sentences. Sensing each other's pain and joy, and causing both. Sharing the ride, claiming the other can't hear, and holding on tight.

I am incapable of imagining my life without her.

I also realize that she and I share something else, a sort of DNA, that defines and binds us now. It probably always has but, at this juncture, it's chronic and incurable.

We are Memphians. Lifelong.

We love our city, warts and all, and we've seen it at its best and worst. While it makes us angry, what we love is never lost. While it can seem cold, the warmth is still there and can still be seen. While we see it every day, what we see every now and then can still take our breath away.

Like the sun on the river, like the woods in Shelby Forest, like music through an open door or laughter across a table. Like the woman who just brought me some cough medicine.

I'm a Memphian, and damn lucky.

— — —

Look for elves | February 28, 2020

Christmas is long gone, but those of us who believe in elves know that work has begun in earnest for the next season. The workshop is busy. Hands and eyes guided by years of experience, by love of the process, by patience and pride, are shaping and sanding and creating magic things.

I know. I've been there.

Years ago, I made a TV spot for a Christmas decoration company in New York. The concept was Santa's workshop – not a huge operation but a place of personal purpose.

We scouted the city and found it – a woodworking shop in Greenwich Village.

Now we needed elves. Santa would only be in the background. Elves were going to speak for the quality of their work. As you're probably aware, elves are shy and hard to find, so we cast about 30 little people to fill the workshop.

I flew up for the casting. The cab driver couldn't find the building because all I had was an address but no cross street. As we looked for numbers, I suddenly told him to stop, paid him, and popped out of the cab.

Walking along the sidewalk side-by-side were two little people with huge portfolios. I just followed them to the address, into the elevator, and into a waiting room full of little people and portfolios. The principal I cast for the major speaking part had actually been a Munchkin in "The Wizard of Oz."

We made the spot and, people, it was Santa's workshop, and those folks were elves if only for the moment, if only for the magic. It even snowed a little in the city while we were shooting.

My friend, Dan Swanson, is an attorney, a member of the choir at Grace-St. Luke's, and, I suspect, an elf. In fact, I believe his wife, Robin, is probably an elf as well.

They both take great pleasure in small things, in things just so, in things made by hand, and in time and things shared with others.

Dan recently finished a dining room table – made by hand, by touch, by feel – from the wood of two oak trees that stood in the front yard of Robin's childhood home in Minnesota. Dan has already made 13 identical boxes from the wood and Robin has given them to family members, each with a personal message inside and a picture of the trees and the house. The table is exquisite, not just because of the skill in making it, but because of the love in the making of it. It shows in the detail. It fills the boxes.

My friend Posey Hedges, master of the mandolin among other things, once hand-crafted radio spots with me. Now he convenes elves at Old City Millwork, meeting unusual needs one at a time ... for St. Mary's Episcopal Cathedral when a 160-year-old piece needed a new section that looked as old as the original ... for brand-new woodwork in UT's oldest buildings in the Medical Center that needed to look like it had been there from the very beginning ... for cabinets that don't just fit but fit the people using them.

Like magic.

Our son, Gaines, is remaking and reshaping a farmhouse in Germantown, parts of it dating from 1872, with his hands and his imagination, all the while living in it, working out of it. His wife, Courtney, and our three grandchildren are all in as well. They are quite literally making a home. There are elves out there and somewhere in our DNA.

In the time of fleeting texts and ceaseless emoji, of tireless and tiresome tweets – in the time of Amazon, porch-delivered culture and impersonal personal communication – look for things crafted over time, words chosen with care, relationships built from deeper places.

Look for the magic. Look for elves.

I'm a Memphian, and I still believe.

—— —— ——

Comfort. Food. | April 17, 2020

When I went off to college to the University of Tennessee, I was braced for change.

I knew I would have to figure out how to do laundry. And that no one was going to wake me up and make sure I got my butt to class, or tell me to do my homework, or to eat more vegetables. And that the last thing I wanted to do was call my father and tell him I needed more money – he'd made that abundantly clear.

But I knew I'd still have what I'd always had to get me through tough spots, to look forward to even in the stress of the moment, to restore order in chaos.

I'd always have barbecue.

In all the vast experience of my 17 years, wherever I was in the city and in the world I roamed, barbecue was never more than three blocks away. Some better than others, but all good, all close, all comforting. That would be the case where I was going.

Wrong. Like so many assumptions about college, so very wrong.

Even though it's in my state, Knoxville doesn't know any more about barbecue than a pig knows about Sunday. Then and now.

However, there were a couple of places that provided affordable consolation in greasy bags, personality unavailable in the chain choices, taste unavailable on the strip below the campus.

In the time of COVID-19, our memories are surfacing, bringing us together in our time apart, reminding us of each other, and of the things and times we shared in our time together.

This week, several friends sent me messages independent of each other, and photos, of those two places that we shared a half century ago – places for comfort food.

One was on University, just a mile or so from campus, but much further in experience and circumstance, the other side of the interstate, the other side of town. By day, the building was shared space between a small grocery and fish market on one side, and a meat market on the other – but I was never there by day.

By night – or very early in the morning depending on what 2 or 3 a.m. is to you – the meat market side was Brother Jack's.

There was pork in there, and hot sauce, and the warmth it brings. It also looked like frat row in there – no women while dorms had hours, and only the bravest of dates after hours were lifted, willing to face the fare.

What I remember, and the visits are as fuzzy as I was at the time, Brother Jack sat in the corner on a stool next to a popcorn machine converted to rotisserie basting God-knows-what was turning in there, and his son-in-law, Sarge, manned the counter in his army sergeant uniform jacket. There were ribs, but ribs weren't the main fare for this bunch.

The frat boys wanted pig burgers – supposedly meat cut from the backs of slabs of ribs, ground, pressed into patties by hand, seasoned, cooked on a flat top, disturbingly white even after being cooked, and served between two pieces of white marshmallow bread ... think Wonder. I think they were a quarter.

We stood packing the small place and overflowing outside, there were no seats, and imploring, "Hit me, Sarge." That meant to douse your pig burger with their hot sauce, a nuclear concoction that set your tongue on fire and melted the roof of your mouth.

When somebody yelled "Hit me, Sarge," Brother Jack would cackle over by the popcorn rotisserie.

The hangover cure value of pig burgers was based on that sauce. You were so busy dealing with the aftermath of eating them, you forgot your headache.

The other place was the Smoky Mountain Market – or the Smoky Mtn. Market as the pole sign said, or the Smoky Mt. Market as the sign on the front said. It was a convenience store on Chapman Highway just across the Tennessee River, but the convenience was the food.

There were hot dogs in there. Better yet, there were Smoky Mountain Market Chili Cheese Dogs in there. Two dogs, split and grilled crispy black on the bottom, slapped on a hot dog bun open face, covered with chili, mustard, onions and a couple of squares of sliced American, and then topped with another hot dog bun. Damn.

Then there was the Full House. Take a big Styrofoam cup, stand two tamales up inside end-to-end, and fill it with chopped onions, grated cheese, and chili. OMG.

Most of the times when I'd visit, weeknights around 10 or 11 on a study break or a what-the-hell, why-not break, the guy running the counter crew was named Red, skinny and about 5-foot-5, the styled eponymous hair about 6 inches of that. I used to order milk just to hear him scream out, "Pint-a-white!" The scream was so the guy on the covered porch out front where the cooler was could hear him. When he had the milk, he'd scream back, "Pint-a-white!" and toss the pint carton 20 feet through the open window to Red.

We remember the food, and what it meant to us.

After this is over, I'm going to remember the windows at Caritas Village turned into takeout, manned by volunteers, and serving those out front kept 6 feet apart by handmade numbered signs. Those who could pay and those who couldn't were all served.

I'm going to remember Elwood's Shack feeding the health care workers, and the Salvation Army feeding the homeless with food bought from local restaurants.

I'm going to remember that each takeout entrée I bought from Mortimer's came with a roll of toilet paper, and every takeout package I bought from Huey's came with a handwritten message of thanks and good wishes from the staff styled on the top.

And there's still barbecue every three blocks or so.

You and I will both remember those who served us and others through all of this.

Remember them when you give, and when you tip for takeout now, and when you tip period.

Comfort. Food.

I'm a Memphian, and as they say, you are what you eat.

— — —

A prom dedication | May 29, 2020

You remember high school ... mine was in the '60s but there are some timeless qualities.

What you wore mattered, who you were with, where you went. What you did, what you didn't do, and when would you do that, and would you ever do that again, and let's please do that again. Pimples and shaving, and baby fat and insecurity, and friends and love, bad decisions and discovery – all that came and went and came back.

All that mattered. And then it didn't. Because I'm a senior now. Because I don't know what's next, really, and I don't know who I am, really. And just when I was getting to know these guys, I've got to start all over again somewhere else. Really?

And somebody I know, somebody who was just here, a senior just a year ago, just died in Vietnam.

A lot of high school was really pretty terrifying.

But we had the prom. The defining party that is both end and beginning, celebration and launch. At least we had that.

Or not.

There was no prom for Johnnie Anderson or Ira Jackson. No rented tuxes and boutonnieres for James Dukes, Ray Leuellyn, or Louis Allen. No long sleeveless dresses and corsages for Jeanne Crutcher, Annie Wilburn, Catherine Exton, or Rosetta Dukes.

They are all African American. They were all in my class, the Class of 1967, the first integrated class to graduate from White Station High School.

There was no prom for all 400 or so of us.

I began this column by asking you to remember high school and its abundant angst. Now imagine you're entering your senior year, your one year at the top, and the powers that be close your school. You and your fellow seniors will be spending your final year in high school with complete strangers.

Now imagine that it's 1966, the handful of you are Black, and every one of the several thousand students in your new school, and every one of your 400 or so fellow rising seniors is white.

I can only imagine the courage that took.

Those students I mentioned above all had the following after their names in my high school annual – yes, I still have my high school annual – "T.W. Patterson High 1, 2, 3."

T.W. Patterson was the all-Black school, elementary through high school, that was closed and its students moved to White Station. It stood where a post office and the Assisi Foundation stand today at the end of Erin Drive in the heart of East Memphis. The neighborhood most or all of those kids came from was called Truse-McKinney, where Home Depot and Kroger stand today between Eastgate and Mendenhall.

The close-knit neighborhood famously stood together as one for years, refusing to sell their homes individually and holding off powerful interests until they got their price for the whole thing in the '80s.

The parents of those students had guts, too.

I got a message last week from Susan Adler Thorp, consultant, former political reporter and commentator, and fellow Spartan from the Class of 1967. Susie (I can call her that; she calls me Danny) was suggesting I should write about this in this No-Prom Time of Plague we're in. A fine writer, she could certainly do it herself, but she knows that The Daily Memphian gives me space every week and that I should use it wisely. Susie can be direct.

As I've thought about those students over the years, I've always been proud of our class and school. There were no incidents, at least none that I heard about, and none in my circle – and I had people far from angels in my circle – did anything to or even talked about the new arrivals.

But I was wrong. We weren't heroes. Exercising common decency, rare as it may seem, doesn't deserve recognition.

Those kids passed a test none of us were given against odds none of us were asked to face.

Which brings us back to the prom.

To all the high school seniors missing their proms this year, it sucks, but you'll get over it. A disease took it from you, and I'm confident a vaccine for that disease will be found, and you now have a story to tell.

A disease took our prom from us, too. Those infected were so concerned that we might mix and mingle with each other, Black and white, that untoward things would occur – you know what music and dancing leads to – and so sure that fights and ugliness would break out, they canceled our prom. Shared joy was never given a chance in the spring of 1967. That disease is racism and there is, extant, no vaccine.

You brand-new graduates should dedicate yourselves to finding the cure.

I would like to dedicate the prom White Station didn't have in 1967 to our classmates – the students of T.W. Patterson High – and to their quiet courage and inner strength. You are an example for the ages.

You mattered.

I'm a Memphian, and Onward Spartans.

— — —

Living through this, killing time | May 22, 2020

I don't cook. Not really.

A Keto diet has limitations. For instance, there's no white or wheat flour allowed, so nothing to sop up all that yellow from all those eggs that are allowed. That won't do.

I've got time so I've been reading cookbooks, and today I made drop biscuits with almond flour. Before COVID-19 and 2020, the Year of the Plague, I didn't know from almond flour. I didn't know anything about coconut flakes and pork dust either, or air fryers, but last night I made coconut shrimp in the air fryer we just bought. I ground up a bag of pork rinds to make the pork dust to coat the shrimp. I made some tomato aspic, too.

All of that required masking up for a field trip. These days, I look forward to a ride in the car so much I should hang my head out the window like my dogs.

I went to Kroger for the almond flour, right there in the baking aisle among a whole collection of weird stuff. Who knew? Then, I went to Cash Saver for a key ingredient for the aspic – Major Peters Bloody Mary Mix. That's the only place I know that stocks it. And, sure, it extended the ride in the car.

Seems I'm cooking. I'm drinking gin and tonics and a little red wine while I'm at it. Sugar's not allowed either, but I choose to believe that what I'm drinking has no sugar. Surviving plague requires some denial. My play list is also helpful.

I don't make things. Not really.

There's a small sculpture of a redbud tree on my screened porch fashioned from wire, its blooms made from tiny pieces of epoxy resin painted red – faded red. I can paint that, I thought, and that will require ... a field trip.

Off to Michael's, head out the window, the second day it was open. Have you ever been to Michael's? A warehouse of what-not, the raw ingredients of arts and crafts and whimsy. If one needs, say, an unpainted rabbit in a three-piece suit, they're right over there – in four sizes. I selected a small bottle of red paint, from a universe of red variations, and a tiny brush, from a forest of tiny brushes.

Seems I can make a redbud tree bloom. By my rough count, I think I painted 250,000 of those tiny tips. Again, the play list comes in handy, and singing along is recommended.

I don't apologize. Not really.

I'm not good at it, and while I recognize the importance of it, I often fail to recognize that I need to be doing it. This morning, I apologized to my wife for biting her head off about absolutely nothing last night. Isolation and misunderstanding and too much information based on too few facts causes stress on all of us, and that's hardest on those closest to us.

Seems saying 'I'm sorry' now and then might just keep us from being really sorry about what's left when this is over.

I don't miss people. Not really.

I miss individuals – friends and family – those who are still here but I can't see because of COVID-19, and those who aren't here, and I won't see again. But those aren't the people I'm talking about. I didn't realize how much I miss you. All of you.

Seems I miss talking to you in lines for hot dogs and beer and coffee, and the charming way you hold up lines with complicated orders for ridiculous variations of all of those things. That cute little trait you have of not using your turn signal. How you just can't park between the lines, bless your heart, or use the crosswalk, or stay in your lane.

I miss you desperately.

You give life to restaurants, buzz to bars, and business to business. You give streets and sidewalks, parks and playgrounds, and the next table over and three seats down personality. You give place to this place.

Much as I miss you, Memphis, I don't want to see you up close for a while yet. And I'm going to keep finding ways to spend time without most of you so that I can see a lot more of you later.

COVID-19 isn't through with us yet, but what kind of city we are when it is will depend on how careful we are in the next few months. For everybody's sake, ease back into the city, don't charge.

I'm a Memphian, and this isn't over. Not really.

—— —— ——

Born lucky | June 12, 2020

A couple of weeks ago in a promless spring amid a season of plague, I wrote about a promless spring 53 years ago and the disease that caused it. Awaiting a vaccine for COVID-19 in the present, we remain in want of a cure for the racism that killed proms all those years ago and took the life of George Floyd just the other week.

As far as we may think we've come, an image that might have been used to define slavery back in the day – the image of a white man's knee on a Black man's neck – became a broad-daylight image live on screens across all platforms in our day.

Just as current events took me back to my high school class of 1967, the first integrated graduating class at White Station High School, marches here and across America have taken me back again, reminding me of just how lucky I am.

In the spring of 1966, I brought my date home from a party about 1:30 in the morning and headed home myself. I was feeling fine and looking fine in my momma's convertible, weaving a bit with the radio turned up and the top down, lit by the moon and several beers.

And lit up by the cop I passed.

As I saw him doing a U-turn in my rearview mirror, I hung a right and a quick left, and accelerated. Add reckless driving and running from the cops to the DUI, and wanton stupidity. Not seeing him back in my mirror, I pulled into a long curving driveway and cut my lights. I figured I'd wait 10 minutes or so, raise the convertible roof, and then make my way....

That's when the cop car pulled right in behind me.

Both cops got out, working their way down either side of my car. When the one on my side got to me, he said, "Son, if you're trying to hide a car in the dark, you might want to take your foot off the brake."

No matter how hard you try, you'll never guess what happened next.

Well, maybe you will if you grew up in East Memphis. Maybe you will if you grew up white.

The cops took my license, backed out of the driveway, and then followed me home to my parents' house, told me to be careful, and gave me my license back.

I was lucky.

And no matter how hard you try, you know that never would have happened had I been a Black kid. Not then. Not now.

I was white.

My life wasn't severely altered, or ruined – or forfeited – because of that stupid, dangerous incident. I wasn't threatened, beaten, arrested or jailed. Or killed. There is nothing on my record. I graduated on time in a few months. I was accepted into college.

I ran from the cops, people. I was driving drunk. The driveway I was parked in belonged to a prominent Memphian, then and now. Then and now, there's every reason to believe if I'd been Black in that driveway, I might never have left that driveway.

The worst part is I've told that story as an amusing anecdote over the years. My run for it. The brake light line from the cop. Lucky kid.

Lucky white kid.

Circumstances of my birth saved me that night, just as those circumstances cost Trayvon Martin his life in 2012 in Sanford, Florida. He was the age I was in 1966.

Those same circumstances cost Ahmaud Arbery his life last February in Atlanta, and Breonna Taylor her life in March in Louisville, and George Floyd his life right in front of all of us in Minneapolis.

And so many more, who have died – died around the country, died right here – no matter the other circumstances, from being born Black.

This is not about guilt. This is about awareness. If you were born white, you did absolutely nothing to deserve the privileges you've enjoyed because of it, any more than those born Black did anything to deserve having to start so far back in the contest of living.

That was true in that driveway in 1966, and still depressingly true 54 years later. It will remain true until white people do the following:

Own it. Earn it.

Own the fact that you have privilege you never earned, and start earning it by giving back what you've taken by using it. Own it by admitting the big things – like what you're doing when you suppress voting, when you send public money to private schools, when you close the borders of a country built by immigrants, when you stack people in prisons like firewood for non-violent crimes, when you deny insurance to the working poor and a living wage to everyone – when you ask a police force to keep order in the face of the disorder big injustice causes.

Own it by admitting the little things – like telling stories like mine and thinking they're funny.

They're tragic.

I'm a Memphian, and I was born lucky.

— — —

Things have come to me | June 19, 2020

There are few benefits to growing old, aside of course from the obvious benefit of growing old itself. However, I have discovered one fairly recently.

If Grandan sits in a chair, things come to Grandan.

In a chair in my son's house, without moving at all, a gin and tonic comes to Grandan. Wheaten terriers come in and cover like hairy thunderstorms, just as loud and sudden and wet, and then back out again.

Things and sounds come bouncing, flying and falling from every direction.

A royal blue Gund elephant comes, too, and other cuddly friends – Gotta Getta Gund. Things done and being done come – things like drawings and letters, things formed from Legos and Silly Putty, things made from imagination from what's at hand, things to be shared.

Grandchildren come to Grandan, and in the midst of the tickling and giggling, in a smile accented by a bit of pizza in the corner, in the twinkle of an eye underlined by a bruise earned on the trampoline, in the shake of hair getting really long – long enough that the pink experiment has just about disappeared – something else comes to Grandan.

It's their turn. They will make of the world what they will.

If you and I can agree on nothing else, if events over the past few weeks have taught us anything, as even causal observation of the last four years will confirm, we're currently making a mess of this country and contributing mightily to the mess the world is making of itself.

So very tired of so many things, I could not be more tired of hearing, both from the left and the right, "I worry about what kind of world we're leaving our grandchildren."

You know exactly what you're leaving them. You made it. You've not only stopped caring about each other, you've stopped talking to each other. You've become so obsessed about avoiding people who don't think or look like you, the world is starting to think and look like you.

So stop worrying. Our grandchildren could not possibly do anything but improve on that.

Mac Conaway, the youngest visitor to my chair, just turned 1. I don't worry when I look at that face, I rejoice.

Almost half of his life has been in some sort of quarantine, in the midst of a modern plague. We've been obsessed with lack of freedom and/or toilet paper, with loss of income and/or bowling and/or pedicures and/or streaming bandwidth, with spread of disease and/or conspiracy theory, with isolation and/or empty Cheetos bags and/or empty days.

And we've been watching, with many eyes truly wide open for the first time, what a white knee on a Black neck has been truly strangling for so long. And we've been seeing, truly focused this time, the beginnings of real change sown at the grassroots level.

Meanwhile, Mac has had his brother and sister at home all the time, and Mom and Dad, and the dogs, and lately, grandparents who bring him stuff. And cousins. And there's this whole walking thing that's pretty cool. And a whole world outside full of discovery.

A wonderful world of possibility.

I don't worry when I look at that face, I hope.

I'm a Memphian, and from where I sit, things are looking up.

—— —— ——

Viva L'Italia | July 3, 2020

Italy died today.

This year, Nora and I will celebrate our 50th wedding anniversary – obviously we were married when we were in elementary school. I gave her a big trip to Italy to mark this seminal milestone in style. Rome, some time in Sorrento and the Amalfi Coast, a visit to Pompei and Capri, and a week exploring Sicily.

In late September, we would see Caravaggio up close again, and drink limoncello above olive groves and the Bay of Naples again. We would spend another morning in the excavated homes of the eerily preserved citizens of Pompeii, and spend another day atop Capri, seeing the impossibly blue Mediterranean just as Tiberius saw it. And in early October, we would see Sicily and its ancient cities and churches for the first time, and I would see another birthday on that storied island.

All of that time would be spent among the warmest and most open people we've seen in our travels, wearing the widest of smiles in genuine welcome.

All of that is officially a victim of COVID-19. We canceled today.

International travel was already scary enough. Customs lines and hassles. Stacking hours over water in a metal tube with strangers, some very strange. Now add a global pandemic, our age, and an impressive list of maladies, aka underlying conditions, and the mix is just too toxic.

But instead of feeling sorry for myself and my first-world problem, I looked at this through the lens of coronavirus, the only way to see things lately.

Italy is alive today.

Just a few months ago, Italy was the poster child for both the threat and reality of COVID-19, the country's hospitals overrun, businesses closed, the economy in shambles, the population shut in and shut off. At their lowest moment, when new cases were rising like floodwater in Venice and death like medieval plague, what did the besieged, isolated and locked down Italian people do?

They went out on their balconies and applauded. They went out on their balconies and sang.

I was reminded today of a piece I saw and posted from The New York Times in mid-March:

"At precisely noon on Saturday, millions of Italians, from Piedmont to Sicily, leaned out of windows or stood on their balconies to applaud the health care workers in hospitals and other front-line medical staff who have been working round the clock to care for coronavirus patients."

On another evening at precisely 6 – no one's sure who called these meetings online or however – they came out on those balconies and in those windows and sang or played their national anthem. If they couldn't sing or play an instrument, they banged on pots and pans.

At precisely 6 the following evening, they sang, played and banged Italian hit songs – "Azzurro" by Adriano Celentano from 1968, and "Ma il cielo è sempre più blu" by Nino Gaetano from 1975.

They didn't deny COVID-19 and science itself. They didn't lie about the number of cases, the number of tests, the number of deaths. They didn't point fingers at each other. They didn't promote false cures. They didn't stigmatize and demonize care and caution.

Then, they stood and faced the problem. Together.

Today, they are past the worst and coming back because of it. Today, they are open to visitors from Europe, and closed to America. Today, we are the problem. Today, with 4% of the world's population we have about 20% of the world's deaths from COVID-19, more than any other country. And rising.

Tomorrow, we celebrate the birth of our nation. Out of respect, dress appropriately.

Wear a mask.

I'm a Memphian, and America could take a lesson in Italian.

— — —

The face of tragedy is smiling | August 14, 2020

Two weeks ago today, Steve Montgomery died.

I cried when I heard the news. His injuries from a tragic biking accident were just too great to overcome.

Steve was the much beloved retired senior pastor of Idlewild Presbyterian Church. He was officially the Reverend Dr. Stephen R. Montgomery, but more than that to me and countless others, he was Steve.

Just Steve.

While thousands considered him a friend, it never felt like thousands when you visited with him, it was just you and Steve. He listened to you, you the homeless, you the wealthy, you the mover and shaker, and you the one being moved and shaken.

His eyes, complete with the twinkle, met yours. They never left yours during the conversation, they never scanned the busy room for more important targets, they never failed to see something in you that made you special.

If you read what my colleagues David Waters and Geoff Calkins have written about Steve, you know how special that could make you feel.

So, after I cried, I smiled.

Any memory of Steve and his smile, any memory of any experience with Steve, can produce a smile even in the midst of tears, even in the midst of life's challenges and losses. He caused us to question our behaviors and beliefs, to address our failures, to act rather than watch, and he did all of that without confrontation and condemnation; he did it with love.

"May God bless you with a restless discomfort
about easy answers, half-truths and superficial relationships,
so that you may seek truth boldly and love deep within your heart."

At Idlewild, before confirmation occurs the confirmands must appear before the Session, the lay leadership of the church. The Rev. Anne H.K. Apple, acting head of staff at the church, told me about 15-year-old twins, Lauren and Andrew Hobson, who appeared before the Session recently.

She said their message was that Steve Montgomery, the man who baptized them, had led them by example. "He was always there," Andrew said. "He was always greeting everyone at the door, always welcoming everyone."

The twins made a prayer flag with an image of Steve in the center that Lauren drew, and messages from Steve surrounding the image:

"God is good all the time. All the time God is good."

"Pray daily and leave the rest to God."

"Live simply. Love generously. Care deeply. Speak kindly."

"All are welcome here."

You've been 15. You may have raised one or two. They're pretty hard to impress.

"May God bless you with holy anger at injustice, oppression,
and exploitation of people, so that you may tirelessly work for
justice, freedom, and peace among all people."

When Steve took over at Idlewild 20 years ago, he embraced and expanded a program called More Than A Meal, not only feeding the homeless, but inviting them into the church for dinner, for company, for grace shared at table.

He inspired another church down the street – mine – Grace-St. Luke's Episcopal Church, to do the same in 2001. To actually bring those most in need within our walls, to serve them and be served by so doing, to share with them and to grow by so doing.

Today and in partnership with other churches, More Than A Meal still happens every Thursday at Idlewild and every Sunday at Grace-St. Luke's.

And Steve will remain in every bite, every smile around every table.

"May God bless you with the gift of tears to shed with those who suffer

from pain, rejection, starvation, or the loss of all that they cherish, so that you may reach out your hand to comfort them and transform their pain into joy."

When Anne walked into the Idlewild offices the Monday after Steve died, she was greeted by a staff member with her arms raised high, "because that's what Steve often did, often involving a little Steve dance."

She paused and added, "That's what we should all do ... a little Steve dance."

"May God bless you with enough foolishness to believe that you really CAN make a difference in this world, so that you are able, with God's grace, to do what others claim cannot be done."

The Sunday after Steve died, the Rev. Ollie Rencher, rector of Grace-St. Luke's, included in the service "A Four-Fold Blessing," written by a Benedictine nun, Sister Ruth Marlene Fox, in 1985. All four parts are quoted in this column.

I don't know if Sister Ruth knew Steve, or if Ollie was thinking of Steve, but Steve is in all four parts of that blessing. In every word.

Smile. We've all been blessed by the presence of Steve Montgomery in our midst.

And, hopefully, enough foolishness will ensue.

I'm a Memphian, and Steve Montgomery was my friend.

—— —— ——

Discovered, again and again | August 28, 2020

Lauren Crews and I were sitting atop the bluff one late afternoon sipping whiskey.

Our view from the wrought iron gazebo behind the National Ornamental Metal Museum was pretty much the view Hernando de Soto had when he first saw the Mississippi right about here in May of 1541. His claim to have discovered the river must have come as a surprise to the Indigenous peoples who had lived here for centuries before he made Spain's claim.

In fact, our view was pretty much the same as Chief Chisca's from atop the ceremonial mound just south of where we sat, one of two mounds still right here, quiet monuments to provenance. The majestic, sweeping turn of the great river before him must have commanded his eye as it commands ours today. Life and death for his people would come from that river, and he could literally see it coming from right here.

This was the view the French had when they built the first European structure here in 1682 and later followed with Fort Assumption in 1739, hence the name of the neighborhood just east today, French Fort.

This was the view when the United States built Fort Pickering here in 1801. This is what the commandant of that fort would see of a late afternoon in 1809, maybe even with a bit of whiskey. That was a decade before Memphis was founded just north of Fort Pickering, and four decades before that commandant, Zachary Taylor, would become the 12th president of the United States in 1849.

This is what Union soldiers would have looked down on from their Civil War battery atop Chisca's mound – the cannon mounts are still up there, the entrance to their powder magazine in the mound still visible.

This particular afternoon, Lauren had asked me to join him following the first column I wrote about this haunting point of origin for this city. He told me a story about paddling the Mississippi from source to mouth in a canoe, just Lauren and his dog.

He told me that on a number of occasions, on yet another hot still night on yet another buggy sandbar, after he had pulled the canoe ashore and had yet again thrown his paddle down and exclaimed out loud to no one but the bugs and the dog that he was done – using adjectives and adverbs best suited to a limited audience – that he was quitting.

He remembered:

"Dan, the dog wouldn't let me."

That visit was almost 10 years ago. I had just written about this place, what was once here and still here in spirit.

In addition to all that early history and all those forts, here also was the pride of Kemmons Wilson's new chain when it was built in the '50s, its glass-walled, fifth-floor dining room affording that stunning view of the river, and now a fading Super 8 Motel.

Here also are the mysterious, abandoned Marine Hospital grounds behind it.

Here is the imposing hospital built in 1936. Here is the deep-porched, metal-roofed elegant Victorian lady from 1883, the nursing quarters of the original hospital.

If it's not haunted, it should be – by Civil War wounded, some say, but that was far earlier, or by yellow fever victims, some say, but that, too, was earlier.

Those who took the air on the porches and the grounds until 1965, who lost a battle in these rooms, were river people. They fought the Mississippi building the original levees, operating the boats, dredging and dragging land and life from the flotsam and jetsam of a nation, and it broke them.

You can feel the river, and hear them in the quiet.

Lauren called that meeting to let me know he had bought the Marine Hospital and had grand plans for it.

In the decade since, the plans have changed course like the river. He has figuratively thrown the paddle down many times in the face of opposing currents and storms, but The Marine Residence at Historic French Fort is rising. The many windows and rooms of the hospital are becoming modern apartments, the wide porches of the nursing quarters are becoming galleries over a courtyard pool. He still fights his battle to make the area more accessible, its significance less of a secret.

Lauren's dog would again be happy to know that he didn't quit.

Chisca and his people, de Soto, Taylor, and the reasons for settlement, for forts, for a city, are all captured and held here, all in the view. Lauren and I will share it again soon, and a bit of whiskey.

Memphis, in fact anywhere, is about connections. There is no more connected place to our beginnings than here. The wrought iron in that gazebo was donated to the Metal Museum by the Waring family, and once stood in Colonel Roane Waring's yard, where my wife Nora played as a child two doors up the street from her house. When I told her what I was writing about this week, she reminded me that she was a candy-striper, a volunteer nurse, in the Marine Hospital just before it closed.

Take a little road trip yourself. Take the last exit before the Memphis-Arkansas bridge as Crump is turning into I-55, the Metal Museum Drive exit, and take a look around.

I'm a Memphian, and you can see all of our history from here.

—— —— ——

The owned perspective | September 18, 2020

There's a French Creole proverb depicting the master/slave relationship in the sugar cane plantations of Louisiana, its origins in folktales of Senegal, where so many slaves came from:

"Bouki fait gombo, lapin mangé li." (He-goat makes the gombo, but rabbit eats it.)

This morning, I got an email from a good friend in Atlanta, Kathie Larkin, remembering a trip Nora and I made with Kathie and her husband Steve to New Orleans a couple of years ago. She wasn't remembering the wonderful food found in such rich abundance there, or the sense of centuries that drapes the city like the Spanish moss that hangs from its live oaks. Any of us who have visited New Orleans remembers those things.

She was reminding me of a place we visited together that relatively few of us have ever seen. She was reminding me to write about it again as we as a region, we as a country, are taking another look at what we've elevated to heroic status, at the monuments we've created.

From 1936 to 1938, as part of the WPA and the Federal Writers' Project, more than 2,000 interviews were conducted with former slaves resulting in the *Slave Narratives: A Folk History in the United States*. Those former slaves were very old by then, but their memories of dark childhoods were clear.

Most of us have never heard of those narratives.

I saw some of those memories engraved in stone, and stood where they were made, surrounded by a reality I had not truly acknowledged before, finding the past alive in the present like nowhere I have been before.

On the wall in front of me, I saw the words of Julia Woodrich, born a slave in Louisiana in 1851, talking about her mother: "My ma had fifteen children and none of them had the same pa. You see, every time she was sold, she had to take another man. Her had fifteen children after she was sold de last time."

Julia's mother was profitable property, and Julia would have some memories of her as a child – if her mother was sold, she would been in the bargain – but at age ten she would have been considered an adult slave, put to work accordingly, and worth $25,000-plus in today's money.

On a sugar cane plantation, she would have had a life expectancy of ten adult years.

The Conaways and the Larkins were visiting one of the plantations along the Mississippi on the River Road between New Orleans and Baton Rouge – a stretch of 50 miles or so of antebellum ascension fronted by massive columns at the end of ancient live oak alleys. This short stretch is said to have produced more wealth from its sugar than all of the plantations north pulled from their cotton.

But this plantation – Whitney Plantation – is unique among those open to the public. This is the only one anywhere dedicated to the history of slaves and telling the story from their point of view.

Here you see where they came from – some of the culture stolen from them that somehow survived in bits and pieces of our language, food and religion – some of the brutal business of human beings as property measured in profit and productivity – some of the horror of grinding cane into sugar and grinding people into the swamp surrounding that cane.

Here are the two-room cabins they lived in, eight to ten to a side in the growing season, double that in the grinding season – October through December, 24 hours a day, seven days a week.

Here is the hell on earth that owners upriver evoked to make their slaves work harder by threatening to "sell them down the river."

Here are monuments to history we don't acknowledge in our Southern parks and on our Southern courthouse lawns and along our Southern boulevards. These aren't statues of romanticized leaders of some ersatz lost cause placed on pedestals; these are memories of the marginalized and brutalized people who made those leaders rich, marked and remembered on the ground they died on, ground in which they were placed largely unknown and unmarked.

Whitney Plantation is in St. John the Baptist Parish and is a very different kind of holy ground if you're looking for it. Revelation, confession, and even redemption have been planted here. The harvest is up to us.

This is a very different kind of plantation experience if you're looking for it.

This tour ends at the master's house instead of beginning there, and leaves you with a fuller understanding of how it was built and how life was lived in and around it.

As we take a hard look at America today, we must still ask how we are building it and at whose expense.

I'm a Memphian, and measuring how far we've come still depends on who holds the rule.

—— —— ——

By OTIS SANFORD

Dedication

To the Sanford and Baptist families.

ON POLITICS

A compassionate governor | January 10, 2019

"It is compassionate to actively help our fellow citizens in need. It is conservative to insist on responsibility and results. And with this hopeful approach, we will make a real difference in people's lives."

—President George W. Bush
April 2002

I don't have photographs of politicians – either neatly framed or as a dartboard bull's eye – on display in my office at University of Memphis. With one notable exception.

That exception is an autographed 8-by-10 glossy shot of a smiling Gov. Bill Haslam surrounded by a group of journalists, including David Plazas of The Tennessean and me, at a Tennessee Press Association luncheon in 2017.

This week, as I sat at my desk to write a column about Haslam's highly publicized and celebrated decision granting full clemency to Cyntoia Brown, the governor's photo was in view. And then it hit me. Haslam is the personification of Bush 43's description of compassionate conservatism.

The popular Republican governor, who leaves office next week after two successful terms, made national news Monday by issuing a clear and convincing statement of why Brown deserved clemency. Her life sentence for murder – imposed in 2006 when she was just 16 and after being forced into a travailing life of prostitution, rape and other abuse by a ruthless pimp nicknamed Cut Throat – was, in Haslam's words, "too harsh."

Here is what the governor said in his commutation order:

"This decision comes after careful consideration of what is a tragic and complex case. Cyntoia Brown committed, by her own admission, a horrific

162

crime at the age of 16.

"Yet, imposing a life sentence on a juvenile that would require her to serve at least 51 years before even being eligible for parole consideration is too harsh, especially in light of the extraordinary steps Ms. Brown has taken to rebuild her life. Transformation should be accompanied by hope."

The governor noted that while in prison, Brown earned her GED and an associate degree from Lipscomb University with a 4.0 grade point average. She is now working to obtain a bachelor's degree. "Over her more than 14 years of incarceration, Ms. Brown has demonstrated extraordinary growth and rehabilitation." And her case "appears to me to be a proper one for the exercise of executive clemency."

And before the law-and-order critics howl, this is not a pardon. Haslam is not wiping Brown's criminal slate clean. She will remain in prison until Aug. 7, exactly 15 years after she fatally shot Nashville real estate agent Johnny Allen while in bed with him at his home.

She also will remain on parole for 10 years and must perform community service, which she has said she will gladly do to help steer other vulnerable young girls from a life of sexual exploitation.

In essence, Haslam did what the justice system failed to do 15 years ago – make the punishment fit the crime. Instead, prosecutors and presiding Criminal Court Judge Randall Wyatt Jr., now retired, considered Cyntoia Brown a throw-away.

They did not do what Haslam did. They didn't look below the surface of a terrible homicide, which also included robbery, to discover a victimized teenager who had the potential to turn her desperately troubled life around.

Now the question becomes, how does clemency for Brown play politically for Haslam, who is still considering a run for the U.S. Senate in 2020 to replace three-term Republican Sen. Lamar Alexander?

"In the Republican Party, you're going to find conservatives who may not like it, and staunch conservatives who really won't like it," said Lee Mills, chairman of the Shelby County GOP. He then added, "Some of those staunch conservatives already didn't like him.

"But a lot of your moderate Republicans, and even moderate and conservative Democrats will say Haslam made the right decision. I'm one of those staunch conservatives and I agree with the decision."

Mills said something else with which I completely agree. Haslam did not succumb to partisan ideology on either side. He was not influenced by the national media or the celebrities who spoke out in support of Brown, including Rihanna, Kim Kardashian West and Ashley Judd.

He was not unduly swayed by political lobbying from leading Democrats in the state, including U.S. Rep. Steve Cohen of Memphis, and state Sens. Brenda Gilmore of Nashville and Raumesh Akbari of Memphis. Nor was he necessarily persuaded by those in the faith community who kept Brown on their prayer list.

Haslam was moved simply by the desire to do the right thing. That has been his aim throughout his two terms as governor. Whether it was expending political capital in a failed attempt to expand health care to more needy Tennesseans, or his noble, but equally unsuccessful, efforts to keep guns out of public parks, playgrounds, bars and college campuses.

This was a governor who led Tennessee as a compassionate conservative, who improved education – particularly higher education – and who helped bring economic prosperity and record low unemployment to the state, who did the absolute right thing in commuting Cyntoia Brown's life sentence, and who charmed us journalists every year at the state press association luncheon.

As the fictional U.S. president said in the closing scene of the movie "Independence Day," "Not bad. Not bad at all."

— — —

Big Mo | January 17, 2019

It is a nickname that just might stick. And Jim Strickland would be wise to embrace it.

Big Mo – as in Momentum.

For the moment at least, the moniker fits Memphis' first-term mayor, and it's not only because he is an imposing 6 feet, 5 inches tall.

In announcing his candidacy for reelection this week, Strickland sought to paint Memphis as a city on the upswing under his leadership. A city experiencing noticeable growth with near-record-low unemployment and a doubling of city spending with businesses owned by women and minorities.

Strickland's email blast Tuesday morning making his reelection bid official carried the heading "Let's Keep the Momentum Going." It signaled that he intends to run on his mayoral record that also includes balancing the city budget with no property tax increase, allocating money for expanding prekindergarten in Memphis, and reducing the city's far-flung footprint to focus more on investing in previously neglected neighborhoods.

But while Strickland, 55, is heavily favored to win a second term, the campaign won't be a yearlong coronation, despite internal poll numbers showing he has an eye-popping job approval rating of 72%. The mayor still has his share of critics, many of whom express their sentiments regularly via social media.

They complain that Strickland has not done enough for disaffected neighborhoods or to reduce crime and the city's poverty rate, which, according to the most recent University of Memphis study, is 24.6% overall, but nearly 30% among African Americans and almost 40% among children.

Just last week, the mayor was sharply criticized for canceling a meeting with members of the Memphis Interfaith Coalition for Action and Hope (MICAH) then later soliciting MICAH members for help with his mentoring and tutoring initiatives.

MICAH is a coalition of faith-based and community organizations that addresses public policy issues such as affordable housing, inequities in the criminal justice system and economic disparities. An official with the coalition said members felt insulted by Strickland. To which Ursula

Madden, the mayor's chief communications officer, responded by telling The Commercial Appeal: "It's hard to imagine that anyone would be insulted by a plea to mentor and tutor children, and to clean our city."

Madden added, "This administration can't get sidetracked over a rescheduled meeting; we're focused on moving the city forward, and collaborating with people who want to help."

Ouch.

That hiccup aside, Strickland is not only buoyed by high poll numbers. He is riding a wave of mostly positive economic news, including low unemployment and successful business recruitment. He also can legitimately claim some credit for figuring out how to rid the city of Confederate statues honoring Nathan Bedford Forrest and Jefferson Davis in December 2017.

If Strickland does adopt Big Mo as his 2019 calling card, he would be borrowing a political term made famous by George H.W. Bush during the 1980 Republican campaign for president.

Bush was a little-known former congressman and onetime CIA director when he launched an improbable presidential run against frontrunner Ronald Reagan. When Bush scored an upset win in the Iowa caucuses, he proudly declared, "I've got the 'Big Mo.'"

Unfortunately for Bush, his Big Mo was fleeting. Reagan regrouped, overtook a stumbling Bush in the New Hampshire primary and went on to win the GOP nomination and the presidency. But Bush's early momentum was impressive enough to earn him a spot as Reagan's running mate, which he parlayed into his own presidential victory in 1988.

So, Mr. Mayor, embrace Big Mo because, despite this city's challenges, positive momentum clearly describes Memphis at the moment.

The city is celebrating its bicentennial this year and stands to reap a gigantic windfall in tourism dollars because of it. The travel website Frommer's included Memphis as one of the best places to visit in 2019. And last year, CNN Travel named Memphis the best city in the world to visit during the month of May.

Just keep in mind, mayor, that as with H.W. Bush, Big Mo can easily fade. The city election is less than nine months away, which can seem like light years in politics.

Plus, though unlikely, Willie Herenton, who still insists he's running, could reclaim the magic that catapulted him to the mayor's office in 1991 and four more times after that.

But for now, the momentum – and most of the available campaign money – are on Strickland's side. His support among African American voters is far stronger than in 2015 when he captured more than 25% of the Black vote in beating incumbent A C Wharton.

A $150-per-person fundraiser for Strickland in December included an impressive list of younger African American elected leaders, including county commissioners Van Turner and Mickell Lowery and state Sen. Raumesh Akbari.

Missing from that list, however, was freshman commissioner Tami Sawyer, who still believes Strickland took more credit than he deserved for taking down the Confederate monuments. Should she keep up the criticism, Sawyer and her supporters could be a small burr under Strickland's reelection saddle.

"I definitely abide by the old saying that you run unopposed or you run scared," Strickland told The Daily Memphian Tuesday. "The only thing I can control are my actions. I can't control any opponents. I can't control the media. I can't control the public. All I can do is control me. I will work harder than anybody else."

Spoken like a guy who is taking nothing for granted in the fickle world of politics, but a guy who is sure the political winds are at his back. A guy who by any objective measure has earned the name Big Mo.

—— —— ——

Poverty in Memphis | January 31, 2019

In an otherwise carefully crafted State of the City address that was full of symbolism and substance, Memphis Mayor Jim Strickland included one line that may have caused more confusion than clarity.

"Poverty is down," Strickland proclaimed as he rattled off a number of positive things that are up and negative things that are down since he took office. "The latest census estimates show (poverty is) down about 17% since 2014."

The mayor moved on to his remaining litany of ups and downs, all designed to show the progress made under his administration on many of this city's major issues.

Police hires are up. Police officers leaving the department are down. Prosecution of violent crime is up. Violent crimes, including gun crimes, are down. Affordable housing units are up. Homelessness is down. And so on.

In total, the speech accomplished Strickland's main goal of recapping not just 2018, but his first three years as mayor, while also making some news with new initiatives to be rolled out later this year. More on that later.

But I was struck by his give-and-go comment on poverty – particularly given the fact that it is consistently the most nagging concern facing Memphis. And the subject did not come up again during the approximately 30-minute speech at the Links at Whitehaven.

The poverty number Strickland used stems from the Memphis Poverty Fact Sheet, produced annually by Dr. Elena Delavega, associate professor in the School of Social Work at the University of Memphis and the leading authority on poverty in the Bluff City.

Technically, Strickland is correct. In 2014, the overall poverty rate in Memphis was 29.8%. By 2017, the overall rate had dropped to 24.6%, according to Delavega's report last year. So if you take the 5.2 percentage-point drop from 2014 to 2017, divide it by the original 29.8%, then multiply that number by 100, you will get a 17.4 percent decrease.

But a serious look at poverty in Memphis requires going far beyond a simple math equation that helps to buttress a well-written and well-delivered State of the City speech. Besides, poverty has had its own ups and downs over the last eight years, according to Delavega's reports.

In 2010, the overall rate was 26.5%; in 2011, it was 27.2%; in 2012, it was 28.3%; in 2013, it was 27.7%; in 2014, it was 29.8%; in 2015, it dropped to 26.2%; in 2016, it was 26.9%; and in 2017, it was 24.6%.

A C Wharton was mayor most of those years, and the largest percentage drop, year to year, occurred during his administration.

Strickland took office in January 2016, which means during his first year, poverty actually increased by seven-tenths of a percentage point before dropping noticeably in 2017. Therefore, he can legitimately claim credit for a decrease of 8.5% instead of 17.4%.

In looking at poverty, "we have to be careful because there may be measuring errors we cannot control for," Delavega told me. "One important thing to observe is trends."

One encouraging number from Delavega's latest report was the poverty rate among African Americans. It decreased to 28.9% in 2017 from 32.3% the previous year. That is an impressive drop of 10.5%.

And yet, all these numbers aside, poverty continues to be a destabilizing problem in our city and the cause of so many other ills. It is responsible for household dysfunction, neighborhood blight, lawlessness and toxic stress, particularly among young women with children who struggle every day to provide food, shelter and normalcy for themselves and their kids.

People in poverty lead complicated lives that many who are not in their world can't understand. Those complications often mean doing what's necessary to survive, from petty stuff such as siphoning electrical service from a neighbor to far more serious crimes.

None of this is meant to critically nitpick Mayor Strickland's treatment of poverty in his speech. The Memphis economy under his watch is getting better. Unemployment is at all-time lows and many of his proposals outlined Monday are promising.

They include the launch of the Memphis Community Catalyst Fund, which the mayor said would provide money for infrastructure improvements in various neighborhoods. "That can be anything from new sidewalks, new pedestrian crossings, new lighting," Strickland said.

The mayor also announced the rollout of Buy901, a searchable website where private individuals and businesses can easily find certified minority-

and women-owned businesses that already do business with the city.

"Need a new roof or fence and want to hire a local or minority contractor? Great. Just visit Buy901.net and you'll be able to pick the same contractors we use," he said.

It was also telling that Strickland gave the speech in Whitehaven, a community that has long felt neglected by city government.

All of that, along with efforts to improve early childhood education and reduce crime, represent tangible things the Strickland administration can cite as the mayor launches his campaign for reelection this year.

When it comes to poverty, the situation is dicier. And numbers can never tell the complete story. We may no longer be the poorest big city in America. That dubious distinction belongs to Detroit.

But we are light years away from the slightest suggestion of mission accomplished.

—— —— ——

Tennessee's man problem | February 20, 2020

Trailblazing political leader Jane Eskind used to tell audiences an anecdote that, while intended to be humorous, clearly defined how male chauvinism operated in media and politics throughout Tennessee.

Eskind was the first woman to hold a statewide office when she was elected to the old Public Service Commission in 1978. She also ran unsuccessfully for other offices, including governor and the U.S. senate. But despite her high profile in Democratic politics, Eskind, who died in 2016, had a difficult time being taken seriously by the old boys' club.

"During the campaigns, there were many people who thought I should go home and have a baby," she once said. "And it was always interesting to go to the newspapers to do the (endorsement) interview and to know that your male opponent had been interviewed by the news editor, and you were going to be interviewed by the society editor."

Thankfully, attitudes at newspapers have changed since those days. But sadly, state politics have not. There has only been one other woman elected to statewide office since Eskind, and that happened 40 years later, in 2018, when Marsha Blackburn was elected to the U.S. Senate replacing Bob Corker.

Even in a so-called progressive bastion like Memphis, there has never been a woman elected city or county mayor. Except for a sliver of east Shelby County that once resided in Blackburn's old 7th Congressional District, the city and county have never elected a woman to the U.S. House.

And currently in the Tennessee General Assembly, women occupy 8 of the 33 seats in the Senate and 12 of the 99 seats in the House. That means women make up just 15% of the state Legislature, while they represent 51% of the state's population of 6.5 million.

All of which tells me that when it comes to politics and public policy, Tennessee has a definite man problem. This in a state that in 2020 is congratulating itself for being the 36th and deciding state to ratify the 19th Amendment giving women the right to vote 100 years ago.

But Tennessee's man problem is about more than just numbers. It's about attitude and optics. Far too many of this state's political leaders have a paternalistic and chauvinistic attitude toward women. And what's worse, these guys just don't care how it looks.

For example, Gov. Bill Lee last month went before television and print news cameras to trumpet the coming of a bill – that is yet to be written – that would outlaw abortions in the state once a fetal heartbeat is detected. Usually that is about six weeks, which is about the time most women discover they are pregnant.

Lee said the forthcoming bill would also require an ultrasound to be shown to a woman seeking an abortion, and the abortion could not be performed based on race, sex or a diagnosis of Down Syndrome or other fetal abnormality.

To ensure that the bill withstands a court challenge, it will include language to automatically increase the abortion ban to 8 weeks, 10, 12 weeks and beyond until it is upheld by the courts.

Lee was accompanied by a large group of like-minded conservative lawmakers. A wide-angle news photo showed nearly 40 men on the stage and four women who stood off to the side.

The optics were that mostly older white men were pronouncing that they know what's best for women and their reproductive health. But the governor and these men didn't think, or care, about the optics.

Meanwhile, earlier this week, an all-male state Senate subcommittee refused to sign off on a proposal, offered by Democratic Sen. Sara Kyle of Memphis, to allow feminine hygiene products to be included in the state's annual sales tax holiday.

Republican Sen. Joey Hensley of Hohenwald, who chairs the Finance, Ways and Means Subcommittee, convinced other subcommittee members to issue a negative recommendation on Kyle's proposal, arguing that he was unsure how the state would make up the estimated $132,700 loss in sales tax revenue.

Hensley is the same guy who earlier worried that a tax holiday on feminine products would lead to abuse, with women buying up and hoarding tampons to avoid paying sales taxes. The statement was reported by national news media outlets and made Hensley a laughingstock.

He is also the same guy who last year sponsored a $435,000 tax break on the sale of ammunition.

What's happening here is easy to see. Our male-dominated Legislature could not care less about the issues around securing feminine hygiene products for people in Tennessee who cannot always afford them.

It is of particular concern in Memphis and Shelby County where access to such products is often difficult for impoverished women and girls. Kyle and Democratic state Rep. G.A. Hardaway of Memphis successfully pushed through a bill in the Legislature last year to make free feminine hygiene products available in eligible public schools.

And sure, Hensley insisted this week that in theory, he supports a tax holiday on tampons, calling it "a worthwhile thing to do." He even promised to work to get the proposal funded. But the old cliché is still true – action speaks louder than words. And the actions of Tennessee's governor and legislative leaders on a range of health care-related issues speak volumes about their arrogant, cavalier and condescending attitude toward women.

The truth is, we are not that far removed from the days when a hardworking, politically astute leader such as Jane Eskind was treated with denigration, derision and chauvinism.

And the other truth is, it won't change until Tennessee's 51% continue to make an even greater impact at the ballot box, and the stage for a major political announcement is no longer dominated by men who think the same, govern the same and, for the most part, look the same.

I don't know about you, but I can hardly wait for that day to arrive.

— — —

Past, present and future | March 21, 2019

If Memphis Mayor Jim Strickland is experiencing stress over a looming battle to win a second term in office, he's not showing it. At least not publicly.

Strickland is just as approachable and jovial as ever, despite a recent, highly-publicized "screw-up" – the administration's term, not mine – over the percentage of city business going to minority- and women-owned companies.

The mayor committed the error during his State of the City speech Jan. 28 at the Whitehaven Country Club. Minority- and women-owned businesses got 12% of city contracts in 2015, the year Strickland was elected, he said. For fiscal year 2018, that figure doubled to 24%.

The cadence Strickland used in announcing the impressive percentage increase made it obvious that this would be a signature accomplishment on which to fuel a strong reelection campaign.

Except, as we now know, the numbers were wrong. Thanks to solid watchdog reporting by the Memphis Business Journal, we learned last week that city officials failed to include $154 million in city contracts awarded during fiscal year 2018, of which about $19 million went to minority firms.

That dropped the percentage from 24% to 17.6%, which actually represented a decrease in minority contracting from 21% recorded in 2017. City spokesman Dan Springer was quoted in The Commercial Appeal's 901 column, calling the error a "screw-up."

The description was appropriate, but not fatal. The mayor immediately owned the mistake. But he was justified in continuing to tout a significant increase in city contracting to minority- and women-owned companies, even though there remains lots more work to be done.

So there was Strickland at high noon Tuesday glad-handing and greeting a receptive audience at the Memphis Rotary Club in his first major speech since the error came to light.

During his talk, Strickland repeated much of the boilerplate language from his State of the City address, including the jump in minority contracting. But this time, he smartly omitted numbers. Racial and gender diversity in city contracting is up, and that's a good thing for everyone.

"Memphis has momentum," Strickland said, reciting his 2019 campaign theme. He later added, "My job as mayor is to not just celebrate our successes, but to be clear-eyed about our challenges."

And with that, the campaign's first faux pas seemed to be over – unless of course his two major challengers, former mayor Willie Herenton and Shelby County Commissioner Tami Sawyer, try to keep it an issue going forward.

This much is clear. The 2019 mayor's race is shaping up as a three-way contest representing the past, present and, perhaps, future of city politics. Herenton, who was elected mayor five consecutive times starting in 1991, told The New Tri-State Defender last week he is running to complete an incomplete agenda.

In a startling bit of candor, Herenton told the newspaper he felt he needed to resign in 2009 amid a federal investigation into a questionable real estate deal.

The investigation, which resulted in no criminal charges, "weighed very heavily on my family and my ability to perform my duties as a mayor in the manner that I wanted to do," he told The Defender. "To make a long story short, I left before completing the agenda."

As for Sawyer, her agenda is to take Memphis in a different direction that focuses on people at the lower rung of the economic ladder.

Sawyer's grassroots activism propelled her to a seat on the County Commission last year. But after just six months in that role, she is looking to energize enough young voters and disaffected Memphians to overtake Herenton as the most viable alternative to Strickland.

"By 2030, economists anticipate that Black wealth will be at net zero dollars," Sawyer told The Daily Memphian in a podcast interview earlier this month. "That means there will be more debt in the Black community than there will be assets. And if that's 2030 across America, imagine when that will be in Memphis.

"Those are the type of things that I looked at when I said we don't have four or five years for basic leadership. What we need now is someone who's going to look at the fact that we are underserving too many Memphians of all identities."

The challenge for Sawyer, however, is convincing voters beyond her core constituency that she is prepared to replace Strickland in the mayor's office, while also fending off criticism from older Memphians that she has not spent enough time working in the trenches.

Herenton, in The New Tri-State Defender interview, appeared to take a subtle swipe at Sawyer – without naming her – when he said today's "so-called activists" don't know "a damned thing about activism.

"We were real activists," said the former mayor, adding that he marched with Dr. Martin Luther King Jr. and risked his job as a school principal by participating in the famous Black Monday protests of Memphis City Schools in 1969. "I put everything on the line when I was very young," he said.

With that kind of rhetoric, Herenton appears to be signaling that he intends to be tougher on Sawyer than on Strickland. All of which could serve to benefit the incumbent as he shows little evidence of a candidate under stress.

So with less than seven months remaining before the city election, the campaign themes are beginning to form. For Herenton, it's unfinished business. For Sawyer, it's new business. And for Strickland, it's taking care of business.

It all promises to be interesting. And, for political observers at least, a lot of fun.

—— —— ——

A crisis mayor | June 27, 2019

At last count, 15 people have filed petitions to run for mayor of Memphis in the Oct. 3 election. Less than a handful of them are considered serious candidates.

And only two of them, incumbent Jim Strickland and former mayor Willie Herenton, can readily attest to this fact: Running for mayor is tough, but being mayor is a lot tougher.

A crisis can strike like lightning. And the mayor invariably will be blamed for everything that goes wrong inside the city limits – from unemployment to damaging straight-line winds and everything in between.

It's how a mayor responds to those crises and effectively communicates with city residents that usually determines success or failure in the job.

The truth is, all mayors face challenging moments that can quickly morph into a crisis. Take, for example, Pete Buttigieg, the mayor of South Bend, Indiana.

Since announcing his candidacy for president, Buttigieg had been rising in the polls as a fresh and unconventional face in Democratic politics. But then it happened. A white South Bend police officer last week shot and killed a 54-year-old Black man who, according to the officer, was suspected of breaking into cars and approached him with a knife.

Now, members of South Bend's African American community, which makes up about 26% of the city's population, are incensed. And they are blaming Buttigieg for failing to address longstanding concerns about racial inequity in policing. Among those concerns is the fact that the police force is only about 5% black.

Because Buttigieg is a presidential candidate, his heated interactions with Black South Bend residents last weekend made national news and, in my view, severely crippled his already remote chances of being a serious contender for the Democratic nomination.

A somewhat similar incident occurred in Memphis 32 years ago that tested the responsiveness and credibility of then-mayor Dick Hackett.

It happened on the morning of Sept. 24, 1987, just days before a city election. Police officers were called to what was then known as the LeMoyne

Gardens housing project in South Memphis.

Once there, officers encountered a 27-year-old mentally disturbed Black man named Joseph DeWayne Robinson who was holding a 12-inch butcher knife. Within minutes, Robinson was dead – shot 10 times in the head, arms and torso.

And just like that, Hackett faced his second colossal crisis involving deadly force by police against Black citizens – the first being the 1983 Shannon Street killings, when officers shot seven people to death after they had abducted a police officer and beaten him to death.

In the 1987 shooting, witnesses disputed the police account that Robinson charged at officers with the knife. They claimed he was already on the ground when officers fired.

Two of Hackett's opponents, Minerva Johnican and Dedrick "Teddy" Withers, immediately attacked the mayor and his police director, John Holt, for running an out-of-control police force. Withers called the shooting an act of murder and said police had declared "open season" on Black men in Memphis.

In response, Hackett – accompanied by well-known attorney and future judge D'Army Bailey – paid a personal visit to Robinson's mother in her LeMoyne Gardens apartment.

They were seen embracing in the doorway after Hackett promised her the city would make changes to how the police responds to calls involving mentally ill residents.

Hackett was reelected in a landslide, receiving about 20% of the Black vote. And the following year, the mayor's administration created the Crisis Intervention Team, which became a national model.

So how have more recent mayors dealt with crisis situations? A C Wharton's crisis moment came in the form of severe cuts to police salaries and benefits.

The City Council, with backing from the Wharton administration, approved cuts to police and firefighters' health care benefits, salaries and pensions in 2014. Wharton said the move was necessary because the city faced rising annual requirements for its pension plan.

Rank-and-file officers and firefighters were livid. Scores of officers quit the force as a result. And in one controversial act of protest in August 2015, some 70 officers walked out of the funeral for slain fellow officer Sean Bolton just as Wharton started to speak.

Some criticized the officers for using the funeral to make a political statement. But coming just two months before the election, the incident contributed to Wharton's dwindling support, and he lost his reelection bid to Strickland.

As for Strickland and his police director, Michael Rallings, their big crisis moment was the July 2016 protest in support of the Black Lives Matter movement that shut down Interstate 40 on the Hernando DeSoto Bridge.

Rallings, who was interim director at the time, personally escorted the protesters – arm in arm – off the bridge without anyone getting hurt. The following day, he and Strickland sat through a televised, town hall-style forum at Greater Imani Church in Raleigh listening to a host of citizens' grievances.

And while Strickland got some credit for how the city peacefully handled the incident, protest leaders said the forum produced nothing in the way of substantial changes to police policies regarding excessive force.

Some of those protest leaders are now backing Shelby County Commissioner Tami Sawyer in her bid to unseat Strickland in the October election.

The point is this: Being mayor of any major city, whether it's South Bend or Memphis, is fraught with unforeseen calamity. It takes someone with political skill to know what to say in response and how to say it.

Most of all, it takes someone with proven leadership skills, who is willing to take criticism without being overly critical themselves. And who will never forget why they are there – to serve the public.

Come Oct. 3, city voters will decide who among the 15 candidates so far meets those requirements best.

— — —

A pivotal endorsement | August 22, 2019

Political campaign endorsements come and go. Usually they don't amount to much unless the person or organization making the endorsement is highly respected by an overwhelming majority of voters and has unquestioned credibility.

When I worked as a reporter for The Commercial Appeal in the 1970s and '80s, the late Terry Keeter, The CA's political writer, once told the story of a well-known elected leader who would repeatedly rail against the newspaper for being biased during his campaign stump speeches. After one such diatribe, Keeter said he told the politician, "You'd better quit complaining about the paper or we'll endorse you."

Reporters often jokingly commented that an endorsement by The CA was the kiss of death for a candidate. Still, most of them were eager to get the paper's editorial page support. But the most sought-after endorsements historically have been those from respected community leaders, other key politicians and influential groups.

For the first half of the 20th century, any candidate endorsed by Memphis political boss E.H. Crump was usually a shoo-in to win. For example, in 1914, Boss Crump orchestrated a write-in campaign for John Riechman, a close friend and political crony, for Shelby County sheriff.

The write-in effort, which targeted mostly Black voters, exceeded even Crump's expectations. Riechman ended up beating entrenched incumbent Sheriff T.G. Tate – who was endorsed by The Commercial Appeal – by nearly 9,000 votes out of 17,946 total votes cast.

Crump's choices for city, county and state offices rarely, if ever, lost at the ballot box from 1909 when Crump was first elected city mayor to his death in 1954 at the age of 80.

Beginning in the mid-1970s, an endorsement from then-U.S. Rep. Harold Ford Sr. became a cherished commodity for local candidates, Black and white. Some candidates paid dearly to be included on the official Ford Ballot, and the congressman often complained that political gadflies were peddling fake Ford ballots to confuse voters and make money.

These days, endorsements are still very much in vogue. But their effectiveness is questionable. Both the Democratic and Republican party organizations in Shelby County publish their choices in partisan races. So do advocacy groups, labor unions, neighborhood organizations and out-of-state special interest groups.

In this year's race for Memphis mayor, Shelby County Commission member Tami Sawyer touts a list of mostly left-leaning groups that have endorsed her campaign to unseat Mayor Jim Strickland.

Local organizations that favor Sawyer include UpTheVote901, Memphis For All and the AFL-CIO Central Labor Council of Memphis and West Tennessee. She also has been endorsed by Nashville-based Women for Tennessee's Future, which uses the acronym WTF.

National groups supporting Sawyer include Washington-based Leadership for Educational Equity, Massachusetts-based Maria's List and Democratic Socialists of America, which is headquartered in New York but has a Memphis-Mid-South chapter. Sawyer, to no surprise, also snagged the endorsement of the 2019 iteration of the People's Convention in June.

Meanwhile, former mayor Willie Herenton, who is seeking to reclaim the office 10 years after resigning, has received support from the leadership of the city's big three labor unions – the Memphis Firefighters Association, the Memphis Police Association and Local 1733 of the American Federation of State, County and Municipal Employees.

On the surface, these endorsements could be problematic for Strickland, whose two major opponents are African Americans in a city with a 64% majority Black population. But endorsements from organizations – especially obscure ones – are one thing. While support from a well-respected individual is another.

Which is why I was struck by a 60-second radio ad that began airing this week on local stations aimed at African American listeners. The speaker is Memphian Elmore Nickleberry. His words, written here in their entirety, sufficiently explain the rest.

"I started working for the Memphis sanitation department during the 1960s. I was part of the 1968 sanitation strike. I marched with Dr. Martin Luther King. I didn't set out to be a part of history, but it was poor conditions for the sanitation workers and I just wanted to feed my family.

"That was 50 years ago. Since that time, mayors have come and gone.

Not one of those mayors made sure that we were taken care of, that we could retire with respect until Jim Strickland came along. Mayor Strickland set up a fund for our retirement and a bonus, and he dedicated I Am A Man Plaza in our honor. Thank you, Mayor Strickland, for your leadership. My name is Elmore Nickleberry. I am a man. I am a voter. On October the 3rd, I'm voting to reelect Jim Strickland as our mayor."

The crux of Nickleberry's comments refer to the city's decision in 2017 to award grants of $70,000 each to the 14 surviving sanitation workers from the 1968 strike. The city also created a supplemental retirement plan for other sanitation workers hired since the strike.

Nickleberry is unquestionably the most visible and celebrated face from the historic strike that led to Dr. King's assassination April 4, 1968. He has been interviewed by The New York Times, the Smithsonian Magazine and CBS News.

Strickland campaign spokesman Steven Reid said Nickleberry volunteered to make the radio ad. "He said he was willing to do anything to help the mayor."

Of course, one ad from one unassuming, 87-year-old, recently retired Black sanitation worker may not turn the tide of an election. In today's heavily saturated social media world, endorsements are not what they used to be. Still, there is something powerful and authentic in Nickleberry's words that made me want to listen intently to his message.

This is not to downplay the support Herenton and Sawyer are receiving from local and national groups or diminish the million-dollar war chest Strickland has at his disposal to flood the airwaves with more commercials and litter the city with huge yard signs.

But while Herenton has the endorsement of leaders of the union representing sanitation workers, Strickland has in his corner the most recognizable sanitation worker ever.

Simply put, the Nickleberry radio ad is campaign gold. He comes across as unpretentious and believable. And his endorsement could go a long way in upping the vote for Strickland.

—— —— ——

A necessary debate | August 29, 2019

In 1999, Memphis survived a bare-knuckles, free-for-all mayor's race that was one for the ages. A race that still evokes hard feelings and hardened resolve 20 years later.

It was a race that explains a lot about the state of this year's mayoral contest and why voters are being denied the chance to size up the major candidates together in a formal debate.

The 1999 campaign included a collection of quirky second-tier candidates — some quirkier than others — who had no real shot at winning, but were great at providing comic relief.

Among them was beloved Memphis wrestler Jerry "The King" Lawler, who was the most credible of the perceived second tier and ended up finishing in a virtual tie for third place on election day. The least credible turned out to be perennial candidate Ernest Lunati, who was eventually kicked off the ballot by the Shelby County Election Commission.

The field also included colorful football coach Pepper Rodgers, who once guided the Memphis Showboats of the short-lived United States Football League. Rodgers promised voters that if elected, he would immediately resign. It never came to that.

But the pre-millennial mayor's race is best remembered for the squabbling and intense sniping by four political veterans, all trying to knock off popular two-term incumbent mayor Dr. Willie Herenton, the first African American elected to the office.

Chief among Herenton's opponents was Joe Ford, a member of the powerful Ford political family who at the time was serving on the Memphis City Council. Others were then-Shelby County Commission member Shep Wilbun, former City Council member Mary Rose McCormick and former County Commission member Pete Sisson.

Ford appeared to be making headway in challenging Herenton with help from his brothers, including former U.S. Rep. Harold Ford Sr., who managed the campaign.

A key moment in the race came when Joe Ford announced in mid-August that, if elected, he would appoint three deputy mayors — one for education, one for business and community development, and one for citizens' services.

The plan quickly started to turn some voters off, particularly when Ford left open the possibility that he might appoint one or more of his brothers to deputy mayor positions.

That led to the campaign's turning point: a televised mayoral debate — in which I served as moderator — at the University of Memphis.

During the questioning, Ford struggled to defend his deputy mayor proposal. Lawler produced the best shot of the night when he said of Ford's plan, "A vote for Joe Ford is (a vote for) Harold Ford and the rest of the Ford family. We're going to get the whole fam damily it looks like."

But the five challengers spent most of the night attacking Herenton. And he was clearly perturbed by it. That was the last time Herenton would appear in a political debate.

Despite Herenton's disgust, the debate, coming just two weeks before election day, helped him. He won reelection convincingly. He got 45% of the vote to Ford's 25% and Lawler's and Sisson's 11%. Everyone else finished in the low single digits in an election that produced a respectable 40% voter turnout.

When Herenton ran for his fifth term in 2007, he pointed to 1999 in explaining why he would not agree to any more debates.

"They had 14 candidates, and I found myself sitting on the stage with all of these guys — everybody shooting at me because I was the incumbent," Herenton said during a half-hour television interview in which he accepted pre-recorded questions from voters. "I said, 'Never will I do that again.' If I'm the incumbent, I have a record. I should be judged on my record."

Fast forward to today and Herenton is again running for mayor. Only now, he is not the incumbent. He quit the job in 2009, and except for a failed run for the Ninth District Congressional seat in 2010, he has been out of politics since.

And yet, the bitterness of 1999 is still there. Herenton has so far declined to take part in any debates, televised or otherwise, with incumbent Mayor Jim Strickland, County Commission member Tami Sawyer and businessman LeMichael Wilson.

It is a grievous error on Herenton's part. Here's why:

In his last political race in 2010, Herenton was trounced by incumbent U.S. Rep. Steve Cohen for the Ninth District Democratic nomination. Cohen, who is white, got 78% of the vote to Herenton's 21% in a district that is overwhelmingly African American.

The result caused plenty of Memphians to conclude that Herenton's political time was over. That the old Doc magic had faded.

More than a few Memphis voters were surprised when Herenton announced in April 2018 that he intended to again seek the mayor's office this year. Others were less kind, saying it was time for him to "go to the house."

But so far, Herenton has run a credible campaign. He still trails Strickland in the mayor's internal polls, but Herenton has overtaken Sawyer as the incumbent's top challenger.

A televised debate would be Herenton's chance to convince skeptical voters that he's still got it. Unlike 1999, he would be the hunter instead of the hunted.

I don't blame Strickland for not wanting to debate just Sawyer and Wilson. The mayor has nothing to gain and everything to lose by agreeing to that. It should be everyone in the top tier or nothing.

The fact is, Memphis voters deserve to see and hear all the serious candidates — side by side — who want to lead this city into the next decade.

This is not about 20-year-old grudges. It's about leadership. Who's got it, who wants it and who's lost it. That should not be too much to ask in exchange for our votes.

—— —— ——

Hurtful words | September 19, 2019

Let me cut to the chase. Shelby County Commissioner Tami Sawyer's race for Memphis mayor is doomed.

She lacks the preparation and, at this point, the credibility necessary to lead a city of some 647,000 diverse residents — the 29th-largest city in the nation, according to 2019 U.S. Census Bureau estimates.

And she has shown no capacity to oversee the plethora of city departments, to offer cogent suggestions on such issues as what to do with Tom Lee Park or to effectively relate to this city's first responders.

In essence, I'm convinced that Sawyer's already longshot quest for mayor has imploded. And the wounds were all self-inflicted.

It gives me no joy to say any of this, because Sawyer had succeeded in energizing a base of mostly young, liberal voters through grassroots activism, a nonconventional agenda and impressive smarts.

Plus, Mayor Jim Strickland, who is seeking a second and final term in the Oct. 3 election, needed to face vigorous opposition beyond former mayor Willie Herenton. Someone from a different generation who could force the incumbent to sharpen his campaign message and make the case that his base of support goes beyond the Poplar corridor and the baby boomers who traditionally show up at the polls.

Sawyer was supposed to be that candidate. At least her enthusiastic supporters thought so. Many of them saw in her another Stacey Abrams, the former Georgia state representative who almost became that state's first African American governor, losing a hotly contested race in 2018 by about 50,000 votes.

But the hard truth is, Sawyer, politically speaking, is no Stacey Abrams, who served 10 years in the Georgia Legislature and was the House minority leader for six of those years.

Sawyer's grassroots activism, primarily through the effort to take down Confederate statues from city-owned parks, gave her plenty of media exposure and helped her win an open seat on the County Commission just last year.

One knowledgeable political source told me that when talk first surfaced of Sawyer, 37, possibly challenging Strickland in this year's mayoral election, she was urged to stand down and get something accomplished on the commission first. Then perhaps look at a race for mayor in 2023 when Strickland would be term-limited.

Clearly, Sawyer did not take the advice, which apparently gave rise to her campaign slogan, "We Can't Wait."

But she was not prepared from the outset to handle the rough-and-tumble atmosphere of a campaign for mayor — or the intense media scrutiny that goes with the territory. Hence at times, Sawyer has seemed to be campaigning against the news media, rather than Strickland or Herenton.

Internal polling from the Strickland camp has consistently shown Sawyer's support for mayor in the single digits. That number dropped even lower after CNN political commentator Angela Rye spoke at a Sawyer campaign event in August and called Strickland a racist and a Dixiecrat.

Then last week, Sawyer found herself in much deeper political trouble after tweets — some of them 10 years old — came to light in which she disparaged police and talked jokingly about killing white babies after watching horror movies.

But the tweet that likely sunk her candidacy was one from five years ago when she seemingly bragged, "We had a teacher that was a closeted lesbian. Decided it was our duty to out her. She quit after a semester." The tweet also included the hashtag #meangirls.

Sawyer's initial response to media coverage of the tweets was one of defiance. "We can examine my decade old tweets out of context and debate what kind of person I was or wasn't in 2009," she tweeted on Friday the 13th. "Or, we can examine what's happening in Memphis today. I'm running because this is life or death for Memphians. The stakes are too high to get caught in this foolishness."

The following evening, however, she posted a lengthy apology on the blog site Medium. But even that statement began with a bit of snobbery aimed at the media. "Over the last week, the biggest news story in Memphis hasn't been our poverty, what's happening in our schools, or what's happening in our neighborhoods. It's been tweets I made about a decade ago," she wrote.

News flash: Some of us in the media and others in Memphis have been grappling with, and searching for, solutions to poverty, failing schools and neighborhood decay for years. That includes the years Sawyer was in Washington or when she was forcing a teacher to resign because of her sexual preference.

Eventually, Sawyer's blog post got around to real contrition. "There are tweets that show a woman who, at that point, still hadn't come to terms with her homophobia, who still wasn't standing up and being a voice for all, regardless of ability.

"I am, not just deeply ashamed, but deeply sorry for those tweets, the harm they caused at the time, and the harm that seeing them now will still bring up, especially for members of those communities, and for all of us."

On Monday, as LGBTQ+ advocacy groups roundly criticized Sawyer, she told The Daily Memphian she is reaching out to those groups and to individuals who are upset over her tweets.

"I fell short in my path," she said. "And that path is something I have to reckon with. I've worked really hard to make sure that they understand that I understand the pain that was caused."

Most important, Sawyer said her focus now is not on getting her campaign back on track. Rather it's about "people who are really dear to me – that they hear me that I see their pain."

Those are laudable words. But with two weeks remaining before election day, are they enough to salvage her campaign? My answer is an emphatic no. I say that not out of malice or ill will. But because from the beginning of her campaign, Sawyer showed a level of political naïveté even as she energized millennial voters.

With the rare exception of a certain occupant of the White House, attacking the news media is not a winning formula in politics.

There also is another lesson to be learned from her mistakes. Be careful what you post on social media. Because hurtful words have a way of coming back to hurt you — sometimes when you least expect it.

—— —— ——

A sobering message | October 5, 2019

Late in the evening of Oct. 3, 1991, as midnight approached, Dr. Willie W. Herenton was surrounded by nervous family members and hundreds of wide-eyed supporters.

They had crowded into The Peabody hotel, the longtime brick-and-mortar symbol of privilege and power in Memphis.

It was election night in the Bluff City. And Herenton, the underdog candidate for mayor against entrenched incumbent Dick Hackett, chose the hotel for his watch party to make a symbolic point of his own. That an African American kid who grew up poor in South Memphis was about to take the reins of power in a city known for its political elitism.

Once word finally came from the Shelby County Election Commission headquarters that Herenton had won by a scant 172 votes – later adjusted to a 142-vote margin – jubilation erupted throughout The Peabody and into the streets Downtown.

Minutes later, Herenton tore himself from the hugs and kisses and addressed the joyous crowd, pledging to unite a racially and politically polarized city.

"This victory tonight represents a new beginning for Memphis," he said. "A new beginning that will move this city toward unprecedented unity and prosperity for all of our city."

Herenton went on to serve nearly 18 years in the mayor's office. And while he never fully achieved the unity and prosperity for Memphis that he promised, he did succeed in earning the respect and admiration of many Memphians for, first, winning the office against tremendous odds, and then maintaining his political strength for so long.

On Thursday, 28 years to the day of his stunning mayoral victory, Herenton gathered again with supporters on election night in Memphis. And again, he was an underdog candidate in the mayor's race.

This time, however, the watch party was in more humble surroundings – storefront space on Third Street in South Memphis. And the election outcome was humbling as well.

Herenton finished a distant second to incumbent Mayor Jim Strickland, who won in a landslide with 62% of the vote to Herenton's 29%.

Unofficially, Herenton received 27,694 votes to Strickland's total of 59,886. Shelby County Commissioner Tami Sawyer finished a disappointing third with 6,666 total votes, or 7%.

In the 1991 race, Herenton amassed 122,596 total votes and the turnout was nearly 65%. On Thursday, only 96,245 total votes were cast in the mayor's race for a turnout of just 25.5%.

Elections are about more than just putting people into office. Elections are about sending messages. And Thursday, Memphis voters sent several.

By an overwhelming margin, voters said Strickland is doing just fine in the mayor's office and the city is indeed moving in the right direction.

Voters also spoke clearly that playing racial politics, whether it's subtle or overt, is not a winning formula in a citywide contest. No, Memphis has not completely unloaded its racial baggage. Far from it.

But in our modern-day local politics, people emerge from time to time with a remarkable ability to transcend racial differences and win political support in every sector of the city.

Strickland is such a person, as is U.S. Rep. Steve Cohen, as was former city and county mayor A C Wharton, and as was Herenton during most of his reelection campaigns.

Sawyer's attempt to paint Strickland with the racism brush was a total failure, particularly among African American women. It, and those awful tweets, very likely cost her some votes and could hamper her future efforts at higher public office.

I'm also convinced that Memphis voters sent another important and compassionate message Thursday – and it was aimed directly at Dr. Herenton.

It was a message of thanks for his public service to Memphis as a city school teacher, principal, deputy superintendent, superintendent and finally as the longest-serving mayor in the city's history.

It was a message of gratitude for all he endured, racially and otherwise, while serving in public life. No, his record is not spotless. It includes plenty of failures along with successes. But there is little doubt among most Memphians that Herenton cares deeply about his hometown and wants it to prosper.

Above all, the message Memphians sent Herenton, who will turn 80 next April, is not that he has nothing else to offer. It is that he has nothing else to prove.

Perhaps it's true that Herenton has long regretted resigning as mayor in 2009. But that was his choice. If he indeed has an unfinished agenda, as he insisted during the campaign, it will have to remain unfinished. It's time for others to move their agendas forward.

Former County Commissioner Sidney Chism, a onetime Herenton loyalist who supported Strickland this year, said it best. "We had an opportunity to be elected to office and make some major changes. That era is over," he told The Daily Memphian.

"We're at a place now where young people want a place at the table. They want to be treated fair and equal and have an opportunity to advance themselves in life. ... You've gotta know when to get out of the way."

I believe Herenton has now gotten that message. At his watch party Thursday, he looked more relieved than disappointed. And his words were conciliatory as he offered congratulations and support to Strickland.

"I think we effectively campaigned," he said. "It's just that the voters made a different decision."

Yes, they did. It was a decision far different from the one 28 years ago that sent a proud and determined Black man to the mayor's office at City Hall. But it was the correct decision, based not on disdain for a man who didn't know when to quit, but out of respect for a native son who already has given a lifetime of service.

— — —

The year of the voter | January 9, 2020

I am usually terrible at predictions. So, I try to avoid making one unless it is a sure thing.

But I am prepared to offer a prediction for the new year that is based on a degree of certainty mixed with hope. I believe that 2020 will be the year of the voter.

I'm convinced voter turnout, particularly for the November presidential election, will be the strongest Shelby County residents – and more broadly Americans – have seen in more than 50 years. Fueling this robust voter participation will be a combination of anger and fear – two emotions that have traditionally driven people to the polls in large numbers.

That's not supposition. It's based on data. A 2011 University of Michigan study found that anger is the top motivator in election participation. And the angrier people are, the higher the turnout will be.

"Anger in politics can play a particularly vital role, motivating some people to participate in ways they might ordinarily not," said Nicholas Valentino, a Michigan research professor and the study's lead author.

A more recent study by Stanford University political scientists also found that voters are motivated more by animosity against candidates they oppose than by candidates they support.

"Today, it is outgroup animus rather than ingroup favoritism that drives political behavior," wrote political scientist Masha Krupenkin, now a professor at Boston College. She co-authored the 2018 Stanford study called "The Strengthening of Partisan Affect." Among its conclusions: "From the 1980s onward, partisans have grown increasingly more hostile toward the opposing party."

While turnout has ebbed and flowed over the last 60 years, voter participation generally has been its highest during years in which the country was in crisis or when the electorate seemed to be consumed by fear and anger over certain candidates and the direction the nation is taking.

Voter turnout historically in Shelby County is a good indicator of this trend. I examined the numbers over the past 66 years based on newspaper archives and Shelby County Election Commission records.

In the 1964 presidential election, Shelby's turnout, according to press reports, was more than 75%. That was the year President Lyndon Johnson, a Democrat from Texas, signed into law the landmark Civil Rights Act. The act banned segregation in public places and outlawed employment discrimination based on race, color, religion, sex and national origin.

The act instantly became the No. 1 issue in the presidential election. Republican Barry Goldwater, who was against the legislation, lost the election, but gained support from angry white voters in the Deep South who opposed civil rights.

Many of them had been longtime Democrats. But the Civil Rights Act started the shift of most white Southerners to the Republican Party. Tennessee, aided by a massive black voter turnout in Shelby County in 1964, went for Johnson, who got 55% of the statewide vote to Goldwater's 44%.

Four years later in 1968, Memphis and the nation were rocked by the assassinations of Dr. Martin Luther King Jr. and Democratic presidential candidate Robert F. Kennedy, while protesters filled the streets to protest the Vietnam War and to continue the push for civil rights. Republican Richard Nixon won the presidency over Hubert Humphrey, and turnout in Shelby County that year was 73%.

Voting decreased slightly during the 1970s. But in 1980, Shelby's turnout was an impressive 74% as Republican Ronald Reagan easily won the presidency over incumbent Democrat Jimmy Carter. Reagan was aided by voter anger over the Iran hostage crisis and massive inflation, including escalating gasoline prices.

In the 1992 election, won by Bill Clinton, turnout in Shelby County again reached 73%. It would be the last election – federal, state or local – to come close to a 70% turnout. The highest turnout in presidential elections since then was 65% in 1988, when George H. W. Bush was elected, and 62% in 2012 when Barack Obama was reelected.

I predict Shelby County will return to a 70% level this year – and it will be close to that number nationwide. Partisan anger for and against President Donald Trump, along with sustained fear over his erratic leadership, will be the primary drivers. But other factors will play a role as well. One of them is health care.

Republicans long ago decided they don't care about accessible health care for millions of working-class Americans who can't afford it. And if Democrats are smart, they will make health care their top political issue this year.

Better yet, they should talk to Dr. Scott Morris, founder and CEO of Church Health in Memphis. In fact, if Democrats are smart, they would put Morris in charge of formulating their health-care platform.

Morris was a last-minute substitute speaker Jan. 7 at the Memphis Rotary Club's weekly luncheon meeting at The Bluffs on Highland Avenue. He delivered a passionate and personal message about the urgent need to make health care available to those who can least afford it. It was the best speech I have heard at a Rotary meeting in the nearly 15 years I have been a member.

Without being partisan, Morris spoke in easy-to-understand language about the travesty of the Tennessee Legislature's refusal to expand Medicaid for the state's working poor. We're talking about some 300,000 Tennesseans, many of whom are Shelby County residents, who have jobs, however menial, but have no employer-provided health insurance and cannot afford it themselves.

Former Gov. Bill Haslam tried to coax lawmakers into expanding Medicaid in 2015. But Republicans who control the Legislature refused to even consider it because by doing so, they would be acquiescing to the Affordable Care Act, also known as Obamacare.

The Republicans' argument is that expanding Medicaid would be too expensive in later years, even though initially 100% of the cost would come from the federal government. And the state's share would rise to no more than 10%.

As Morris pointed out to Rotarians, Tennessee taxpayers are sending about $1.5 billion annually to the federal government that is being used for Medicaid expansion in other states. "The poorest people (in Tennessee) get nothing," Morris said.

But instead of Medicare for all, which some 2020 Democratic presidential candidates are pushing, Morris suggests we should consider lowering the age of Medicare eligibility to 55.

Once Morris finished, I was angry that many of our state and federal elected leaders have given only lip service to improving health care when in reality they are turning their backs on the working poor.

Others should be angry also. And they should channel that anger into activism by making sure they and those they know are registered to vote.

Anger, fear and a demand for change drove more than 70% of registered voters to the polls in the 1960s. My prediction in 2020 is that it will happen again.

—— —— ——

Lamar's lack of courage | February 6, 2020

His statement contained 467 words, which was 437 words too many.

U.S. Sen. Lamar Alexander needed only 30 of them to tell the nation what most of us already knew – that President Donald J. Trump was dead wrong to attempt a shakedown of a foreign government for his personal political gain, but that Alexander is not courageous enough to demand that we learn the truth under oath.

Instead of the word salad that came from Tennessee's senior Republican senator late on the evening of Jan. 30, all we really needed was this single sentence: "There is no need for more evidence to prove something that has already been proven and that does not meet the United States Constitution's high bar for an impeachable offense."

Fine. That should have been it – period, paragraph, end of statement. The rest of Alexander's treatise only showed that, in addition to courage, he needed an editor.

I have spent the last week reading and re-reading the senator's protracted statement searching for clarity and pearls of wisdom from a gentleman who has seen it all in politics. I got neither. What I did get was the picture of a partisan guy pretending to be someone he no longer is – a statesman who puts country ahead of party.

This is a man who for more than a generation has carefully cultivated a reputation as a moderate Republican, an independent thinker and a strict constitutionalist. But when America needed him most to be all of that, Alexander caved.

He caved to pressure from Trump, caved to allegiance to buddy Mitch McConnell and caved to the threat of retribution from Trump loyalists that would follow and hound him into retirement at the end of the year.

Sure, Trump's acquittal was a fait accompli before the Senate impeachment trial even started. There was no way 67 senators were going to vote to convict this president when Republicans hold the majority and every GOP member – except outcast Mitt Romney and cautious Susan Collins – is expected to toe the line at all costs.

Hence, Alexander should have just let those 30 words represent his sincere belief that what Trump did was wrong, just not impeachable. Instead, he began his statement with the self-serving claim that he had been fighting all along for a trial that included evidence.

"I worked with other senators to make sure that we have the right to ask for more documents and witnesses," he insisted.

But after House managers, in opening arguments, presented a convincing case against Trump, Alexander concluded, "There is no need for more evidence to prove that the president asked Ukraine to investigate Joe Biden and his son Hunter....

"There is no need for more evidence to conclude that the president withheld United States aid, at least in part, to pressure Ukraine to investigate the Bidens; the House managers have proved this with what they call a 'mountain of overwhelming evidence.'"

Later in the statement, Alexander attempted to show somewhat of a break with the president's defense, while also trying to minimize the seriousness of Trump's actions.

"It was inappropriate for the president to ask a foreign leader to investigate his political opponent and to withhold United States aid to encourage that investigation. When elected officials inappropriately interfere with such investigations, it undermines the principle of equal justice under the law."

No, senator. Inappropriate is not the appropriate word. Calling certain African nations "s---hole countries" was inappropriate. Implying that the late Congressman John Dingell is looking up at us from hell was inappropriate. Pointing out a Black supporter at one of his rallies and calling him "my African American" was inappropriate. And calling pro football players who knelt during the national anthem SOBs was inappropriate.

Withholding duly appropriated government aid in order to force a country to do his political bidding is more than just inappropriate. It's illegal.

But here is where Alexander's statement really flies in the face of logic. "The question then is not whether the president did it, but whether the United States Senate or the American people should decide what to do about what he did. I believe that the Constitution provides that the people should make that decision in the presidential election."

That's pure political doubletalk. The best way for the people to determine if what Trump did makes him unworthy of a second term is to hear from witnesses, under oath, who know firsthand what happened.

Voters deserved to hear from John Bolton, the former national security adviser; Mick Mulvaney, the current White House chief of staff; and others who were in the room.

If they had refused a Senate subpoena or if the president had blocked their trial testimony, the people could take that into consideration at the ballot box.

Alexander then ended the statement with a patronizing history lesson on the Constitution. "Our founding documents provide for duly elected presidents who serve with 'the consent of the governed,' not at the pleasure of the United States Congress. Let the people decide."

Except let's withhold vital evidence from the people that would make their decision more informed.

I'm not the only one who found Alexander's weak excuse for siding with the party over the people a sad moment in history. Presidential historian Douglas Brinkley, appearing on CBS Sunday morning, said, "The day of John F. Kennedy's 'Profiles in Courage,' at least temporarily, is over."

He added, "Bipartisanism has for the time being gone the way of the dodo – extinct."

Alexander was supposed to be different. He was supposed to be that guy who got elected Tennessee governor in 1978, and then stepped in several days before his scheduled swearing-in to save the state from the reckless and criminal behavior of his predecessor Ray Blanton.

He was supposed to be the same guy who went to Washington as education secretary in 1991, who ran a respectable campaign for president himself in 1996, and who easily got elected senator three times with a streak of independence mixed with thoughtfulness.

The reality is, despite straining to justify not hearing from relevant impeachment witnesses, Alexander and his GOP compatriots have been willing to overlook Trump's trampling over our system of checks and balances because this president has given them tax cuts, conservative judges – some of whom are unqualified – and a reversal of many Obama-era policies.

In the end, I guess I expected more than the man from Maryville could give. I was hoping for political courage.

All I got was 467 words that said nothing.

A voter at 105 | Feb. 27, 2020

Her name is Charlotte Robertson. But on the Shelby County Election Commission voter registration rolls, she is listed as Lindsay Robertson.

Lindsay was her husband's first name. He passed away in the 1980s after working for years as a photo engraver for Memphis Publishing Co., helping to produce the afternoon Memphis Press-Scimitar newspaper.

Charlotte and Lindsay were married in the early 1940s, probably 1941, she believes. She can't recall for sure. And at age 105, she can be forgiven for a small lapse in memory, even if it's about her wedding day.

Back then, it was commonplace in Memphis for married women to be identified only by their husband's first and last names. And yes, by today's standards, it was a sexist practice, perpetuated by the newspapers and other places, including the election commission.

But Charlotte – or Mrs. Lindsay – Robertson was not about to let a little thing like a name discrepancy deter her from voting. Over the years, poll workers have questioned her about it a couple of times. But she has lived in the same house for 65 years, and has never been denied the right to cast her ballot.

And after all these years, she figures it's not worth the time and effort to correct the name. As long as she's allowed to vote, who cares what they call her?

As Shelby County voters prepare to head to the polls March 3 for the 2020 presidential primary, there can be no better example of someone who cherishes the constitutional right to vote than Robertson. Someone who won't let age, or the wrong name, stand in the way.

Records I received from the election commission show Robertson has participated in every presidential election going back to the 1970s – and no doubt long before that. She has been a routine early voter since 1996. Plus, she rarely misses a Memphis municipal, county or state election, including primaries.

Robertson will turn 106 in July. And the good Lord willing, she says, she intends to vote in the November presidential election. To put it bluntly, Charlotte Robertson is darn serious about voting. As serious as life itself.

"And life to me is serious to the end," she told me in a brief telephone interview this week.

But believe it or not, Robertson is not the oldest active registered voter on the Shelby County rolls. That honor goes to Brunette Nelms, who will be 110 on March 9.

Nelms, an accomplished pianist and former schoolteacher, is a transplant from Mississippi, and first voted in Memphis in the 2007 city election. Since then, she – like Robertson – has not missed a presidential election.

Harold Morrison, 104, and Mary Robinson, 103, are the third- and fourth-oldest voters still listed as active. Both have lengthy voting histories, and last participated in the 2018 midterm election.

My point is simple and direct. Voting should be automatic and as routine as waking up each day. Our political leaders should be working continuously to make it easier to vote, not more difficult.

Too many people have fought and died for the right to vote to let the opportunity to cast a ballot go for naught. And especially in a politically volatile year such as this one, voter turnout in the November general election should be 70%, or even 80%. And the Super Tuesday primary should approach at least 50%.

That's wishful thinking, I know. But really, it should not be. As I was speaking with Robertson about her commitment to voting and researching the oldest voters in Shelby County, I naturally thought about my own late mother, Bertha Sanford, who lived to be 101.

My mother, who spent all but about seven years of her life in Mississippi, was not allowed to vote until she was in her mid-50s. On Aug. 10, 1964, she was among a small group of African Americans in Panola County who challenged the state's refusal to register Black voters.

When she showed up at the county courthouse that day, Mom didn't have to pay a poll tax, which was one of the tactics used to keep Black people from registering. But she was forced to read and interpret language from the state's Constitution.

That was child's play for my mother, who went to college for two years, studied English and French and taught school for several years. She did as instructed with ease, and the clerk reluctantly signed her up. For the next 46 years, Mom never missed a state or federal election. And I don't either.

So, who are the real role models in our lives? Teachers, coaches, faith leaders, yes. But I submit great role models are also those people who understand what it means to practice good citizenship. People who involve themselves in the political process, who study the candidates and the issues, and who believe that voting is more than a civil right. It's a duty.

My parents will always be my heroes and top two role models. But now, I am adding a few other names to my list – such as Mary Robinson, 103; Harold Morrison, 104; Charlotte (aka Lindsay) Robertson, 105; and Brunette Nelms, 109.

When you go to the polls on Super Tuesday or for a future election, remember those folks – along with my mom. Perhaps then you will keep going back routinely for decades to come.

—— —— ——

No national unity | April 23, 2020

It was a moment most proud, peace-loving Americans should never forget.

In the early evening of Sept. 11, 2001, mere hours after the horrific terrorist attacks in New York, Washington and rural Pennsylvania, about 150 members of Congress gathered on the east front steps of the U.S. Capitol.

They stood shoulder to shoulder – senators with representatives, Democrats with Republicans – to speak with one voice in condemnation of that day's tragic events.

"When America suffers ... we as a Congress and a government stand united and we stand together to fight this evil threat," said then House Speaker Dennis Hastert, a Republican from Illinois, to unanimous applause.

Hastert was joined front and center at the podium by Democratic Sens. Harry Reid and Tom Daschle, Democratic Rep. Richard Gephardt and Republican Sen. Trent Lott.

After a moment of silence that lasted 17 seconds, the lawmakers were starting to disperse when spontaneously some in the group began singing "God Bless America." Congressional leaders at the front froze in place and joined the chorus.

One headline later described the scene as a "beautiful moment" that was noted by news organizations around the world. "One of the most poignant images as the symbols of U.S. economic and military power burned was the spontaneous singing of 'God Bless America' by members of Congress," wrote a reporter for the Australian, one of that country's leading newspapers. "They stood shaken and tearful on the steps of the Capitol, their love of nation and all that it symbolizes plain for the world to see."

In 2020, America is suffering again. Not by sinister people perpetrating evil acts, as Hastert described the Sept. 11 attacks. This time, the perpetrator is a silent, invisible killer known as COVID-19.

But it has proven to be deadlier by far than the 9/11 terrorists. And no section of America, the land we all love, has been spared. Yet, the bipartisan unity from our elected leaders is noticeably missing.

They may not be able to gather on the Capitol steps because of social distancing guidelines. But where are the images on Zoom of Mitch McConnell, Nancy Pelosi, Chuck Schumer, Jim Clyburn, Kevin McCarthy and others – if not singing – speaking with one voice that America stands united in its fight against this menacing pandemic?

They are nowhere to be found.

Instead, we have a buck-passing president who, without legitimate contradiction, failed initially to take the spread of the coronavirus seriously. He is now constantly lurching from one policy position to another with just two things on his mind – getting showered with praise and getting reelected.

Those in President Trump's administration who are trying to provide aid and comfort to the nation are being undermined and hamstrung by an ill-equipped leader. A leader who every day seeks to shift blame to his predecessors, to the Democrats – particularly Democratic governors – and the news media, while refusing to shoulder any responsibility himself.

As a result, the dissension has filtered down to statehouses, local governments and finally into the streets with thoughtless protesters thumbing their noses at social distancing and demanding that states end stay-at-home orders. What's worse, Trump is encouraging the rallies because the participants are part of his base, and he needs their energy, however misguided, as he sees his poll numbers dropping.

Some protesters, however, were themselves confronted – at a safe distance – by health care workers who realize their safety is at risk from these selfish demonstrations.

But governors such as Bill Lee in Tennessee, Brian Kemp in Georgia and Ron DeSantis in Florida – all Republicans and Trump loyalists – bowed to the pressure and are canceling their respective states' stay-at-home orders.

At least Lee had the good sense to exempt Tennessee's four largest population centers. And Memphis Mayor Jim Strickland is extending his stay-at-home order to May 5. My hunch is the extension will last even longer.

Lee's decision to reopen the state's economy May 1 was met with harsh criticism by the state House Democratic Caucus, who accused the governor of lifting restrictions too quickly and putting people's lives at risk.

Getting Tennesseans back to work "needs to be done in a manner that protects the lives of residents during this unprecedented humanitarian crisis," the House Democrats said Tuesday, April 21.

To no surprise, Republican Lt. Gov. Randy McNally is defending Lee's decision as being "flexible and data-focused." McNally insists the state is doing an exemplary job of testing and the curve of cases is flattening.

The saving grace for Memphis and its suburbs has been the swift local response to the pandemic, particularly by elected leaders and the local coronavirus task force.

Local mayors, led by Strickland, were well ahead of the governor in issuing emergency orders closing nonessential businesses and urging residents to stay home. Local schools and universities were also more proactive than Lee. They shut down classes in early March. Sporting events and, eventually, Memphis In May were put on hold.

And when scores of Memphians decided to trek to local parks without regard to social distancing, Strickland shut them down.

The federal, state, local and individual responses to COVID-19 should never have been an us-versus-them proposition. Unlike the 9/11 attacks, the federal government had plenty of advance warning that a major pandemic was not just possible, but probable. And when the deadly cases in Wuhan, China, became public late last year, the Trump administration should have done much more than it did. Instead, Trump kept telling Americans as late as February that the virus was under control and the few cases that had been discovered in the U.S. would quickly be reduced to zero. In essence, this administration's COVID-19 response has been a colossal failure.

And no, I don't expect any Kumbaya moments such as the one on the Capitol steps after 9/11. Our politics today are too toxic. And sadly, we have a president who enjoys fighting rather than leading.

Hopefully, we will get past this scourge with as few lives lost as possible, and our economy will start to rebound. But regardless, things will inevitably change. It would be great if those changes include our political divide.

—— —— ——

Votes for Bertha | August 20, 2020

Peg Watkins and I are friends on Facebook. I don't personally know her that well, but we do have 145 mutual friends on the social media site.

Judging by many of her Facebook posts, our political views are somewhat similar. I believe Watkins cares about politics, and cares even more about the precious right to vote.

Which is why her recent suggestion to me via Facebook of an informal get-out-the-vote campaign has an appealing ring to it. And it's one that I hope catches on – "Votes for Bertha."

She sent the suggestion to me Aug. 13, the day I posted a photo of my late mother, Bertha Lee Sanford, along with information marking the 56th anniversary of the day she first registered to vote in Panola County, Mississippi.

Mom, who was 53 at the time, was among the first African Americans in the county to register, and my post briefly explained the ordeal she went through just to exercise her constitutional right to cast a ballot in Mississippi. More on that later.

This is what Watkins wrote in response: "I can only imagine what she went through to register and vote. 50 [years] and the struggle continues. We should start a campaign — 'Votes for Bertha!' I'll be the first."

And just like that, I am ready to launch #VotesforBertha in memory of a courageous woman who faced down indifferent and bigoted workers in the Panola County Circuit Clerk's office in August 1964 so she could add her name to the voter registration rolls.

Watkins is 100% right. The struggle continues. We now have a president who is waging an all-out campaign to undermine voting in the November general election because he's seen the polling numbers. And they show him on the verge of losing big time.

So with President Trump pulling the strings, Postmaster General Louis DeJoy instituted a series of cutbacks in mail delivery and equipment, all aimed at making it more difficult to vote absentee by mail.

DeJoy, a major Trump fundraiser, had ordered reduced hours at post offices, some mail sorting machines taken out of service and truckloads of those familiar blue mail collection boxes hauled away and stored.

But bipartisan pushback against the changes became so strong, that DeJoy was forced to reverse course. He announced Tuesday, Aug. 18, that Postal Service changes will be suspended until after the Nov. 3 election.

And yet, other efforts to stifle voting continue. Tennessee officials, including Gov. Bill Lee, Secretary of State Tre Hargett and others, spent plenty of time and taxpayer money to block an extension of absentee voting in the state. A Davidson County chancellor ruled in July that fear of contracting or spreading the coronavirus was a valid reason to vote absentee this year.

But the state appealed the ruling directly to the state Supreme Court, and earlier this month, the high court reversed the decision. It said Tennesseans with underlying health conditions that make them susceptible to catching COVID-19, may vote absentee. But a mere fear of catching the virus is not reason enough to vote by mail.

Add in past voter suppression efforts, such as rejecting a valid college student ID as acceptable to vote while approving a handgun carry permit, and it's clear. Elected officials, mostly Republicans, want to make it more difficult to vote, rather than easier.

Yes, the struggle continues.

But it is a struggle that we must overcome. Not since 1964 has voting been as critical as it is this year. In 1964, the country was at a dangerous crossroads in a fight between civil rights and continued racial oppression.

In the presidential race that year, Democrat Lyndon Johnson was on the side of civil rights, including the right of every American — regardless of race — to vote. His Republican opponent, Arizona Sen. Barry Goldwater, aligned himself with Southern segregationists — most of them disaffected Democrats — who remained violently opposed to allowing African Americans to vote.

And that brings me back to my mother, a college-educated and politically-active former schoolteacher, who was waiting for the right moment to challenge Mississippi's closed society. That moment came Aug. 10, 1964, five weeks after President Johnson signed into law a landmark Civil Rights bill that started the dismantling of segregation laws in the country.

When Mom showed up at the circuit clerk's office that day, she was handed the Sworn Written Application for Registration, along with a copy of the Mississippi Constitution. She was told only to find Section 43 and write down what it says.

It took her mere seconds to find it. And she copied it word for word using stellar cursive penmanship. The impressed clerk took the application, marked through the requirement that Mom write an interpretation of what she had written and approved her as a legitimate voter. The clerk then wrote an N, for Negro, at the top of the form.

That November, my mother cast her first ever ballot, voting for Johnson in the presidential election. Then on Feb. 15, 1965, my father, Freddie J. Sanford, registered for the first time at the age of 54. He also was given a copy of the state Constitution and told to find and write down Section 51, which he did with ease. The notation C-M, presumably for Colored Male, is handwritten at the top of his application.

In 2007, after I wrote a column about voting, a clerk in the Panola County office dug through old files, found the original applications signed by my parents and mailed them to me. I am so appreciative that she did.

So, Peg Watkins, I am on board with #VotesforBertha. America deserves a turnout this year of nearly 70%, which nearly rivals 1964. Forget the suppression attempts. All eligible voters should make sure they are registered. And then, by all means, vote either by absentee, during early voting or in person on election day.

My mom would be pleased.

— — —

Tennessee's felony squad | August 27, 2020

As a kid, I was addicted to television. I still am, to a point. But my TV fare these days involves mostly news and sports.

Back then, it was westerns, comedies and police dramas. One of my favorites was an obscure crime show called "Felony Squad." In it, a dogged team of investigators took only 30 minutes each week to track down and bring felony charges against assorted miscreants and misfits.

I was reminded of that show recently after Tennessee's vengeful state Legislature – with a go-along governor as an accomplice – decided to make protesting on state property a felony.

And not just a felony, but one punishable by up to six years in prison, which also carries an automatic loss of voting rights. Think about that for a second. Exercising your First Amendment right to peacefully assemble after hours on state property to demand, for example, more voting rights could get you a prison stretch and banishment from the ballot box.

The Republican-controlled state House and Senate passed the anti-protest bill with relative ease during a three-day special session in mid-August. And Gov. Bill Lee signed it into law Thursday, Aug. 21, despite saying earlier that the bill contained provisions he "would have done differently."

But then, this is a governor who has done more following than leading since taking office in January 2019.

In June, protesters began an around-the-clock occupation of War Memorial Plaza in front of the state Capitol. Their goal was to bring attention to a host of grievances, mostly involving police brutality and systemic racism in the aftermath of the police killings of George Floyd, Breonna Taylor and other African Americans.

They also wanted a meeting with the governor, which never happened, to press for removing a bust of Confederate General Nathan Bedford Forrest from the Capitol Rotunda.

Then on June 12, Lee issued a statement pretending to support the right to protest. "We encourage Tennesseans to exercise their First Amendment rights and have seen many examples of peaceful protests across our state in recent weeks," the governor said.

"As demonstrations continue, we will continue to protect Tennesseans' right to peaceful assembly, while also reassuring citizens that lawlessness, autonomous zones, and violence will not be tolerated. Further, Tennessee law expressly prohibits camping on state property not expressly designated as a campground area, and that law will be enforced."

Lee was referring to a law passed in 2012 during the Occupy Nashville protest – an offshoot of the Occupy Wall Street movement – at the state Capitol. That law made camping out at the Capitol a class A misdemeanor.

So there was no need for another law this year to address the same offense. Except GOP lawmakers who hold the majority in 2020 have a much stronger and deeper vindictive streak than their 2012 counterparts.

Sen. Kerry Roberts, a Republican from Springfield, acknowledged as much as the recent bill was being debated. He didn't like being shouted at by protesters as he walked along the sidewalk.

"The thing is, what I wish I could convey to people is that it's really hard to be sympathetic to what someone is saying when they are yelling at you, when they're trying to shame you, when they're calling you names and so forth," Roberts said.

Other Republicans felt the same way, as the few Democrats in the Legislature tried to make the case that the bill was an overreaction to sporadic acts of violence and intimidation. The bill also applies to protesters who spit on law enforcement officers or vandalize government property.

"We are using a bazooka to go after a house fly here," argued Nashville Democratic Sen. Jeff Yarbro, the Senate minority leader. "Are we really saying that a citizen in this state can be punished with a year in prison and have a felony record because they camped on public property?"

Yes, senator, we are. And that's not all.

While it's doubtful that anyone arrested, tried and convicted solely under this law will serve six years in prison, they will lose their voting rights. The Tennessee Constitution "denies the right to vote (to) persons convicted of an infamous crime. (And) any felony is considered an 'infamous crime' and disqualifies a person from exercising the right of suffrage."

What's worse, once you lose your voting rights in Tennessee because of a felony conviction, you must petition a court to have those rights restored. That runs counter to most other states which automatically restore voting rights after release from custody or after completing probation or parole.

"As I stated on the Senate floor, legislation like this would have made Rep. John Lewis and Dr. Martin Luther King Jr. convicted felons," said Democratic state Sen. Raumesh Akbari of Memphis. "This is ridiculous."

Akbari joined U.S. Rep. Steve Cohen of Memphis this week in condemning the new law and predicting it will be overturned in court.

Believe me, I get it. No one wants to be screamed at while going about their business. But no one forced any of these lawmakers to run for office. And criticism, even offensive criticism, comes with the territory. The job of governing is not always an easy walk down the street.

But turning what should be – and what already was – a misdemeanor offense into a felony is, as Sen. Akbari says, ridiculous, particularly when it comes with a loss of voting rights.

Everyone who reads my weekly column knows that I am a staunch defender of the right to vote. It's personal to me because of my family's history in the struggle to win access to voting. And for Tennessee legislators to use that right as a weapon against protesting on public property is reprehensible.

America is at an inflection point. The ongoing injustices around policing in America must be addressed in government, in the courts and, yes, in the streets. That's not an excuse for violence. It is a call for systemic change.

The last thing we need are tone-deaf politicians in Washington, in the halls of the state Legislature and in the Tennessee governor's mansion ignoring the cries for justice while demonizing and seeking to punish the criers.

We don't need legislators who easily get their feelings hurt, and in return hastily try to turn in-your-face protesters into wanton criminals.

We need lawmakers who are public servants for all Tennesseans, not a modern-day felon squad.

— — —

ON RACE

Defiance in Mississippi | November 15, 2018

"Everything is not about race," Mississippi Gov. Phil Bryant boldly proclaimed this week while struggling to defend an indefensible comment from the person he handpicked to be an interim U.S. senator.

And, of course, Bryant is correct. Not every thoughtless remark or crude slight that comes, particularly, from a white politician is about race. But in Mississippi, past and present, everything regarding race seems to be about defiance.

From the days of pre-Civil War secession to the backlash against Reconstruction, to the rise of the Ku Klux Klan, to the assault on civil rights, to the resistance to desegregation and finally to the preservation of Confederate symbols, defiance has been my home state's political buzzword.

Or to borrow loosely from the onetime governor of neighboring Alabama, defiance today, defiance tomorrow, defiance forever.

So it's no surprise that interim Sen. Cindy Hyde-Smith is resisting all calls to repudiate – or even explain – her outlandish joke about being willing to sit on the front row of a public hanging. In the age of Trump, the operative stance is never let them see you apologize.

For those who thought the 2018 election year was mercifully over, and are unaware of what's happening across the state line in Mississippi, Republican Hyde-Smith is locked in a runoff battle against former Democratic Congressman Mike Espy, who is African American, for the right to complete the remaining two years of retired Sen. Thad Cochran's term.

With control of the Senate remaining in Republican hands after the Nov. 6 midterm election, Mississippi's Nov. 27 runoff quickly became a ho-hum affair, with Hyde-Smith the clear favorite in a deep red state that has not elected a Democrat to the Senate since John Stennis in 1982.

But last weekend, a now-infamous video surfaced on Twitter showing Hyde-Smith with Tupelo supporter and fellow cattle rancher Colin Hutchinson as they addressed a small crowd in front of a statue of Elvis Presley.

A passing train makes her words difficult to decipher. But while thanking Hutchinson for his support, Hyde-Smith says, "If he invited me to a public hanging, I'd be on the front row."

And just like that, a Senate race that had become an afterthought instead became national news. The obvious question became, why would a person seeking elected office say such a thing, even in jest, in a state with a sordid history of lynchings of African Americans?

Several news organizations reported the fact that from 1877 to 1950, Mississippi had the highest number of lynchings of any state in the U.S. And the Jackson Free-Press magazine, which has done an excellent job covering the Hyde-Smith story, reported that 654 lynchings occurred in the state during that 73-year period, including two in Lee County, where Hyde-Smith made the remark.

But adhering to Mississippi's other history of defiance, Hyde-Smith refused to cave to pressure to apologize. In a brief statement released Sunday, she said the comment was "an exaggerated expression of regard" and that any attempt to make it otherwise is "ridiculous."

The following day in an awkward appearance with Gov. Bryant, she refused to say more. Her repeated response to a barrage of questions from reporters was, "We put out a statement yesterday, it's available and that's all I'm going to say about it."

Bryant's attempt at cleanup only made things worse. "All of us in public life have said things on occasion that we could have phrased better," he said.

He then immediately pivoted to criticism of some African American political leaders for boycotting the 2017 opening of the Mississippi Civil Rights Museum in Jackson after Bryant invited President Trump – who has repeatedly made racially insensitive comments – to the event.

"Absolutely, we have been sensitive to race relations in this state," Bryant insisted this week before adding, "Everything is not about race."

This from a governor who is a dues-paying member of the Sons of

Confederate Veterans. A governor who flatly refuses to entertain removing the Confederate emblem from the state flag and who has continued a tradition of signing state proclamations designating April as "Confederate Heritage Month" every year since he took office in 2012.

That kind of defiance defined Mississippi when it became the second state – following South Carolina – to secede from the Union on Jan. 9, 1861, just over two months after Abraham Lincoln was elected president.

It defined the state when then-Gov. Ross Barnett vowed in 1962 never to allow a Black person to enroll at the University of Mississippi.

And sadly, that defiance continues to this day. Hyde-Smith had a chance to buck the trend simply by saying, "I apologize for my unfortunate choice of words." But she refused.

Even state Rep. Karl Oliver of Winona had the good sense to apologize after saying last year that anyone advocating for the removal of Confederate monuments should be lynched.

So yes, it's true. Everything is not about race. But because of a defiant Cindy Hyde-Smith, most voters who show up Nov. 27 for a Senate runoff election will have race on their minds when they cast their ballots.

—— —— ——

Healing racial discord | December 4, 2018

I am willing to give the nearly 500,000 Mississippi voters the benefit of the doubt.

Their support of Republican Cindy Hyde-Smith in Tuesday's special Senate runoff was about issues dearer to them than race relations.

I will concede that their votes giving Hyde-Smith an 8-point win over Democrat Mike Espy were about defending Brett Kavanaugh, maintaining unfettered gun rights, ending abortion, building a wall, erasing the Obama legacy and every other political talking point in the conservative playbook.

And I am willing to wager a week's pay that, if asked, none of Hyde-Smith's voters will acknowledge that Mississippi's shameful racial history or the candidate's racially insensitive comments during the campaign played a role in their ballot decision – except possibly as defiance against the national media that viewed this as solely a contest about race.

From northernmost DeSoto County to southernmost Harrison County on the Gulf Coast, Hyde-Smith's voters – including some who cringed at her quip about attending a public hanging – will insist their vote was about policy, not prejudice.

As a result, what was expected all along came to pass. Deep red Mississippi remained true to its political colors. Hyde-Smith defeated Espy by 69,181 votes out of 887,929 total votes cast, according to the unofficial count.

The runoff fell five days after Thanksgiving, but the turnout was robust. Both candidates worked hard. And the outcome by all accounts was fair and square.

Hence, the state's first woman senator, described in a Washington Times column this week as a "nice lady with a gift for saying graceless things," becomes the 53rd – and arguably the most reliably conservative – GOP vote in the Senate. And an extra cushion that Senate leader Mitch McConnell and President Trump can use to counter rogue votes by more moderate Republicans.

But as much as Hyde-Smith's voters and the candidate herself insist otherwise, the specter of race hung over this election like an ominous storm cloud over a Delta Blues festival.

How could it not? Espy was the first serious African American candidate for either the Senate or governor in Mississippi since the Reconstruction era when two black men – Hiram Revels in 1870 and Blanche Bruce in 1875 – were selected by the state Legislature to serve in the U.S. Senate.

Since then, African Americans have been shut out of statewide, nonjudicial offices. And most of the governors and senators elected from Reconstruction until the late 1960s campaigned as staunch segregationists. They mostly looked the other way as racial violence, particularly lynchings, were carried out against Black residents seeking equal rights, including the right to vote.

Some of that history hauntingly returned to the public's consciousness with Hyde-Smith's remarks captured on video that if one of her Tupelo-area supporters invited her to a public hanging, she would be on the front row. She was also caught on video saying voter suppression is "a great idea" for some liberal college students.

Once the remarks became national news, Hyde-Smith's campaign decided a half-hearted apology during the sole runoff debate Nov. 20 would be sufficient. Otherwise, she would say nothing else, assuming correctly that her supporters would stick with her regardless.

Plus, she had sufficient cover from Gov. Phil Bryant, who handpicked her to be the interim senator after Thad Cochran resigned for health reasons earlier this year. She also had backup from Sen. Roger Wicker and especially the president, all of whom brushed aside her tasteless remarks as being innocent misstatements taken out of context by the media.

So now, Hyde-Smith is no longer an obscure appointed interim lawmaker. She is the duly elected senator for at least the next two years. In her victory speech Tuesday night, she made no direct mention of her controversial remarks.

"The reason we won is because Mississippians know me and they know my heart," she said, later adding, "No matter who you voted for today, I'm gonna always represent every Mississippian."

Those were nice, if predictable, words. But allow me to suggest something more.

At her earliest opportunity, Hyde-Smith should meet personally with constituents who did not vote for her – including perhaps the relatives of Mississippians who were victims of lynchings – to gain an understanding of why her public hanging comment was so hurtful.

Then she should give a heartfelt speech recognizing Mississippi's sordid racial past, reflected in her enrollment in an all-white private school that was set up solely to avoid mandatory public school desegregation.

She should use the speech to point out things she has done as a public official, in the Legislature and as agriculture commissioner, that advanced the cause of race relations in Mississippi.

And she should commit to hiring a racially diverse staff and working as a senator to improve conditions in the Mississippi Delta, where some of the state's poorest residents live.

Of course, I don't believe Hyde-Smith will do any of this. Few past senators and governors in my home state – with the exception of William Winter – have even considered it.

But until someone in authority does, Mississippi will remain trapped in its own twilight zone of racial discord.

And the stagnant polarization that defines the state's politics will continue.

— — —

A Capitol bust | February 7, 2019

When Gov. Bill Lee addresses the Tennessee Press Association winter convention Thursday, Feb. 7 – seven days into Black History Month – he almost certainly will be asked about the Nathan Bedford Forrest bust on display in the state Capitol rotunda.

Judging by his most recent remarks on the subject, Lee's response to the statewide group of journalists and journalism educators likely will not produce any surprises.

He is dead set against removing the bust of Forrest, a Confederate general, early Ku Klux Klan leader and ruthless slave trader, from its lofty place of prominence in the halls of state government.

It would be a mistake, Lee said during last year's gubernatorial campaign, to "whitewash history" by moving the Forrest bust to the State Museum where it could be explained with greater context.

Weeks before his Jan. 19 swearing in, Lee reiterated his stance during an interview with USA Today Network. "I've said often times I think the removal of monuments is not the best approach to resolving the challenges that are presented with that conversation. Wiping out history wipes out also the history that we're not proud of."

Lee also added this: "The Ku Klux Klan is a part of our history that we're not proud of in Tennessee, and we need to be reminded of that and make certain that we don't forget it."

So to the governor's way of thinking, the best way to remind us of Tennessee's shameful history is for a copper image of that shame to be looking down on everyone who enters the halls of state government where decisions impacting Tennesseans of all races and cultures are made.

It's easy, and frankly counterproductive, to simply criticize Lee for maintaining an antiquated position that's rooted in loyalty to the Old South and to mid-20th century defiance to racial reconciliation.

So I will offer a different approach. It's an alternative bust, financed with private dollars, that would be more appropriate for the Capitol rotunda and represent the antithesis to Forrest's shameful history.

My first choice for such a bust was World War I hero Alvin York, who grew up in Fentress County, Tennessee, near the Kentucky state line. York's bravery was immortalized in the 1941 Gary Cooper film "Sergeant York." It told the story of how York, who was drafted into the Army, reconciled his Christian beliefs in non-violence with his desire to serve his country.

With help from some of his outnumbered fellow soldiers, York miraculously silenced 35 German machine guns, killed 25 German soldiers and captured 132 prisoners in October 1918 on a battlefield in France.

A statue of York aiming his rifle was erected on the state House grounds in 1968, and a bust of him already stands in front of his historic Fentress County home.

My second choice would be one of the supporters of the Women's Suffrage Movement who led the effort to gain passage of the 19th Amendment in the Legislature in 1920, making Tennessee the decisive 36th state to ratify the amendment giving women the right to vote.

But choosing a single person from that historic effort to be memorialized in the rotunda would be difficult. Plus, the Tennessee Woman Suffrage Heritage Trail already identifies monuments, busts and markers across the state that honor the women who were vital to the movement's success.

So that leaves Lt. George W. Lee of Memphis as my third choice to replace Forrest at the rotunda. A portrait of Lee was placed at the Capitol in 1973. But this genuine American hero deserves much more.

Lee, a Mississippi native who came to Memphis at age 18, was decorated for bravery in battle while serving in the 368th Infantry in France during World War I. During a firefight against the Germans on the night of Sept. 25, 1918, Lee managed to escape a barrage of enemy artillery and machine gun fire, including trading gunfire with a German sniper in a tree, to carry out orders from a superior.

After the war, Lee became an influential business leader and arguably the most prominent African American citizen in Memphis. In addition, he became a highly respected national figure in the Republican Party. He also was a splendid orator and wordsmith who wrote the most complete history of Beale Street.

Despite being stripped of his influence in the local party during the contentious 1964 presidential campaign, Lee maintained allegiance to the Republican Party until his death in an automobile accident in 1976.

So the least that the 2019 iteration of the Tennessee Republican Party, which controls the Legislature, can do is support a more meaningful way to recognize this authentic patriot who has never gotten his due.

And the best way to do that is to find the political courage to move a blatant symbol of Tennessee's shameful history out of the Capitol rotunda and into the museum, and make way for a proper honor for Lt. George W. Lee.

Former Gov. Bill Haslam said many times during his eight years in office that state property is not the best home for the Forrest bust. "If we are going to honor a limited number of Tennesseans in the Capitol, Forrest should not be on that list."

Replacing Forrest with Lt. Lee probably won't happen, of course. But at the very least, Gov. Lee should be asked about it at Thursday's press association luncheon. Who knows? Maybe he'll surprise us and say he's all for it.

In politics, strange things occasionally do occur.

Column update

In my column last week, I encouraged someone to question Tennessee Gov. Bill Lee, during his appearance Feb. 7 before the Tennessee Press Association, about his opposition to removing a bust of Confederate Gen. Nathan Bedford Forrest from the state Capitol Rotunda.

I ended up being that person, and Lee appeared to backtrack slightly from his earlier stance. Here is our exchange during a brief question-and-answer session with the news media.

Q: Could you elaborate a little bit more on your decision against removing the Nathan Bedford Forrest statue from the rotunda?

A: That isn't a decision that I make. That is up to the (Tennessee) Historical Commission. That decision is not a governor's.

Q: Are you willing to make a recommendation or even get involved in the discussion?

A: I certainly want to have a discussion, and listen and talk to folks around their decisions and why they are making that decision.

Q: But you made a statement to the USA Today Network that you were opposed to it because it would be removing history.

A: I am concerned about removing history and not allowing us to have conversations around those parts of history that we are ashamed of and those parts of history that we are proud of. And I want to continue conversations in that direction as substantive conversations unfold.

—— —— ——

Frat boys | February 14, 2019

It took five days of negative press before Mississippi's Lt. Gov. Tate Reeves finally spoke up for himself.

But he still may need another human lifeline. Someone willing to step forward and explain away Reeves' college years spent palling around with overtly racist fraternity brothers.

Someone who can paint Reeves as a sympathetic figure – rather than a cohort of those in blackface – and diffuse another racially charged political dust-up in my home state.

Paging Gov. Phil Bryant.

Reeves, like Bryant, is a staunchly conservative Republican, who is running to succeed Bryant in this year's state election. Normally, Reeves is a talkative guy.

But for days, he was mostly silent amid a growing controversy over his membership in the Kappa Alpha Order at Millsaps College in the 1990s when fraternity members posed for yearbook pictures wearing blackface and other racially offensive garb. They also are seen glorifying the Confederacy, with total reverence for Confederate Gen. Robert E. Lee.

A rather bland statement from a Reeves spokesperson late last week generally addressed the lieutenant governor's college days as a Kappa Alpha member. "Like every other college student, he did attend costume formals and other parties, and across America, Kappa Alpha's costume formal is traditionally called Old South in honor of the Civil War veteran who founded the fraternity in the 1800s."

But about fraternity members wearing blackface and shouting racial epithets at Black Millsaps students, we heard nothing until Tuesday when Reeves finally met with reporters.

He said he had never dressed in blackface or worn a Ku Klux Klan costume. He acknowledged the obvious – that he was a member of Kappa Alpha in college. But he did not address the fraternity's documented racist history at Millsaps while he was there.

"I condemn racism because that's the way I was raised, and I will tell you that's the way I have governed as lieutenant governor," Reeves said.

Sorry, but that's not enough. Which is why Reeves may need a helping hand from the governor.

Bryant has become quite adept at taking a political crisis – particularly one involving race – and insisting it is a nothingburger, then deflecting to a side issue that often makes whatever or whomever he's defending the real victim.

For example, Bryant has successfully shunned all efforts to remove the Confederate battle emblem from the state flag. He insists that changing the flag by government fiat would be disrespectful to Mississippians who voted years ago to keep the flag as it is.

Critics, by and large, have now given up asking. Hence, Mississippi is the only state that still includes a semblance of the Confederacy in its flag.

Then last November, Bryant came to the rescue of Sen. Cindy Hyde-Smith, who created a national firestorm during her campaign for the seat by saying that, if invited, she would eagerly sit in the front row of a public hanging.

When she repeatedly refused to answer a barrage of questions from reporters about making such an insensitive comment in a state infamous for lynching black people, Bryant intervened on her behalf. He downplayed the remark as merely a poor choice of words, then pivoted to the question of why there is not similar outrage "about 20 million African American children that have been aborted." Where the governor got the 20 million figure is anyone's guess. He did not cite the source.

But thanks in part to Bryant's intervention, Hyde-Smith was able to run out the clock and comfortably defeat African American Democrat Mike Espy in the special Senate election.

Bryant's ability to diminish and deflect has defined his political style throughout his seven years as governor.

While defending Hyde-Smith's public hanging remark, Bryant boldly proclaimed, "We have been sensitive to race relations in this state."

As proof, he pointed to the Mississippi Civil Rights Museum that opened in 2017. Bryant invited President Donald Trump to the opening ceremonies, then played the victim when African American political leaders such as U.S. Reps. John Lewis and Bennie Thompson chose to stay away precisely because of Trump's racially offensive rhetoric.

Now, Bryant may be needed once more to help a fellow conservative and the GOP's heir apparent to the governor's seat wiggle out of the fraternity blackface controversy. Because Reeves' comments Tuesday will likely not put this issue to rest.

Mississippi is a state that still has not come to terms with its sordid racial past. As a native Mississippian, I know that firsthand, and I'm a lot older than Reeves. How he behaved in college, hanging around with racist frat brothers, is a relevant matter as he seeks to be the next governor – even if it's true that he never dressed up in blackface.

At some point, Reeves should acknowledge the state's shameful history and explain what his racial views are today. That includes clarifying his affection for the Sons of Confederate Veterans, a group that still maintains the Civil War was fought over state sovereignty, not slavery.

And yes, Democratic gubernatorial candidate Jim Hood's college fraternity at Ole Miss also took yearbook photos dressed in blackface. But unlike Reeves, Hood is not pictured in the photo spread.

The fact is, Reeves is running to be the chief executive of a state where nearly 40% of citizens are African Americans. They and everyone else in Mississippi deserve to hear directly from him a definitive statement on race relations in 2019.

Only then can we start to paint an accurate picture of the man who wants to be Mississippi's next governor.

—— —— ——

Sugarmon's legacy | February 21, 2019

It was one of those typical sweltering July days in Memphis. The temperature reached 96 degrees in the mid-afternoon, and it was not much cooler by nightfall.

None of that mattered, however, to hundreds of black Memphians who made their way to Mason Temple by car or on foot the evening of July 31, 1959. They came hoping to witness political history in the making, and ended up listening to one of the world's quintessential history makers.

A 30-year-old Martin Luther King Jr. was at Mason Temple that night to support attorney Russell Sugarmon Jr., also 30, in his improbable quest to win elected office in Memphis. The two had met and become friends while attending Morehouse College together, and Dr. King eagerly said yes when Sugarmon and fellow Memphis lawyer Ben Hooks asked him to speak at the huge get-out-the-vote rally.

As present-day Memphians pay tribute to the life and legacy of Sugarmon, who died Monday at age 89, it is important to remember the man beyond his brief service in the Tennessee Legislature, his lengthy tenure on the Shelby County General Sessions Court bench and his uncanny abilities as a behind-the-scenes political strategist.

It is also important to remember with gratitude and respect the early years of Sugarmon's political and professional life that served as turning points for racial and social change in Memphis.

I was fortunate to sit down with Sugarmon four years ago at his Downtown Memphis residence for lengthy interviews about his early career as a civil rights attorney and trailblazing political leader.

The interviews became a key part of my research on the political and racial history of Memphis from the rise of longtime political boss E.H. Crump to the historic vote for Dr. Willie Herenton as the city's first elected African American mayor.

Sugarmon played a crucial role in what I consider to be two seminal moments in the city's political evolution. One was the Volunteer Ticket of African American candidates who ran for city offices in 1959. Sugarmon led the ticket as a candidate for the powerful position of city commissioner of public works.

Other members of the ticket were Hooks, who ran for Juvenile Court judge; Rev. Roy Love and Henry Bunton, who sought seats on the Memphis City Schools Board of Education, and Eliehue Stanback, who ran for city tax assessor.

Sugarmon was the group's primary strategist, and together they shook up white Memphians, most of whom could not envision a Black man holding any elected office.

But Sugarmon, more than others on the ticket, had a legitimate shot at winning because of the effectiveness of the campaign organization and because he had five white opponents in a race that required no runoff.

After Dr. King's highly publicized visit to Memphis that steamy July evening, white political leaders, including outgoing commissioner and future mayor Henry Loeb, started to worry.

Loeb was unopposed for mayor that year, and he could not stomach the idea of Sugarmon – or any other Black candidate – assuming his commission seat. So Loeb, with help from the city's two daily newspapers, urged at least two of the white candidates to withdraw.

Eventually, one of them, Will Fowler, dropped out "for the good of Memphis," he said. That was enough to keep Sugarmon from winning. He received 35,237 votes, but finished second to William Farris, who got 58,951 votes.

The Commercial Appeal's editorial board, in trying to justify its opposition to Sugarmon and the Volunteer Ticket, said it was "opposed to bloc voting" by Black Memphians as a matter of principle. "Of course, minorities want to make their views known, and in this election Negroes got together, flexed their muscle and showed a capacity for using the election processes."

Sugarmon noted in our interview that the editorial marked the newspaper's first acknowledgment that, because of him and his running mates, Black voting strength was here to stay.

The other historic moment that Sugarmon discussed with me was his legal representation of a group of Black college students who staged sit-ins at lunch counters and public libraries in Memphis in March 1960.

Claude Armour, then the city commissioner of public safety, had warned the students – mostly from LeMoyne College and Owen Junior College – that they would be arrested if they went through with the demonstrations.

But on Saturday, March 19, 1960, nearly 40 male and female students sat down in the Cossitt Library Downtown and the main library at Peabody and McLean. They were promptly arrested and charged with loitering, disorderly conduct and disturbing the peace.

The arrests mobilized Black Memphians like never before to step up their push for desegregation. Sugarmon and attorney H.T. Lockard represented the students the following Monday before City Court Judge Beverly Bouche.

Sugarmon argued during the hearing that, under Supreme Court rulings, the students had a legitimate civil right to enter the libraries. But Bouche made his bigoted feelings clear. "I'm not concerned at all with civil rights," he said. "I'm not here to listen to arguments over integration or segregation."

The sit-ins, he said, were "an attempt at mob rule (and) an open invitation to violence. There is no doubt in my mind that this was a concerted effort to use this court as a platform for your propaganda," he told the students and their lawyers. "I have said many times from this bench, and I will repeat, we will not tolerate anything in this city that smacks of mob rule or gangsterism, and race, creed and color has nothing to do with it."

Although Sugarmon and his co-counsels failed to get the charges dropped, they were successful in exposing blatant racism within local government and the judicial system. Six months after the sit-ins, a biracial group of business and community leaders secured an agreement from city officials to desegregate public libraries, the city zoo and Downtown lunch counters.

Of course, there are countless other significant events in Sugarmon's life of public service. They include forcing the desegregation of city schools. Sugarmon often said one of his proudest moments was helping to walk African-American first-graders into previously all-white elementary schools in 1961.

With his death, hundreds of Memphians – perhaps even a few who were at Mason Temple that night in 1959 – no doubt have other Sugarmon stories to share. They will be doing that in the coming days as we offer thanks to a man who spent his life making Memphis a better and more equitable city.

Editor's Note: Portions of this column are excerpted from Otis Sanford's book, "From Boss Crump to King Willie: How Race Changed Memphis Politics."

—— —— ——

Flashback to the '60s | April 10, 2019

Must every major dispute in local and state politics turn into a mini-race war? For some people, the answer is an absolute yes.

Racial fights are as much a part of our history as blues, country and bluegrass. They mobilize all parties involved, inflame passions to the nth degree and produce sensational headlines. They force combatants to dig in their heels and try to score political points by demonizing the opposition.

And the side wielding the most political clout – in this case the Tennessee Legislature – gets to set the rules and make things intolerable for the other side.

The case I'm referring to is a bill steamrolling through the Legislature that would penalize groups that sponsor voter registration drives and end up turning in hundreds of "incomplete" forms.

The Republican supermajority in the state House approved the bill with ease Monday, despite a chorus of complaints from opponents who see this as tantamount to voter suppression, primarily against people of color.

Supporters say House Bill 1079 is intended only to eliminate the practice of groups paying people based on the number of voter registration forms they collect, and that most of those forms contain incomplete names, phony addresses and other fake information.

Critics, including most Democratic lawmakers, view the bill as overkill, particularly an earlier version of the proposal that said violators could be charged with a Class A misdemeanor, which carries 11 months and 29 days in jail. The criminal penalty was amended to apply only to those who do not take the required registration training.

Despite the amendment, Democratic state Rep. London Lamar of Memphis did not mince words. She called the bill a form of "voter disenfranchisement" and a "very lazy and punitive way of doing something."

Race is a key ingredient in the dispute because the bill's sponsors acknowledge that it stems from efforts last year by the Black Voter Project in Shelby County to register large numbers of voters for the 2018 midterm election. Many of those forms, which were turned in at the registration deadline, were indeed incomplete and created an expensive headache for the Shelby County Election Commission, which had to sort through and verify them.

In addition, a lawsuit filed by the Shelby County Democratic Party and the local branch of the NAACP sought to force the election commission to put the applicants collected by the Black Voter Project on the voter rolls.

Robert Meyers, the outgoing commission chairman, vigorously supports the bill to cut down on what he viewed as fraud by the Black Voter Project.

In a March 25 letter addressed only to the county's Republican legislative caucus, Meyers said, "I saw firsthand how disruptive third-party voter registration drives can be…. Of the tens of thousands of voter registrations received by the SCEC in the few days before the close of voter registrations, most were incomplete and many were clearly fraudulent.

"It could be argued that the combination of the way these voter registrations were handled prior to their delivery to the SCEC and the filing of the lawsuit were designed to sow fear, uncertainty and doubt into the election process," Meyers wrote.

Linda Phillips, administrator of elections for Shelby County, told me this week that dozens of forms turned in by the Black Voter Project were in the same handwriting. Others contained addresses that were vacant lots or housing projects that had long been torn down.

Although Phillips stopped short of outright endorsing the bill passed by the House, she implied that it would make the election commission's job easier.

Of course, no one should knowingly turn in incomplete voter registration forms, let along fraudulent ones. There are laws on the books already that address those issues. But here's the problem I have with this new legislation. It is clearly targeted at groups trying to register African American voters, who are predominantly Democratic voters.

And why must we resort to using the threat of jail time when trying to address an issue that mostly involves African Americans?

Republicans, including Secretary of State Tre Hargett, can try to make the argument that this legislation seeks only to protect and enhance voting. But if it passes the Senate and is signed by Gov. Bill Lee, which seems likely, it will put a chill on Black voter registration drives. That's the ultimate definition of voter suppression.

Instead of fueling another racial fight over the right to vote, lawmakers should be promoting better ways to help individuals and groups with the registration process.

One good way is about to be rolled out soon by the Shelby County Election Commission. The commission has purchased six new Android tablets that will be loaned out to groups to register people online.

Online registrations improve accuracy and significantly reduce the time-consuming process of checking whether the applications are valid. Phillips said the tablets, which are programmed only for voter registrations, can be checked out just like a book at the library.

The information will be fed directly into the commission's data base to make verification much simpler.

"I don't want people to go to jail," Phillips told me. "I want people to register to vote."

I believe she is sincere. I cannot say the same for GOP lawmakers who think the only way to resolve thorny political issues – particularly those involving race – is with heavy-handed, 1960s-style tactics.

—— —— ——

Forcing desegregation | July 4, 2019

When I was growing up in North Mississippi in the 1960s, my ideal celebration of Independence Day revolved around two things: sharing ice cream and cake with my sister Doris, who was born on July 4, and taking a holiday afternoon trip to Sardis Lake.

It was a thrill just seeing the expansive dam, the people fishing at the spillway and the water skiers being pulled by fancy speedboats.

But the other unmistakable feature about the lake was that it was racially segregated.

Everyone knew the rules. No African Americans were welcomed at any of the beach areas and campgrounds frequented by white visitors. That included the John W. Kyle State Park located at the lake.

African Americans instead were relegated to the Cypress Point public use area on the far west side of the lower lake. In essence, the lake's back side was also the Black side.

The segregation slowly diminished as African Americans decided enough was enough. As I recall, there was no formal decree. Black patrons just began showing up at the lake's other recreation areas that had been reserved for whites.

Eventually the icy stares and racist comments evolved into acceptance. And official segregation at Sardis Lake became a thing of the past.

As we celebrate our country's 243rd birthday, I bring this up only as context for the renewed debate over the use of forced busing in the 1970s to desegregate public schools. The issue got the most attention during the second night of the Democratic presidential debates last week.

California Sen. Kamala Harris put former Vice President Joe Biden on the defensive for his fierce opposition to busing in the 1970s when he was a young senator from Delaware. Specifically, Harris chided Biden for working in concert with James O. Eastland, the Mississippi senator and outspoken segregationist, to undermine busing efforts across the country.

"There was a little girl in California who was part of the second class to integrate her public school, and she was bused to school every day. That little girl was me," Harris said in what became the defining moment of the debate.

Biden insists he did not oppose voluntary busing, only that which was imposed by the federal government. And lots of people, Black and white, have come to his defense.

For me, busing was never an issue growing up. My family lived on a farm outside Como, and I was bused to school all 12 years, including my senior year in 1970-71. That also was the first year of full school integration in Mississippi, more than 16 years after the landmark Supreme Court ruling in Brown vs. Board of Education that outlawed so-called separate but equal public schools.

In Memphis, however, busing was this city's most divisive issue during the 1970s. Like most Southern cities, Memphis simply ignored the Brown decision. Members of the all-white school board convinced themselves that neither Black nor white Memphians wanted school integration, so why bother?

"We believe our Negroes will continue using their own school facilities since most of them are located in the center of Negro populated areas," school board president Milton Bowers said shortly after the Brown decision was announced.

The problem was Black and white schools in Memphis were separate, but they were far from equal. So in March 1960, a group of Black lawyers, led by future Supreme Court Justice Thurgood Marshall, filed suit in U.S. District Court in Memphis demanding full integration of city schools.

Presiding Judge Marion Boyd initially sided with the school board, which claimed it was doing all it could to achieve integration as quickly as possible. But the U.S. 6th Circuit Court of Appeals took a different view. It declared that the board was in fact illegally running a segregated school system and ordered Boyd to oversee swifter changes.

Boyd continued to slow-walk the case until he left the district court bench in 1966. It was then assigned to his successor, Judge Robert M. McRae Jr.

The lawsuit lingered several more years until the Court of Appeals and McRae finally lost patience. After a contentious hearing in December 1971, McRae ruled that busing would be imposed to bring about full integration of schools.

The decision sent shockwaves across Memphis. White residents were incensed, a group called Citizens Against Busing buried an old school bus in Frayser in symbolic defiance of the ruling, and McRae was the target of constant death threats.

The first wave of busing started in January 1973. It involved some 7,000 students – almost all of them Black – who were bused to previously all-white schools. But the backlash grew stronger.

White Memphians by the thousands abandoned the city and moved to the suburbs in Shelby County or across the Mississippi state line to DeSoto County. The result was a dramatic demographic shift in school and city population from majority white to predominantly Black.

The city's tax base was adversely affected and broad-based support for Memphis City Schools diminished. Those and other negative outcomes are among the reasons that Biden objected to busing in the 1970s.

"I oppose busing," Biden said in a 1975 interview, according to The New York Times. "It's an asinine concept, the utility of which has never been proven to me."

Biden said in the interview that court-ordered school integration plans were "really just quota systems to assure a certain number of Blacks, Chicanos, or whatever in each school. That, to me, is the most racist concept you can come up with."

He added, "The problem, you see, is that the courts have gone overboard in their interpretation of what is required to remedy unlawful segregation. It is one thing to say that you cannot keep a Black man from using this bathroom, and something quite different to say that one out of every five people who use this bathroom must be Black."

Lots of people, then and now, agree with him, which is why the confrontation between Harris and Biden resonated around the country. Of course, hindsight is easy. Busing, by and large, was a failure.

But in Memphis, as in many other communities, white resistance to school desegregation was so intense that judges, such as McRae, felt they had no other option except busing to try to end a clearly racist system.

Because unlike what they did at the segregated areas of Sardis Lake during my childhood, African Americans were not about to just show up and waltz into all-white public schools and trust that they would be accepted. It required the power of the federal courts – and in some instances the muscle of the federal government – to force change.

After all, the demand for change is why we celebrate Independence Day.

— — —

Who's in the room? | September 3, 2019

How many people were in the room?

Of those who were, did anyone voice an objection? If so, how strongly?

How much time was spent discussing the almost certain negative reaction and whether that reaction should affect the decision to publish or not publish?

And above all, how diverse, racially and otherwise, were the people around the table?

Those are just some of the questions that instantly came to my mind after viewing what is now universally considered an atrocious cover on the September issue of Memphis magazine.

There are plenty of appropriate descriptors for the cover, which shows caricatures of Willie Herenton, Tami Sawyer and Jim Strickland, the three leading candidates for Memphis mayor. None are flattering, either of the cover itself or of those in leadership at the magazine who approved it.

Some of the kinder ones include unfortunate, insensitive, inappropriate and objectionable. The harsher ones include disgusting, demeaning, outrageous, grotesque and, yes, racist.

All three candidates have reasons to fume. Herenton, the former mayor, looks like an aging member of the Vice Lords flashing gang signs. And Strickland, the current mayor, is depicted with his right eye nearly closed and his upper lip twisted, resembling the old western TV character actor Jack Elam wearing glasses and a suit and tie.

But Sawyer is treated the worst. Her caricature is a throwback to an era when Black women especially were depicted in cartoons as horribly unattractive and with exaggerated facial features that suggested the subject is subhuman.

Call that hyperbole if you will, but it is the depiction of Sawyer, a member of the Shelby County Commission, that has created the most pushback from Memphians and widespread cries of racism.

All three candidates have denounced the pencil-drawn caricatures as offensive and divisive. The artist who drew them is former Memphian Chris 'Honeysuckle' Ellis, who's also an actor, now lives in Los Angeles, and has appeared in movies including "My Cousin Vinny" and "Apollo 13."

Once the criticism intensified, Ellis took to social media himself to defend his work, but succeeded only in adding more insults. "The facial images I drew of a monstrously obese female of color were traced," Ellis said in one post, referring to Sawyer. "They are an almost exact representation of the photographs sent to me by the magazine," he said, adding in a later post this is the price the candidates "must pay for local celebrity."

The issue hit newsstands Friday and immediately became the focus of outrage by people who called the magazine's offices or posted responses on Facebook and Twitter.

Facing a barrage of criticism, the magazine posted a 200-word statement on its website at 9 a.m. Saturday that tried to pass for an apology. But if the statement was aimed at falling on a journalistic sword, somebody replaced the sword with a butter knife.

"In publishing that cover, we were following a long-standing satirical tradition," the unsigned statement read. "It was not our intention to demean any of the candidates or to satirize one more than the others, but we are sympathetic to the perceptions our readers have shared. We regret and apologize for any pain this caricature of public figures has caused."

In other words, Sawyer, Strickland and Herenton are in the public eye and should have thicker skin. The magazine did nothing wrong, but if readers think otherwise, accept the apology and move on.

But wait, there's more. The statement went on to praise Memphis magazine for being "a progressive voice in this city, a city which has historically had very few such voices of that persuasion. With every issue we publish, we hope we are building upon that progressive tradition."

The statement invited readers to see for themselves at memphismagazine. com/archives. I did, and found nothing remotely resembling the horrible caricatures in question.

There was a tasteful portrait of Strickland on the cover in September 2018, an equally impressive one of University of Memphis basketball coach Penny Hardaway in December 2018, Pat Kerr Tigrett in September 2017 and a statue of Elvis in June 2016.

But the Saturday statement was itself an insult. And exactly 24 hours later, at 9 a.m. Sunday, the magazine's top leader did a complete about-face.

Anna Traverse, chief executive officer of Contemporary Media, the parent company of Memphis magazine, posted a signed statement of her own.

It was 543 words under the headline, "We Failed Memphis." It began with this: "The first thing to say, and the only thing I ask you to hear if you do not read past this first sentence, is that I am profoundly sorry for the cover of the September issue of Memphis magazine and the pain it caused."

Traverse acknowledged that the Saturday statement from the magazine's editorial team referencing the history of political caricatures was inadequate. "This is not about that history, or about our attempts to explain why our team approved the cover. This is about the fact that we published a magazine whose cover image was taken, justifiably, as playing into a long history of racist, demeaning tropes, a history of marginalizing African American women in particular."

Hear! Hear!

But wait. There's more from Traverse. "Our intentions are immaterial right now. It is true that we did not mean to depict Tami Sawyer in a harsher light than either of the other candidates – but who cares, now? No one at (the magazine) should have attempted to tell our audience how to interpret this illustration; if you are offended, you have every right in the world to be offended. We take responsibility for the cover."

Traverse said the company has stopped circulation of the September issue, and the staff is trying to collect all unsold copies from retail outlets. The cover has also been dropped from the website.

But in her apparently sincere *mea culpa,* Traverse admitted that she viewed the cover before it went to print. And while she had "serious misgivings" about it, she now wishes she had been more vocal.

And that takes us back to one of my original questions. Where was the racial diversity in the room that would have, and should have, said we cannot publish this cover?

The answer is obvious. There is no person of color in the decision-making process at Memphis magazine. So instead of having the benefit of diverse voices with varied backgrounds and experiences, the editorial team is in an echo chamber.

Let me be clear. There are some fine, experienced journalists, and fine people, working at Contemporary Media's publications. Some of them have been colleagues of mine in the past. But this is what often happens when media organizations fail to place emphasis on diversity, in all its forms, when assembling a staff – particularly in leadership roles.

The magazine's original statement was true in one respect. Many local news organizations in the past were anything but progressive. They did not see the need for racial, gender or any other kind of diversity. Everyone in leadership looked the same.

In 2019, that is long past unacceptable, especially in a racially diverse city such as Memphis. But honestly, it should not have required a Black person sitting at the table for the editorial team to conclude this magazine cover should not be used because it's offensive, not just to the candidates, but to nearly all Memphians.

I hope that Traverse, who took over the CEO job this summer, and others at Contemporary Media now understand that. In her statement, she said she is "eager to make changes within our company, including diversifying both our staff and our coverage."

It has been a painful, but necessary, lesson for her. Hopefully others inside and outside the news media, will learn something from this as well.

—— —— ——

Trump's Twitter bombs | October 24, 2019

Let's not take the bait.

Let's not be distracted by the P.T. Barnum-like antics of an ethically challenged – some would say corrupt – president who is a master at shifting America's attention from one shiny object to another.

Above all, let's not fall for his unceasing efforts to sow more racial division and animosity, all while perpetually portraying himself as the real victim. In other words, this time let's keep the main thing the main thing.

And the main thing is mounting evidence that Donald Trump abused power, obstructed justice and engaged in other illegal behaviors that qualify as high crimes and misdemeanors worthy of impeachment and, yes, removal from office.

It's clear to me that Trump started his day Tuesday realizing it would be a bad day for the future of his presidency. He realized that he was powerless to stop the damaging congressional testimony of William Taylor Jr., the top U.S. diplomat to Ukraine.

Under subpoena and under oath, Taylor told impeachment investigators that Trump made investigation of his political rivals a condition for granting government aid to Ukraine.

Knowing that Taylor's testimony was forthcoming and would be released to the media, what did Trump do? What he always does when he's in trouble – toss out a bomb, usually containing racial shrapnel, in hopes of distracting and dividing the public.

Using Twitter, his weapon of choice, Trump wrote, "So some day, if a Democrat becomes President and the Republicans win the House, even by a tiny margin, they can impeach the President, without due process or fairness or any legal rights.

"All Republicans must remember what they are witnessing here – a lynching. But we will WIN!"

A lynching? Really?

Of course, the term was racially incendiary. Trump meant it to be. How else to get reporters, pundits, politicians and ordinary people talking about something other than Taylor's bombshell testimony?

Here is my theory of how the president came up with lynching as the divisive buzzword for the day. Last weekend in Glendora, Mississippi, a two-hour drive from Memphis, yet another memorial was erected on the banks of the Tallahatchie River in recognition of Emmett Till, an African American teenager from Chicago, who was in fact lynched in August 1955.

Till's tragic story is now legendary. Even Trump, who has no understanding or respect for history, has heard it. Till, 14, was abducted, beaten and shot in the head by two white men who then tied Till's body to a gin fan and threw it into the Tallahatchie River.

The wife of one of the men claimed that Till whistled at her, grabbed her, made obscene comments and asked her for a date. The men were acquitted by an all-white jury, but they admitted later in a Look magazine interview to carrying out the lynching.

According to the 2017 book, "The Blood of Emmett Till," the woman decades later recanted most of the story, particularly the accusation that Till grabbed her and used sexually crude language.

Till's horrific murder helped spark the civil rights movement. But it was one of hundreds, perhaps thousands, of lynchings of Black people, mostly in the South, since before the Civil War.

The ceremony last Saturday in Glendora, Mississippi, marked the fourth time that a marker in memory of Till has been placed at the site where his body was recovered. The other three were either stolen and discarded or riddled with bullets.

The new $10,000 marker is bulletproof. It weighs 500 pounds, is made of reinforced steel and encased in protective glass. The site is also monitored by video cameras linked to the Internet.

Although apparently no statewide elected officials in Mississippi attended Saturday's event, it was covered extensively by The New York Times and The Washington Post. Both newspapers used the words "lynching" or "lynched" prominently in their articles.

I believe Trump saw the national news coverage of the Till marker and thought, "There's my word."

Except it is not. In fact, it would be laughable if it were not so insulting. There is no debate about it, despite what Republican Sen. Lindsey Graham is saying. And to say otherwise is to denigrate the names and memories of those who were lynched, often by marauding mobs, with the intent of creating a reign of terror against Black people.

What's happening to Trump is a legitimate attempt to get at the truth, to hold him accountable for his actions and to uphold the U.S. Constitution.

Invoking the word "lynching" was designed merely to divert the conversation from the cascade of damaging testimony that is slowly but surely shifting public opinion toward the inescapable conclusion that this man is wholly unfit for the presidency.

The good news is that, despite a divisive president and a few trigger-happy Mississippi miscreants, our society is finally coming to grips with its racist past. In Memphis and elsewhere, we are dismantling monuments to slave traders and racial oppressors and erecting markers to those who lost their lives as a result of hate.

It's not just the tweets. Trump's actions have allowed us to see what America would really look like with an unchecked despot as its leader. And most of us do not like what we see.

Hence, the impeachment inquiry must proceed, not so that vindictive Democrats can save face. But so that a weary nation can save itself.

—— —— ——

Race and a pandemic | April 10, 2020

There is no tiptoeing around it. The coronavirus outbreak, that has brought life as we know it to a virtual standstill, is now a defining issue of race.

Some will not want to hear that, and I get it. Why bring up race when we all are suffering through an unprecedented pandemic, the likes of which this country has not seen in 102 years?

When we all are being told to stay home, and leave only for absolute essentials such as food and medicines. To go alone, wear a mask and keep our distance from others when we do venture out.

Why talk about race now when the virus itself and job losses are impacting us across the board?

I get all that. But the data that is just now being collected is telling a horrendous story about the disproportionate impact COVID-19 is having on African Americans. We are catching it at a much higher rate than other racial groups and dying from it at rates even higher than that.

Equally alarming is the fact that health officials and political leaders didn't think early on that it was important to keep track of the spread and mortality rate based on race.

In Memphis and Shelby County, for example, Health Department officials, school administrators and elected leaders have done a commendable job trying to stay ahead of the outbreak by shutting down schools and businesses, closing parks and issuing emergency stay-at-home orders. Our local leaders were much more proactive than Tennessee's governor, who has been leading from behind all along. It's why I believe Shelby's number of cases has not spiraled out of control.

But even in the Bluff City, the foresight apparently wasn't there to collect and disperse real-time information on the racial breakdown of coronavirus cases as they were occurring. Only after national news media organizations, such as ProPublica and The Washington Post, started reporting on the racial disparities with cases, did officials rush to address the issue.

Alisa Haushalter, director of the Shelby County Health Department, acknowledged as much during a daily media briefing by the local task force April 7. "Unfortunately, much of our race data has been missing for a variety of reasons. That's one of the pieces of data that's not necessarily on the report," she said before assuring the public the information is now being collected.

The following day, Health Department officials announced that Shelby County, which has a Black population of about 53%, indeed has a disproportionately higher rate of COVID-19 cases among African Americans.

The sample size at that time was still small, about 30% of all confirmed cases. But it showed that Black residents made up 68% of the cases, and 71% of deaths. And as the sample size increases, there is no reason to expect that the disparity will decrease.

The findings mirror what's happening in other large, racially diverse cities, including Chicago, Milwaukee, New Orleans, Detroit and Philadelphia.

So the automatic question is, why is this happening? The answers are simple in their complexity. We know that longstanding health disparities between Black and white Americans mean Black people are more at risk for negative outcomes from a pandemic than white people.

The life expectancy of Black men has long been about four years less than that of white men because of a variety of health, economic, environmental and lifestyle factors, according to the Centers for Disease Control and Prevention.

Add in the issues of poverty, which include everything from lower educational achievement to food deserts in many Black neighborhoods, and the disparities around who suffers the most from COVID-19 come into focus.

Then there is the issue of employment. Other than health care workers and first responders, many of the frontline employees, who must work while the rest of us abide by safer-at-home orders, are people of color. They are your bus drivers, grocery clerks and delivery people.

And of course, there is the issue of coronavirus testing. Memphis and Shelby County leaders, working with various health care agencies, have done a credible job expanding testing across the city. But the fact that the Trump administration was woefully slow in mobilizing a coordinated battle plan against the virus means even the most aggressive measures locally are merely playing catch-up.

All that, along with apathy and perhaps a degree of defiance mostly by younger Black people, explains why this virus is attacking African Americans at a greater rate. But I believe the biggest cause, without question, is our political attitude around access to health care in this country.

It's why Families USA, a Washington-based nonpartisan health care advocacy organization, was quick to criticize the Trump Administration for refusing to reopen enrollment for the Affordable Care Act as the coronavirus was spreading.

"This shows that the administration is not all in when it comes to fighting this deadly virus," the organization said in a statement March 31. "Millions of people are losing their jobs – which often results in them becoming uninsured. It is essential that they promptly get health insurance; otherwise, they will hesitate to come forward and seek care when they get sick – which slows the detection of disease and spreads the already rampant epidemic."

Unfortunately, that has been the case all along for millions of African Americans – inadequate access to decent health care which leads to a reluctance to attend to potential serious ailments. Health officials agree that African Americans are not more susceptible than others to getting the virus. But they are more likely to have worse outcomes when they do get it.

Dr. Anthony Fauci, the country's leading expert on infectious disease, who has emerged as the most reasonable medical voice during the coronavirus crisis, deserves credit for honestly addressing the health disparity issue from the White House podium on April 7.

"I couldn't help sitting there reflecting about sometimes when you're in the middle of a crisis like we are now with the coronavirus, it really does ... ultimately shine a very bright light on some of the real weaknesses and foibles in our society," he said.

"Health disparities have always existed for the African American community," Fauci said, referencing diabetes, hypertension, obesity and asthma — all of which are disproportionately higher among Black people.

"But with the crisis, it's shining a bright light on how unacceptable that is. When all this is over ... and we will get rid of coronavirus, there will still be health disparities which we do need to address in the African American community."

So yes, this crisis is now as much about race as anything else. Black Americans must demand a better response on health care. And we can only hope that our politicians and policymakers have the courage to address those disparities.

Because if a rampaging pandemic won't force a change, nothing will.

—— —— ——

Ida B. Wells Park? | May 21, 2020

I can envision it clearly without a hint of impossible dreaming or wishful thinking.

The park along Union Avenue just east of Downtown Memphis that was once named in honor of Confederate general and slave trader Nathan Bedford Forrest being rechristened as Ida B. Wells Park.

What better way to honor the life and legacy of a courageous journalist, civil rights icon and now a Pulitzer Prize winner? A strong, educated and fearless Black woman who is without question one of this city's most underappreciated historic figures.

Plus, it would be a storybook ending to a decades-long battle to remove the images of slavery, racism and oppression from a place of conspicuous reverence in Memphis.

I can visualize it all. The official dedication would be heavily attended by a racially diverse crowd – assuming coronavirus-imposed social distancing by then would be over, or at least greatly relaxed.

Hopefully those in attendance would include descendants of Wells, notably Michelle Duster, Wells' great-granddaughter who, like her famous ancestor, is an award-winning writer, speaker and educator.

Students and staff from the Ida B. Wells Academy, a K-8 public school on South Lauderdale, could be special guests.

Perhaps there would be a statue of Wells unveiled that day. Women are grossly under-represented among monuments in Memphis. But if not a statue, at least there should be some visible symbol of her fight for racial justice and equality, and her relentless crusade to end lynchings of Black people in Memphis and throughout the South.

"I think that would be a wonderful tribute to her," said City Court Clerk Myron Lowery. "People tend to appreciate greatness after it's gone. And she seems to be a part of the forgotten history of this city."

In 2013, as talk of renaming Forrest Park was renewed, the Sons of Confederate Veterans, without approval, erected a marker in the park identifying it as Nathan Bedford Forrest Park.

The city immediately removed the marker and the push to rename the park gained steam. Lowery, a Memphis City Council member at the time, suggested renaming the site Forrest-Wells Park. He also proposed adding a monument to Wells as a way of providing balance and context.

Lowery's idea went nowhere. But on Feb. 5, 2013, the council approved a resolution giving three Civil War-themed parks in Memphis new temporary names. Forrest Park became Health Sciences Park, Confederate Park became Memphis Park and Jefferson Davis Park became Mississippi River Park.

Local and state courts later ruled that the City Council was perfectly within its rights to rename the parks. But the hostilities were just beginning. They came to a head on the evening of Dec. 20, 2017, when statues of Forrest and Davis were removed mere hours after the City Council approved a plan proposed by Mayor Jim Strickland to sell the three parks to a private nonprofit group known as Memphis Greenspace.

That only created more anger from Republican state lawmakers, along with Forrest's descendants and the Confederate group that filed suits saying the statue removals were illegal.

But here we are in May of 2020, and the lawsuits have been settled. The statues have been turned over to the Sons and Confederate Veterans and relocated out of town. Soon, the remains of Forrest and his wife, which were exhumed from Elmwood Cemetery and placed in the park in 1905, will be exhumed again and given – one would hope – an absolute final resting place, most likely in Columbia, Tennessee, with the statues.

All of this means now is the right time to consider the official renaming of Health Sciences Park to Ida B. Wells Park. Shelby County Commissioner Van Turner, president and CEO of Memphis Greenspace, told me the idea of naming the park in memory of Wells has been discussed.

"I think it would be an appropriate finale, an appropriate ending for that park," he said.

Appropriate is an understatement. Wells was born into slavery in Holly Springs, Mississippi, in 1862. Her parents died in the yellow fever epidemic in 1878, leaving Wells to care for her younger siblings. She studied at what later became Rust College, and at 18 landed a job teaching at a country school.

At age 20 in 1882, she came to Memphis to live with an aunt and continue teaching. She also continued her studies at Fisk University in

Nashville, but she was growing increasingly resentful of the outright racism she and other African Americans were forced to endure.

Wells found a perfect avenue for her writing ability and growing activism when she became co-owner of the Memphis Free Speech and Headlight newspaper, which had an office Downtown on Beale Street. She used the pages of the newspaper to expose the horrors of lynchings, none more stunning than the killings of three Black men – one of them a close friend – who owned the People's Grocery in a section of South Memphis known as the Curve.

How Thomas Moss, Will Stewart and Calvin McDowell were taken from their jail cell by an angry white mob and shot to death just outside the city limits is now a legendary story that exemplifies the brutal racism that existed in Memphis in the late 1800s.

Wells wrote extensively about the killings and exposed the real motive behind the terror. "She was the first one ... to realize that lynching had its base, not in the myth of Black men being attracted sexually to white women, but that it was an economic means to keep Black folks down," said longtime Memphis civil rights activist and author Miriam Decosta-Willis, who was interviewed for the documentary "Ida B. Wells: The Lynching at the Curve."

"I mean this woman had some brains."

Wells' journalism angered white Memphians, including the editors of the white-owned newspapers. An editorial in the Memphis Commercial after the Curve lynchings said, "There are some things the Southern white man will not tolerate, and the obscene intimations of (Wells' editorials) have brought the writer to the outermost limit of public patience."

Soon after that editorial appeared, a mob destroyed Wells' newspaper office while she was out of town and threatened to lynch her if she returned. She never did.

Eventually settling in Chicago, Wells married, had children and became an international figure advocating against lynchings and other injustices. She also was one of the founders of the NAACP in 1909.

Earlier this month, she was posthumously awarded a special Pulitzer Prize citation "for her outstanding and courageous reporting on the horrific and vicious violence against African Americans during the era of lynching."

The citation comes with a $50,000 award that will go to an organization or cause that supports Wells' lifelong mission.

Aside from the school on South Lauderdale, I know of no visible tributes to Wells in Memphis other than a marker on Beale Street near where her newspaper office once stood.

Renaming Health Sciences Park would send a resounding message of gratitude for her commitment to justice and human rights. It would be an ideal and long overdue Memphis tribute for Wells – 158 years after her birth and 89 years after her death.

Because it's never too late to do the right thing.

—— —— ——

A metaphor for the Black experience | May 28, 2020

Before I get too deep into this column, let me make it clear. I am deeply disturbed by the rash of violence that plagued Memphis during the extended Memorial Day weekend.

I am particularly disheartened by the death of a worker at the Dixie Queen ice cream and fast-food joint on Bellevue in South Memphis.

The victim was a 20-year-old man trying to earn a living on meager wages. The shooter was an angry man who felt no hesitancy about firing a weapon through the restaurant's front windows before his cowardly escape in a white sedan.

The incident is tragic and sad, as are the other fatal holiday weekend shootings in the city, along with several non-fatal ones, from Hickory Hill to Cordova. I am simply at a loss to explain the brazenness of shooting up a restaurant, shooting into a car at Jesse Turner Park or the circumstances that led to an apparent murder-suicide in the Windyke area of Southeast Memphis.

Just as I continue to be baffled to the point of anguish over repeated instances of heavy-handed policing of Black men in America.

I spent part of Memorial Day watching back-to-back episodes of "Live PD," a real-life crime show on the A&E Network that showcases real-time policing in America in both large and small cities. Several of the episodes featured encounters by white officers with white suspects, including one guy brandishing a knife and another one being belligerent and refusing commands before finally walking away, mooning the officers and then spitting on one of them.

In each case, the perpetrators weren't even handcuffed until things started to get out of hand. And even then, the officers treated the suspects with kid gloves.

The next morning, I woke up to the news that a handcuffed Black man in Minneapolis died while in police custody after a white officer kept his knee pressed down on the man's neck for several minutes despite the man pleading that he could not breathe.

Now the cellphone video of the incident has gone viral on social media.

And national news organizations are reporting the heinous act of police brutality by comparing it to the 2014 death of Eric Garner, who was put in a chokehold by New York police officers.

Garner's alleged crime was illegally selling single cigarettes on a street corner. Once officers took him down, Garner repeatedly told them, to no avail, that he could not breathe. And he later died.

In the Minneapolis case, the victim, identified as George Floyd, was suspected of forgery. Yes, forgery. He apparently matched the description of a Black man who tried to use forged documents at a local deli.

When cops spotted him, he resisted arrest, they said. Although surveillance video from a nearby business shows no such resisting. Officers then took down Floyd, who was handcuffed, beside a police squad car. But what happened next amounted to a death sentence.

One officer put his knee on Floyd's neck and kept it there despite Floyd, with his face pushed into the pavement, begging for air. "Please, please, please, I can't breathe. Please man," Floyd is heard on cellphone video taken by a bystander, who along with others also pleaded for the officer to remove his knee.

"Relax," the officer is heard telling Floyd.

A moment later, Floyd goes silent. But the officer kept his knee on the man's neck several more minutes until an ambulance arrived and took Floyd to a local hospital, where he was pronounced dead.

And if this does not create sustained national outrage from the halls of government to the smallest police force in America, if this does not convince you that the Black Lives Matter movement had it right all along, nothing will.

"Being Black in America should not be a death sentence," Minneapolis Mayor Jacob Frey said at a press conference and posted on his Facebook page Tuesday, May 26, the morning after Floyd's death. "What we saw was horrible and completely and utterly messed up. This man's life matters. He was a human being and his life mattered.

"For five minutes, we watched a white officer press his knee into a Black man's neck. Five minutes. When you hear someone calling for help, you're supposed to help. This officer failed in the most basic, human sense," said Frey, who is white.

That the four responding officers were fired Tuesday provides only a modicum of relief. But it does little to address the systemic problem that in far too many instances, African American men especially are viewed as threats who must be taken down by law enforcement.

Even a completely unrelated incident Monday morning in New York's Central Park involving an encounter between a Black man bird-watching and a white woman walking her dog is emblematic of the belief that Black men are threatening and must be controlled.

The bird watcher's name is Christian Cooper. The dog walker's name is Amy Cooper. That's as far as the similarity goes. When Christian asked Amy to comply with park rules to leash her dog and started recording her when she refused, Amy got agitated, said she was calling police and injected race into the encounter.

"I'm going to tell them there's an African American man threatening my life," she warned.

When she reaches a dispatcher, Amy says, "There is a man, African American, he has a bicycle helmet, he is recording me and threatening me and my dog."

Growing more irate, Amy says, "I am being threatened by a man in the Ramble (a section of Central Park). Please send the cops immediately."

"Thank you," Christian tells Amy. He then stops the recording.

Thankfully, no arrest was made. But after that video went viral, New York City Mayor Bill de Blasio responded with the obvious. "The video out of Central Park is racism, plain and simple," the mayor tweeted.

"She called the police BECAUSE he was a Black man. Even though she was the one breaking the rules. She decided he was the criminal and we know why."

Yes, we do.

Amy Cooper later apologized. But this issue is about more than one privileged white woman walking her dog, or one ill-trained cop taking down a suspected forger. And please, let's not forget the vigilante former cop and his son in Georgia who decided to hunt down a Black jogger and execute him on site for being a suspected burglar.

In a way, the death of George Floyd in Minneapolis is a metaphor for the Black experience in America. One way or another, most African Americans have had a foot or a knee on our necks for centuries. Through slavery, post-Reconstruction, the rise of the Ku Klux Klan, Mississippi's oppressive closed society, the civil rights movement and now the resurgence of angry white nationalism in the Trump era.

If it sounds as if I'm angry, in many ways I am – about all of it. I'm angry that a young man cannot work at a Dixie Queen without senselessly losing his life. I'm angry that too many Memphians, almost exclusively African Americans, prefer to settle scores with a gun.

And I am angry that the police encounters I saw Monday on "Live PD" do not apply to the average African American citizen.

Still, I continue to hope and pray that we find ways to stop, or at least reduce, inner-city gun violence. And that those across the country who take a solemn oath to protect and serve, do it without deference to race or color. I also wish that all people of good will would speak out against racial injustices – whether by police, dog walkers or vigilantes.

Because Black and brown lives matter.

—— —— ——

A Lyndon Johnson moment | June 11, 2020

It all started with a video. A black-and-white and somewhat grainy piece of news film that depicted the horrors of racial injustice for the entire nation and world to see.

Hordes of local and state police, including some on horseback, are seen descending on about 500 civil rights marchers at the foot of the Edmund Pettus Bridge in Selma, Alabama, on Sunday morning, March 7, 1965.

The marchers were beaten with nightsticks, tear gassed and some trampled by the horses, all in a racist effort to stop them from walking 53 miles to the state capital of Montgomery to register Black people to vote.

The footage was aired on that evening's national newscasts by NBC, ABC and CBS television networks. And perhaps for the first time, all of America was simultaneously repulsed by the viciousness of racism and police brutality.

I can recall vividly, as an 11-year-old, watching the news coverage of what became known as "Bloody Sunday" and rhetorically asking myself, how could the police be so cruel?

I asked that same question more than two weeks ago as I watched 21st-century cellphone video of another horror against an African American man. This video shows now fired Minneapolis police officer Derek Chauvin with his knee planted firmly for 8 minutes, 46 seconds on the neck of George Floyd – who was in handcuffs, face down on the pavement and literally begging for air before taking his last breath.

In both of these harrowing instances, America desperately needed a leader with the ability – and credibility – to say and do the right thing to calm an angered nation. We had that in 1965. We don't have it today.

Like millions of others, President Lyndon B. Johnson watched the news coverage of Selma's Bloody Sunday from the White House. And he was incensed.

Johnson, a Texan, had been lukewarm to civil rights and voting rights legislation as a member of the U.S. Senate. He presided over watered-down civil rights legislation in 1957, mostly because of his desire to one day be president and his reluctance to alienate Southern white Democrats who were decidedly anti-civil rights.

Then came John Kennedy's surprising decision to name Johnson as his running mate in 1960, a move that was more tactical than genuine. Kennedy, a Massachusetts liberal, needed to win at least some Southern states if he had any hope of defeating then-Vice President Richard Nixon.

The tactic paid off as the Kennedy-Johnson ticket carried Texas, Arkansas, Louisiana, North Carolina and South Carolina en route to winning the election.

Kennedy's assassination in 1963 elevated Johnson to the presidency just as the civil rights movement was becoming more intense and bloodier. There had been plenty of racial violence before Bloody Sunday, but the scenes from Selma struck a nerve with Johnson, and he knew it was time for congressional action to ensure voting rights for African Americans.

So on Monday evening, March 15, eight days after the Selma attack, Johnson gave the most moving speech of his presidency. Some historians have called it one of the greatest presidential addresses of all time.

It was written by Johnson's 33-year-old speechwriter, Richard Goodwin, who in interviews years later said he had only a few hours to craft the speech, and he barely finished it in time for Johnson's televised appearance before a joint session of Congress.

The key phrase in the speech was taken from the popular African American protest song, "We Shall Overcome." But the question became would Johnson, a white Southerner, utter those words.

The New York Times reported that as Johnson's motorcade was headed toward Capitol Hill that evening, it drove past a group of protesters standing outside the White House gates. They were singing "We Shall Overcome" in defiance of Johnson, obviously not knowing that those words were in his speech.

Johnson's message was powerful as he urged Congress to pass voting rights legislation. Goodwin may have written it, but the president seemed to wrap himself in every word. Midway through the address, he uttered the enduring lines.

"But even if we pass this bill, the battle will not be over. What happened in Selma is part of a far larger movement which reaches into every section and state of America. It is the effort of American Negroes to secure for themselves the full blessing of American life.

"Their cause must be our cause too. Because it is not just Negroes, but really it is all of us, who must overcome the crippling legacy of bigotry and injustice. And we shall overcome."

Johnson was interrupted 40 times with thunderous and standing applause, according to news accounts of the speech. Dr. Martin Luther King Jr., who watched the speech from Alabama, cried. And on Aug. 6, 1965, Johnson signed the Voting Rights Act into law.

So what of today's crisis? In the aftermath of the senseless killing of George Floyd, I've seen heartwarming images of police hugging citizens, comforting children, kneeling with protesters, praying in a circle of believers and walking arm-in-arm with marchers.

But I've also seen disturbing images of police tear gassing and beating peaceful protesters, pushing an elderly man backward to the pavement, slashing tires, smashing car windows and forcibly pulling innocent people from their vehicles and tasing them. And I have asked myself, where is our Lyndon Johnson moment?

Where is that someone at the highest level of government who can stand up and say with conviction, "The cause of those peacefully protesting across the nation must be our cause too. Because it is not just African Americans, but really it is all of us who must overcome the crippling legacy of bigotry, police brutality and injustice. And we shall overcome, because black lives matter."

The sad truth is, that person does not exist today. The current president has proven that he is incapable of giving such a speech, and any attempt to read it from a teleprompter would be unconvincing at best and insulting at worse.

Instead, Donald Trump would rather traffic in conspiracy theories, tweet pithy insults against his critics and demonize the news media. Hence, we must rely on past presidents, Democrats and just one Republican in the Senate, retired leaders in government and the military, and our collective selves to speak out and press for change.

What happened to George Floyd is an American tragedy. But what keeps happening to undermine American ideals of justice and equality for all is equally tragic.

Lyndon Johnson answered his moment. Our only hope now is to elect someone else who can answer theirs.

—— —— ——

The 'Redskins' offense | July, 16, 2020

Diehard fans of the Washington Redskins, I feel your pain.

Your angst, frustration and – for some – disgust over the decision by the owner of the storied National Football League franchise to drop the Redskins nickname are understandable. Change is difficult, often traumatic. And somehow it seems to hurt even more when it involves a beloved sports team.

I will tell you my own story with a painful name change later. But first, we must examine the reasons behind Washington's historic move. The Redskins name, frankly, is offensive to many. And Native American activists have been pleading with team owner Dan Snyder for years to drop the moniker.

But Snyder ignored the pleas, telling USA Today in 2014 that he would never change the team's nickname. Apparently Snyder has since watched Sean Connery's last James Bond movie, "Never Say Never Again." It was released 12 years after Connery reportedly vowed to never again play the role of the super-sophisticated British spy.

For Snyder, the economic and social pressure became too much to ignore. It started with the May 25 murder of George Floyd, a Black man who died after a white Minneapolis police officer kept his knee on Floyd's neck for nearly nine minutes.

Floyd's killing, along with those of Rayshard Brooks, Breonna Taylor, Tamir Rice and many other African Americans by police, finally sparked a reckoning across the country over racial injustice, racial stereotypes and white supremacy, past and present.

Then Memphis-based FedEx made its powerful voice heard when it called on the Washington Redskins to drop the nickname and mascot. FedEx owns the naming rights to the suburban Washington stadium, where the team plays, under a 27-year, $205 million deal. And company founder, chairman and chief executive Frederick W. Smith owns a 10% share of the team, which has won three Super Bowls.

That's enough clout to get the team's attention. And when other companies, including PepsiCo, Nike and Bank of America joined in the pressure campaign, Snyder had no choice. The Redskins name had to go.

I get it that some fans are unhappy. As are members of the Blackfeet Nation in Montana. According to media reports, the team mascot, adopted in 1971, pays tribute to John "Two Guns" White Calf, a Blackfeet chief. White Calf, who died in 1934, is also said to be the image on the buffalo nickel.

The Redskins nickname has been around since 1933 when the team played in Boston before moving to the nation's capital in 1937.

But times change. And so do team names. The Washington Bullets of the NBA changed their name to the Wizards in 1997 because team owners no longer wanted to be associated with violence. I don't recall if there was a protest from the National Rifle Association.

In 2014, the NBA's Charlotte Bobcats dropped that name and resumed being the Hornets after New Orleans, which relocated from Charlotte in 2002, changed its name to the Pelicans.

Other professional team names have been changed without so much as a single boo from fans. Major League Baseball's Florida Marlins dropped the state name and became the Miami Marlins in 2012. Baseball's Los Angeles Angels switched to the California Angels, then switched again to Anaheim Angels and are now known as the Los Angeles Angels of Anaheim.

And the NBA's Golden State Warriors once only belonged to San Francisco.

In the college ranks, Arkansas State University in Jonesboro once called its sports teams the Indians. Now they are the Red Wolves. And St. John's University in New York once called its teams Redmen. It now uses the name Red Storm.

As for my own experience with a traumatic name change, it happened in 1970 when I entered my senior year of high school. That was also the first year of full forced integration of public schools in Mississippi, 16 years after the Supreme Court ruled in Brown vs. Board of Education that separate but equal schools were unconstitutional.

Prior to my senior year, I attended North Panola Vocational High School in Como. Our mascot was the eagle and we loved it. For us, the eagle represented strength, determination and soaring grace.

Most of us African American students had attended substandard schools for years, with used books and other supplies handed down from all white schools in the county. But we took pride in our sports, particularly basketball, and loved our beautiful purple and gold colors. I was more than a fan. I was a player, although just an average one.

Then came 1970 when grades 10-12 were transferred to the previously predominantly white North Panola High School in Sardis. Instead of Eagles, we suddenly became Raiders. Our majestic purple and gold became a rather dull red and gray. And we hated it.

The name change was bad enough. But the tension from being the school's first truly integrated senior class was ever present, and most of it came from teachers and administrators.

African American students outnumbered white students two to one in my senior class. Yet, of the seven class sponsors, only one was African American. We were forced to have two homecoming queens, one Black, one white. And all other senior class officers and honors had to be biracial pairs. Even the student newspaper had co-editors.

Still, we got through it. Because after all, it was only a name. So, disgruntled Redskins fans, I understand. But as much as I disliked the name Raiders, it was not nearly as offensive as the nickname you have championed for years.

America is now in a different place than it was before George Floyd's murder. And the time has come for significant societal change – by ending our love affair with Confederate monuments in public spaces and by realizing that offensive racial stereotypes no longer deserve to be glorified in movies, in music or, yes, on the football field.

— — —

John Lewis in Memphis | July 22, 2020

On a chilly mid-December evening in 1967, some 30 to 40 mostly like-minded people – Black and white – gathered in a private meeting room at Memphis' main library at Peabody and McLean.

All but a handful of them were affiliated with the Tennessee Council on Human Relations, an interracial group devoted to civil rights, social justice, improving race relations and fighting poverty. The rest were covert observers.

They were there to hear a keynote address by John Lewis, who at just 27, was already a veteran in the fight for voting rights, equal accommodations and equal justice. And he had plenty of scars to show for it.

The speech ended up being a pivotal moment in Lewis' evolution from a teenager in the movement with a streak of militancy in his soul to an ardent believer in nonviolence as the most effective way to counter vicious racism.

Much has been said in recent days celebrating the extraordinary life and legacy of Lewis, a 17-term Democratic congressman from Georgia, who died of cancer at age 80 on July 17.

Arguably the most respected member of the U.S. House, Lewis made numerous visits to Memphis over the years. He was appropriately treated like civil rights royalty each time, with extensive media coverage, photo ops with admirers, and warm greetings from local and state political leaders from both parties.

But on that Wednesday night in 1967, Lewis' visit to the Bluff City went virtually unnoticed – except by the FBI. Four years earlier, Lewis, then 23, had been the youngest speaker at the August 1963 March on Washington, where Dr. Martin Luther King Jr. gave his iconic "I Have a Dream" speech.

And in March 1965, Lewis, who had just turned 25, was nearly beaten to death by Alabama police at the Edmund Pettus Bridge while attempting to lead a group of marchers from Selma to Montgomery to demand voting rights for African Americans. The incident marked a turning point in the movement. Images of the beating were broadcast on national television news and led to a shift in public opinion over forced segregation and the right of African Americans to vote.

But despite his budding fame, the local news media ignored Lewis' speech to the Council on Human Relations. "We actually wanted some media coverage," said longtime Memphis attorney Mike Cody, who at the time was vice president of the council. "But the only ones who covered it and wrote a report about it was the FBI."

Details of the meeting are contained in an FBI surveillance document prepared by Special Agent William H. Lawrence. And no, Lawrence wasn't at the meeting. He relied on information supplied by renowned civil rights photographer Ernest Withers, as well as Memphis police lieutenants E.E. Redditt and E.H. Arkin, who were there.

Cody, years later, obtained a copy of Lawrence's report from someone who was doing research on FBI surveillance activity. The agent's account of what was a totally innocent and benign meeting actually painted Lewis in a positive light. Plus, it was remarkably accurate, Cody told me.

Lewis had been working for several months throughout five rural West Tennessee counties – Fayette, Hardeman, Haywood, Lauderdale and Tipton – gathering information about poverty and substandard housing conditions among Black residents. The young civil rights worker had also met with state lawmakers seeking their help in addressing rural poverty in Tennessee.

But the moment that sticks out most for Cody that evening was when Lewis explained that he had been removed from his leadership role in the Student Nonviolent Coordinating Committee (SNCC) after he objected to the group's growing confrontational stance led by Stokely Carmichael, who later changed his name to Kwame Ture.

According to Lawrence's surveillance memo, "Lewis added that he resigned from SNCC and was deposed as its chairman in 1965 because key people in SNCC were chanting violence and he felt those methods and tactics were wrong.

"He said much more good could be accomplished through non-violent methods. He said the only way poor people, both black and white, can stop the wrongs done to them is to work together speaking against the type of government where only the few at the top are satisfied."

The comments, to me, were striking because if anyone had a legitimate reason to want to fight back against racial oppression, it was Lewis. He had been arrested dozens of time for participating in sit-ins and peaceful protest marches. And he had been beaten routinely by police and others.

In May 1961, when he was 21, Lewis was taking part in Freedom Rides across the South to challenge racial segregation. When the group arrived in Rock Hill, North Carolina, Lewis attempted to enter a "whites only" bus terminal waiting area when he was savagely attacked by a member of the Ku Klux Klan.

Years later, the Klansman personally apologized to Congressman Lewis and Lewis accepted the apology.

In November 1960, Lewis and another demonstrator were sitting at The Krystal lunch counter in Nashville when employees sprayed their faces with insecticide. He was arrested numerous times at other lunch counters and segregated establishments in Nashville and elsewhere.

Yet, he never fought back. And when he gave that moving address at the Memphis library in 1967, Lewis had become an unwavering devotee to Dr. King's nonviolent movement. Which makes it all the more troubling that the FBI felt it had to keep tabs on him and track his movements.

In addition to Cody, Lawrence's memo lists several others who attended the library gathering. They included well-known activist Rev. James Lawson; attorney David Caywood; former police officer, educator and activist Roscoe McWilliams; the council's executive director Braxton Bryant; Memphis War on Poverty Committee director Washington Butler; and community activist Jesse Neely.

The report also identifies a member of the ultraconservative John Birch Society who sat in the back of the room taking notes and hiding her face from Withers' camera. The woman, identified as Betty Eastman, later turned over her notes on the meeting to Memphis police.

Speaking of Withers, his work as a paid FBI informant has been well documented. And people can make their own judgments about that. Frankly, I don't believe Withers, who I got to know pretty well late in his life, intended to put people in physical danger by feeding information about them to federal agents.

But it's clear that FBI surveillance, under ruthless director J. Edgar Hoover, caused plenty of harm to law-abiding citizens whose only goals were equal rights, freedom and justice for everyone.

As for Lewis and his mentor, Lawson, now 91 and living in Los Angeles, they will always be considered "secular saints," Cody said, "for trying to make a change for the better in the world."

—— —— ——

Implicit bias is real | October 1, 2020

On Nov. 18, 2016 – 10 days after our Electoral College process saddled us with Donald Trump as the president – an assemblage of legal scholars, jurists and journalists gathered in Downtown Memphis to dissect the issue of implicit/unconscious bias in American society.

The day-long event at the University of Memphis Law School was no rush job caused by Trump's election. It had been in the works for months, spearheaded by now-retired lawyer Maurice Wexler and federal appeals court Judge Bernice Donald.

Until recently, Wexler was a senior partner in the Baker Donelson law firm. That's Baker, as in the late iconic Republican Sen. Howard Baker, and Donelson, as in the late Memphis City Council member and longtime Republican Party leader Lewis Donelson.

Donald, meanwhile, has been a trailblazer for racial diversity in the local and federal judiciary. She was elected against tremendous odds as a General Sessions Court judge in 1982. She later became the first African American woman appointed as a local U.S. Bankruptcy Court judge, then a U.S. District Court judge before being elevated to the Sixth Circuit Court of Appeals bench.

That Donald's and Wexler's impressive journeys through the legal profession had vastly different starting points is an understatement. But they have at least one thing in common. Both believe that unconscious racial bias is an issue worth getting out in the open.

I think so too, and it's why I agreed in 2016 to join them, as well as Juvenile Court Judge Dan Michael, U of M law professor Demetria Frank and others on a planning committee for the event titled "Implicit (Unconscious) Bias: A New Look at an Old Problem."

The notion that people harbor deep-seated biases, mostly on race but also on age, sex and other factors, has long been an accepted view. But it was not until the late 1990s that social scientists began to collect data on the issue and turn it into a legitimate exercise for businesses and governments to present to their workforce.

But now that Trump is in office – and is looking for any wedge issue on which to energize his far-right base – implicit bias discussions are in danger of being ended in the federal workplace.

The president issued an executive order Sept. 22 that appears to prohibit federal contractors from, as the National Law Review put it, "engaging in many forms of diversity, inclusion, and implicit bias training that have gained popularity in recent months."

Trump's order makes it federal policy that contractors and agencies receiving grants from the government cannot "promote race or sex stereotyping or scapegoating."

On Sept. 28, CNN reported that the president's budget director Russell Vought took the order a step further, saying federal agencies could no longer conduct any "divisive training" that the White House deems anti-American propaganda.

CNN described Vought's directive as including training on critical race theory and unconscious bias.

Both Trump's executive order and the budget office memo are so vaguely worded that their meaning is open to interpretation. Which, after all, is the intent. If the Trump administration can discourage discussions around implicit/unconscious bias without banning it outright, so much the better for them.

It's yet another example of this president realizing that he must continue to stoke the culture wars in society to keep his supporters worked up enough to flood the polls Nov. 3.

It's why, earlier in September, he dog-whistled that the idea of Democratic vice presidential candidate Kamala Harris possibly becoming the first woman president "would be an insult to our country."

It's why he repeatedly excoriates the Black Lives Matter movement. And it's why, in a rare moment of honesty, he told author and journalist Bob Woodard that he does believe in white privilege.

So who should be surprised that, as Trump sinks deeper into disfavor with most Americans, he is attacking this country's reckoning with race as an undermining of American values?

Granted, not everyone agrees that implicit/unconscious bias is a valid legal concept. Wexler, who organized the 2016 event in Memphis, is one of them.

"Implicit bias no longer is an accepted legal theory," he told me this week. "There is no credible evidence that it leads to demonstrable behavior."

Wexler does believe the discussion over whether we have biases lurking subconsciously in our hearts and minds is one worth having. But he says it's impossible to determine what a person is thinking, so we must instead focus on explicit bias. "It's the behavior," he said.

Judge Donald, of course, disagrees. She says there is a mountain of evidence that shows, for examples, "sentencing disparities based on race; employment interview call backs that are higher for people with Eurocentric names and lower for people with Afro-centric names; the hiring memo study that points to implicit bias; and a host of other evidence.

"The research shows that the associations in the brain start very early, around the age of 4 or 5. I vehemently disagree with my friend Maurice."

Apparently, so does Anthony Greenwald, a psychology professor at the University of Washington who helped pioneer studies into implicit/unconscious bias.

"Most people have multiple implicit biases they aren't aware of," Greenwald told the PBS News Hour in June, more than two weeks after the police killing of George Floyd sparked our reckoning with race.

"The problems surfacing in the wake of George's Floyd's death include all form of bias, ranging from implicit bias to structural bias built into the operation of police departments, courts and government, to explicit, intended bias, to hate crime."

Greenwald likens implicit bias to "being the carrier of a disease you don't know you have."

I tend to side with Greenwald and Judge Donald. Implicit bias is a thing, and it's reflected in virtually every aspect of our society. Without meaningful discussions of the issue, in public and private workplaces, we can never fully address the scourge of systemic racism.

Those discussions need not be exercises in white guilt. It serves no purpose to accuse all white people of being inherently racist. Plus, it's not true. But Greenwald, who spoke to me by phone Tuesday, said his studies show a larger percentage of white people possesses implicit bias tendencies than any other group.

I don't expect anything different from Trump. He is who he is – a white man of privilege who sees everyone else, particularly people of color, as beneath him.

As for my friends, Wexler and Judge Donald, both are well-meaning, thoughtful and open-minded people. They are scheduled to conduct implicit bias discussions with city of Memphis employees. From the looks of it, these sessions will be more point-counterpoint.

Should be interesting.

—— —— ——

ON CRIME AND JUSTICE

Trenary's final moments | October 4, 2018

What might he have been thinking? And what was he saying?

Was he reflecting on the success of Move It Memphis, the Memphis Regional Chamber's four-mile walk/run around Downtown that began and ended at Loflin Yard, a hidden gem of a restaurant with a patio full of greenery on West Carolina Street?

Or was he merely making plans for the next day, and what he intended to do to help make Memphis – and particularly Downtown – a better place, a safer place, a more welcoming place.

All those things could easily have been going through Phil Trenary's mind the evening of Sept. 27 as he walked north along Front Street, apparently heading home after the Move It Memphis event ended.

Video gleaned from an apartment building's surveillance camera at 610 S. Front, shows Trenary talking on a cell phone as he slowly walked along the street. One hand is holding the phone to his ear, the other hand is in his pocket.

The 39-second recording also shows, rather ominously, a white dual-cab pickup as it passes by Trenary and parks out of camera view. Trenary then walks out of view as well. Seconds later, Trenary is fatally shot. And the pickup speeds away north on Front Street.

The violence, thankfully, is not captured on the recording. But it is still painful to watch because you know that you are witnessing the final seconds of a man's life. A man who for years helped infuse new life into the city in general, and Downtown in particular.

As I watched those 39 seconds tick away, I almost found myself wanting to shout, "Phil, watch out! Phil, stop! Phil, run away! Phil!"

Phil Trenary and I were not close friends. But like thousands of

Memphians, I knew him, mostly through his visibility in the community, his civic leadership and his footprint on the economic well-being of this city. So, like virtually everyone else in the Bluff City, including family members of those now charged in connection with his death, I am deeply saddened and troubled by his murder.

And while the words 'homicide' and 'Memphis' are used quite often in the same sentence, this homicide has touched a particular nerve, mostly because of the brazenness of the crime and the way Trenary, a beloved individual, was unsuspectingly stalked by his assailants.

Which explains the unprecedented comments from General Sessions Court Judge Bill Anderson at the start of an initial court hearing Monday for Quandarius Richardson, 18, and McKinney Wright Jr., 22, two of the three people charged with Trenary's murder.

Anderson acknowledged that he did not personally know Trenary, the former president and CEO of Pinnacle Airlines and, since 2014, president of the Greater Memphis Chamber. But like the rest of us, Anderson knew his reputation as a force for good.

"It seems his sole agenda was to make this city and county a better place," the judge said. "He crossed racial lines, he crossed monetary lines. He probably could have retired when he sold his airline, but instead he chose to stay in Memphis.... It's just a terrible tragedy."

And then there is this from Wright's mother, Celestine Wright. "I am sad. Very sorry that it happened to him like that, especially to him knowing what kind of man he is helping Memphis, the community, fixing it up and stuff like that. It is a shock and I am sorry."

There remains a lot that we don't know about Trenary's death, including who actually fired the fatal shots and whether, as it appears from police accounts, Trenary was shot from behind execution style.

That lack of details has fed wild speculation, mostly through social media, that others were involved and that Trenary may have been more than just a random target by three lawless young people.

Others simply don't want to believe that teenagers and a 22-year-old that cold and ruthless are living among us and bent on striking fear in the minds of innocent Memphians.

It's obvious to me that the three people charged with Trenary's murder had no idea who he was and how much he meant to this city. All three, including Racanisha Wright, 16, who is now in Juvenile Court custody, have told investigators they were driving around Downtown looking for someone to rob.

That someone ended up being Trenary, whose life and legacy are being celebrated today (Oct. 4) during services at Christ United Methodist Church on Poplar Avenue.

We will never know what Trenary was thinking in his final moments captured on video as he walked along Front Street in the adopted city he came to love.

But strangely, it's almost as if he did speak to us one last time through the words of Judge Anderson, who also said this on Monday. "Let's carry on. Let's do what he tried to do in this community.

"We all have an obligation, every single one of us in this community. We can't sit back on our rear-ends and expect somebody like Mr. Trenary to do it all for us."

Amen.

—— —— ——

A code of silence | October 18, 2018

Picture this scenario: A man with a gun is chasing on foot another man, who may or may not be armed.

As the man being chased reaches the front door of a home and tries to enter, the man in pursuit opens fire. He critically wounds the fleeing individual as other bullets pierce the front door and outer walls of the home.

Two other people, who are associates of the shooter, witness the incident. But as law enforcement officers later try to figure out what happened and whether the shooting was justified, neither the shooter nor the witnesses will cooperate with investigators. And the inquiry is seriously hampered.

Sadly, this is not a hypothetical situation. It basically describes what's taking place as a result of the September officer-involved shooting of Martavious Banks, although some of the details are in dispute.

A month later, Banks, 25, remains hospitalized. But the good news is he is recovering from being shot twice in the back, a family attorney told reporters last week.

"He's doing well," said Billy Murphy, an attorney based in Baltimore. "He's able to talk, he is able to articulate what he remembers."

If that's true, Banks is the only one talking. This week we learned that the Memphis Police Association has advised the three officers linked to the shooting not to speak with the Tennessee Bureau of Investigation, the outside agency looking into the incident. The directive also applies to any other officer-involved shootings that are turned over to the TBI.

So much for police-community relations.

Keeping quiet may make sense for officers who pull the trigger in a questionable shooting. They have a right to protect themselves against self-incrimination just as any other citizen. But what about witnesses who also happen to wear a badge? As the community presses for answers, should they be encouraged to maintain a code of silence?

Yes, says police association president Mike Williams, whose son, Michael Williams II, was one of the three officers at the scene when Banks was shot. "Not that they're trying to hide anything," the elder Williams said. "But their rights have to be protected."

Before we draw any conclusions about a possible cover-up, obstruction of justice or simply a righteous adherence to the thin blue line, let's remember – for background and context – how this highly contentious and murky story has unfolded.

The initial police report said Banks was pulled over Sept. 17 for a routine traffic stop in the 1200-block of Gill in South Memphis. Police said Banks reached for a gun in his vehicle, but then jumped out of the car and fled on foot as officers chased him.

Banks was shot moments later. Police have not said if he had a gun in his possession when he was shot. Family members insist he did not.

The officer who shot Banks was later identified as Jamarcus Jeames, 26, who has been with the department 19 months. Officers Christopher Nowell, 27, a member of the department for four years, and Williams, a member for three years, were present when the incident happened.

Adding to public suspicion was the disclosure by Police Director Michael Rallings that Jeames did not have his body camera on when the shots were fired, and the other officers either switched off their body and dashboard cameras or never turned them on.

Since then, we've heard nothing from police officials as an internal investigation continues into why the cameras were not in use and the TBI looks into the shooting. And now the police association is telling officers to invoke what is known as the Garrity rule in refusing to speak to TBI investigators.

Garrity vs. New Jersey is a 1967 Supreme Court ruling that officers cannot be coerced into answering questions about alleged misconduct under threat of losing their job if those answers are later used in a criminal prosecution.

The Garrity case involved an investigation into ticket fixing, not use of deadly force. And the Supreme Court decision does not apply to officers who witness questionable activity.

Simply put, "the Garrity Rule does not apply in situations where one officer is asked to give a statement against another," wrote retired corrections expert and author Carl Toersbijns in a 2015 article about the Garrity case for the web site Corrections.com. "No officer has a right to protection against incriminating another person."

But regardless of what the Supreme Court ruling says or does not say, the police union presenting rank and file officers is advising its members, including those who are mere witnesses, not to answer when the TBI comes knocking.

How is that any different from the code of silence that police routinely encounter when trying to solve gang-related crimes? And how is it different from the deafening silence of the three witnesses in the car the night 2-year-old Laylah Washington was shot to death while riding in her mother's car more than two years ago?

I get it that police officers under suspicion enjoy the same rights as other citizens. But I agree with former City Council member TaJuan Stout Mitchell, who wrote on Facebook this week that the police association telling officers to keep silent amounts to undermining investigative institutions and a crippling of justice.

"I know (police) feel vulnerable, but they must trust the same institutions they use to convict people," Mitchell wrote. "A young man was shot in the back and if a police officer was shot in the back they would want answers and I would too. I want 'law and order.'"

We all do. Which is the very reason we should call out anyone who intentionally protects those suspected of doing wrong, whether they wear a badge or a bandanna.

—— —— ——

Reforming justice | March 7, 2019

With politics at both the national and state level as divisive as ever, the bipartisan "Kumbaya" sentiments over criminal justice reform are refreshing.

Elected officials and public-policy advocates across the political spectrum seem to be united in favor of the need to reduce our staggering prison population, get rid of most mandatory minimum sentences and help those getting out of prison be successful, thereby reducing recidivism.

From the White House to various statehouses, the push for reforms is quickly gaining momentum as Republicans and Democrats vow to work together to achieve results. It is by far the most encouraging thing I have seen politically in years.

And yet, there is one facet of this newfound political consensus that bothers me. The effort around criminal justice reform, in my view, is becoming a Black thing.

Call me overly sensitive, but I am starting to conclude that when political leaders talk about mentoring those in prison and giving them the education and training they will need once they get out, the faces of those imagined recipients are African American.

After President Donald Trump signed the much-acclaimed First Step Act, designed to reduce recidivism and lower mandatory-minimum sentences, he talked as if it was an altruistic act exclusively for Black inmates.

"This legislation reformed sentencing laws that have wrongly and disproportionately harmed the African American community," Trump said. "The First Step Act gives nonviolent offenders the chance to reenter society as productive, law-abiding citizens. Now, states across the country are following our lead. America is a nation that believes in redemption."

While it is true that African Americans are saddled with disproportionately lengthy prison sentences, white inmates in federal prisons represent 58% of the total population, according to January numbers from the U.S. Bureau of Prisons.

Just last month, Mississippi Gov. Phil Bryant, a supporter of criminal justice reform, candidly admitted at the National Governors Association meeting that white conservatives would never have supported prison reform legislation under former President Barack Obama.

Bryant implied that conservatives would have seen it as Obama, the nation's first Black president, releasing mostly African American criminals "out on our communities, and there's going to be pillaging and crime."

But since Trump is championing the reforms, mostly to score points with African Americans, many conservatives are now fine with it.

And during his first State of the State address Monday, Tennessee Gov. Bill Lee spoke at length about his desire to "build a criminal justice system that is tough, smart, and above all, just."

Lee proposed a series of steps aimed at reducing the state's prison population and lessening recidivism. They include community supervision for nonviolent, low-risk offenders rather than locking them up, eliminating the fees for getting criminal records expunged, and a Volunteer Mentorship Initiative to counsel inmates.

"It's past time that our state's elected leaders speak with one voice on this issue," Lee said. "When it comes to reforming our state's justice system, the cost of doing nothing isn't zero."

Lee then introduced Marcus Martin to the assembled lawmakers and a statewide television audience. Martin, who was seated in the gallery, was incarcerated for five years and, according to the governor, "was on a quick path back to prison."

That trajectory shifted thanks to Men of Valor, a Nashville-based nonprofit that provides spiritual counseling to prison inmates. Martin, who is African American, has now been out of prison 16 years and is a full-time prison minister.

It was a heartwarming story of redemption. But as I listened to the governor's words and watched the handshakes and standing ovation given to Martin, it reinforced my belief that even the most well-meaning politicians see the images of crime through an African American prism.

To be fair, Tennessee's felony inmate population during fiscal year 2018 was 40% African American, according to the state Department of Corrections. That number is hugely disproportionate considering that Tennessee's overall Black population is 16.8%.

But the undeniable fact is, the majority of inmates serving time for felonies in Tennessee are white, representing 57% of the total inmate population.

During his address, Lee introduced and spotlighted two other people besides Martin. Both were white. One was Dan Smith, a horticulture and agriculture teacher from Dyer County and a former agriculture teacher of the year. The other was state Highway Patrol Lt. Travis Plotzer of Dickson County, who helped rescue stranded motorists during recent flooding.

Both men are no doubt well-deserving of the governor's recognition. But in politics, optics are important. And I could not help but notice the subliminal message. All three of the special guests were men. Smith represented education, Plotzer represented courageous law enforcement, and Martin represented redemption from crime.

None of this is meant to criticize these men, nor is it meant to trash what was a fine gubernatorial address. Perhaps my racially sensitive tentacles are raised too high. I'm sure some will think so. But the face of crime has many shapes, sizes and colors.

And while we should encourage and applaud all efforts to reform our criminal justice system, those reforms will affect more than African Americans.

—— —— ——

This is America | June 6, 2019

For 21 days in May, I taught and traveled in Germany. I got around with ease in the city of Mainz – and traversed other parts of the country using a very efficient public transit system.

I also visited two of Germany's major broadcasting centers – the regional DWR, which includes both radio and television, and the much larger ZDF, Germany's national public TV broadcaster.

As I stood in the DWR television control room watching one of its daily 15-minute newscasts, and as I traveled around Mainz and other cities, I did not hear a single word about gun violence, homicides or mass killings.

But within minutes after setting foot back on U.S. soil last Friday, my cellphone exploded with notifications of yet another deadly mass shooting; this one in scenic Virginia Beach, Virginia, took 12 innocent lives.

As writer-musician Donald Glover, aka Childish Gambino, says, this is America.

The experts tell us that the overall homicide rate in the U.S. dropped significantly in 2018. But mass killings, defined by the FBI as the slaying of four or more people in a single incident at one place, have been steadily rising since the Columbine school massacre in 1999.

And while the Virginia Beach shooting produced the largest number of fatalities so far this year, it joins a long list of senseless mass killings in recent years at workplaces, night clubs, concerts, malls, movie theaters, houses of worship and, of course, schools.

All of this is completely foreign to most of the people I encountered in Germany, particularly students at Johannes Gutenberg University in Mainz. And the reason is simple. Gun ownership there is considered a privilege, not a right.

After a deadly shooting at a high school in eastern Germany in 2002, in which a 19-year-old expelled student took the lives of 16 people, the German government instituted more stringent gun laws. They included raising the legal age for having a weapon for sport from 18 to 21, and requiring gun buyers under 25 to certify that they are fit, medically and psychologically, to own a weapon.

The laws were further tightened after a 2009 mass killing at a southwest Germany school that claimed 15 lives. Those restrictions included random checks of gun owners.

According to the website German Culture, the country's gun control laws are "among the most stringent in Europe. It restricts the acquisition, possession and carrying of firearms to those with a credible need for a weapon."

German law bans fully automatic weapons and "severely restricts the acquisition of other types of weapons. Compulsory liability insurance is required for anyone who is licensed to carry firearms."

The Gutenberg University students also told me that there is never a fear of a deadly encounter with police, because – unlike in the U.S. – police officers don't automatically assume that the person they stop is carrying a gun.

"Nobody carries one," several journalism graduate students said, almost in unison. "Why would we?"

All of that is totally foreign to Americans. Most of us believe the Second Amendment gives us the unfettered right to own practically any type of weapon – high powered or otherwise – along with unlimited ammunition and accessories to go with it.

Which brings us back to Friday's killings in Virginia Beach.

The shooter used a .45-caliber handgun, but had several extended magazines that allowed him to continuously fire at his victims and responding police officers.

An extended magazine "allows someone to shoot more rounds before they're forced to reload the gun," former ATF special agent David Chipman told National Public Radio.

NPR also reported that extended magazines were used during some of the worst mass shootings in American history, including the 2012 killings of 20 elementary school children and six adults at Sandy Hook.

A 2013 investigation by Mother Jones reported that of 62 mass shootings it examined, high-capacity magazines were used in at least half of them.

And yet, any effort to restrict or outright ban some of these tools for mass murder continues to face strong resistance from the National Rifle Association and other pro-gun organizations. And that means most

Republican lawmakers – state and federal – who are beholden to the gun lobby will continue to do nothing except spout the same meaningless rhetoric after every massacre.

By now, you know the drill. They will offer thoughts and prayers for the victims, praise the brave first responders, implore the media not to even utter the killer's name, then move on and hope the public does the same.

Until the next inevitable act of carnage.

Indeed, this is America, the land that I love. The land that I was ready to come back to after visiting a country that 80 years ago made mass killing an official government policy. A country that owns up to its shameful past, and no longer has the stomach for mass violence.

This is America, home of the brave. And, thanks to our unwillingness to pass sensible gun control laws, a haven for deadly homegrown terrorism.

—— —— ——

A voice missing | June 6, 2019

It all started with a routine post to Facebook Marketplace.

A snazzy red Infiniti was available for sale by someone in the Hernando, Mississippi, area. Interested buyers could contact the seller by responding directly to the Facebook post.

Twenty-year-old Brandon Webber did, using a phony Facebook account. He agreed to meet the owner on the evening of June 3 at a common area on Hernando's west end, off U.S. 51 southwest of the town square.

Webber was dropped off by a friend, chatted briefly with the owner, then got behind the wheel of the Infiniti and took it for a brief spin. When the test drive was over, Webber made a second request. "I want to see what this car can do." And he asked the owner to take the wheel.

But when the owner got out and walked around the rear of the car, Webber met him with a .22-caliber handgun and, without saying a word, allegedly fired five bullets into his upper torso at near point-blank range.

Webber then hopped back into the driver's seat and fled, leaving the victim sprawled on the pavement, fighting for his life.

A lot has been said and done in the aftermath of Webber's death during an encounter with members of a U.S. Marshals' task force on the evening of June 12 in Frayser. We've heard from Webber's family members; his former school mates; his former high school principal; political, religious and community leaders in Frayser; other clergy from across Memphis; the city's mayor; a Shelby County commissioner who wants to be mayor; and countless others on social media.

The one important voice that we have not heard from directly is the owner of that red Infiniti. He is still recovering in the hospital, and authorities are declining to release his name.

But I do know this much about him. He is a young African American man in his early to mid-20s – just like Webber.

Most of what we know about what happened in Mississippi on June 3 is coming from District Attorney John Champion. But he is not serving as a P.R. spokesman for the U.S. Marshals Service or any other law enforcement agency.

Champion is speaking out for the Hernando shooting victim, whose ordeal has mostly gotten lost amid the violent unrest, the finger pointing and vigils that occurred after Webber was killed.

Champion is reminding us that Webber was not picked out haphazardly by trigger-happy officers and marked for death. A painstaking investigation, that included subpoenaing information from Facebook, led authorities to Webber as the creator of the bogus Facebook account.

The victim, in his hospital bed, was shown a photo spread of possible suspects, and he identified Webber as the man who shot him, stole his car and left him for dead.

Mississippi authorities then issued warrants for Webber's arrest on charges of aggravated assault, conspiracy and armed robbery. The person who drove Webber to Hernando that evening is also being sought. Because Webber likely fled across the state line to Memphis, the U.S. Marshals' Gulf Coast Regional Fugitive Task Force was deployed to apprehend him.

The task force is made up of specially trained deputy marshals and local law enforcement officers. It focuses mostly on violent fugitives and those accused of sexual assaults, and it has the authority to cross state lines to make arrests without notifying local police.

When Webber was eventually spotted in Frayser on June 12, he still had the red Infiniti. And, according to a statement from the Tennessee Bureau of Investigation, he "rammed (the) vehicle into the officers' vehicles multiple times before exiting with a weapon." A source tells me it was a different weapon from the .22 that was used in Hernando.

That's when the task force officers fired the shots that killed Webber. Not long after that, chaos erupted with protesters throwing bricks, cans, even tree limbs at Memphis police officers and sheriff's deputies, who were summoned as backup after the fatal shooting occurred. Other protesters smashed the windows of police cars and shattered the window of a nearby fire station.

And just like that, Memphis became a focus of national news as the summer's first hot spot for frayed relations between police and the community.

Some of the community sentiment is understandable. Why couldn't Webber have been taken alive, just as white suspect Dylann Roof was after he massacred nine African American churchgoers four years ago this week in South Carolina?

Why is it that when Black suspects are involved, deadly force is used more often than not? And why is it that even in cases when unarmed Black suspects are killed by police, criminal charges are almost never filed?

Those are legitimate questions, and no doubt played into some of the reaction to Webber's death. This week, the nation is again debating excessive force after Phoenix police officers drew their guns and roughed up a Black family when a 4-year-old girl shoplifted a doll from a store.

Champion, the North Mississippi district attorney, says he understands the frustration. "I get the distrust in the Black community of police officers," he told me.

But Champion says despite all the comments to the contrary, the evidence clearly shows that Webber was a violent felon. "And I stand by that one million percent," he said. "I just wish that people could sit back, lower the temperature and let all the facts come out."

Indications are that is now happening. There have been no further disturbances, the national media have moved on to other topics and the calming voices are outweighing the critical ones.

But as we continue to heal, let's not forget the other young Black man in this sad case – the Hernando shooting victim whose voice also deserves to be heard.

—— —— ——

ICE in Mississippi | August 15, 2019

In the state of Mississippi that I knew as a child, cotton was king.

This was in the 1950s and '60s. And every available patch of land, it seemed, was covered during harvest season with row after row of the fluffy white cotton bolls that were the state's No. 1 economic driver.

Even before Mississippi became the 20th state in 1817, and in the decades that followed, cotton allowed a select group of plantation owners to amass enormous wealth. That was thanks first to the enslaved laborers who harvested the crops during the antebellum era, and later to the sharecroppers who worked in the fields for meager or no pay during the post-Civil War period.

Today, Mississippi still ranks third in cotton production, behind Texas and Georgia, according to the U.S. Department of Agriculture. But cotton is now the Magnolia State's fourth leading agricultural industry.

No. 1 is poultry, which was a nearly $3 billion industry last year, according to the Mississippi State University Extension Service. That makes Mississippi the fifth largest chicken processing state in the U.S.

Just as cotton made a few people filthy rich at the expense of slave – and later cheap – labor in years past, chicken processing plants are doing the same for their owners today. These owners have brazenly and illegally used hundreds, perhaps thousands, of undocumented immigrants as a vital part of their cheap labor force to turn huge profits.

All of which makes last week's massive roundup of some 680 undocumented immigrants at chicken processing plants spread across Central Mississippi disturbing on many levels.

The raids by federal Immigration and Customs Enforcement agents occurred on the first day of school for many families, resulting in hundreds of children returning to a home minus their parents. The Los Angeles Times explained the raids this way: "Some locals said the workers — immigrants without papers to live in the U.S. legally — had been rounded up with little more dignity than the chickens that enter the plant in rumbling 18-wheelers."

The Clarion-Ledger in Jackson reported this week that, five days after the raids, many children still had not been reunited with either one of their parents.

That is bad enough. But what's really insulting is that not a single owner, director or hiring manager for the seven targeted chicken processing factories was detained – or as far as I know – even questioned extensively by federal authorities, although reportedly some company records were seized.

This despite reports that some of the plants had been under ICE investigation for years, and federal authorities knew that hundreds of undocumented immigrants were working at the plants – some using phony identification.

The seven plants that were targeted last week are owned by four companies – Peco Foods, Koch Foods, P H Food Inc. and Pearl River Foods. But when the largest single-state raid in U.S. history went down last week, only the low-paid workers were scooped up.

Welcome to immigration law enforcement in the era of Donald Trump.

Of course, conservative politicians in Mississippi see it differently. Gov. Phil Bryant praised the raids, adding that the state's Southern District U.S. Attorney Mike Hurst "is doing exactly what he should be doing."

In a statement via Twitter, Bryant said, "If you are here illegally violating federal laws, you have to bear the responsibility of that federal violation." The governor said nothing about the chicken plant owners who clearly broke the law by hiring undocumented workers.

Hurst, a Trump appointee, said at a press conference that the owners are not off the hook. "We will follow the evidence where it leads, and if there is evidence beyond a reasonable doubt, we will prosecute the case," he said.

The problem with that statement is that investigators already knew that the owners were acting illegally by hiring undocumented workers. If they had intended to make this crackdown an example of equal justice, they would have pulled owners out of their cushy offices and detained them the same day that they snatched immigrant workers away from their unsuspecting and frightened children.

Yes, being in the country illegally is a crime. But so is knowingly hiring undocumented workers. The fact is, this was not about equal justice or holding plant owners accountable. It was about selective law enforcement.

Since last week's raids, news reports have revealed an aggressive effort for years by processing plant operators to recruit Latin American immigrants from as far away as El Paso and Miami to work in rural Mississippi for between $10 and $12 an hour. The Washington Post reported that one company even had a code name for its recruiting effort – the "Hispanic Project."

According to The Post, recruitment was so successful, it resulted in a 1,000% increase in rural Scott County, Mississippi's Latino population – home to two of the processing plants that were raided – within a decade.

And, of course, most of these companies have a history of workplace discrimination and labor violations. Some have even been sued by the federal government – the same government, now run by the Trump Administration, that last week tried to send a message that the crackdown on illegal immigration is continuing without doing too much damage to processing plant owners who are high-dollar contributors to Republican politicians.

In many ways, it all reminds me of the Mississippi of my youth. When wagons full of freshly picked cotton traversed the gravel roads on their way to the nearest gin. And when plantation owners reaped all the profits while exploiting African-American laborers who were paid practically nothing.

Only now, the plantations are full of cackling chickens and flying feathers instead of cotton sacks and mule-drawn plows. But they are still plantations.

And undocumented or not, the people with little or no voice are the ones hurt the most.

—— —— ——

Police are spying | November 7, 2019

As a 25-year-old newspaper reporter in 1978, I was fortunate to cover some of the most important stories of that era in Memphis.

My assignment was the federal beat. And the cases that came before the federal grand jury and the U.S. District Court judges were a reporter's dream because they meant stories with impact and lots of bylines.

One of them was the landmark lawsuit accusing the City of Memphis and the Memphis Police Department of spying and keeping secret files on citizens who were thought to be involved in street protests and other demonstrations.

The case has returned to the headlines some 40 years later, because city police were violating the 1978 consent decree that prevents them from conducting illegal surveillance on law-abiding citizens. Now, city leaders want a federal judge to modify the decree, arguing that technology that was not around in 1978 makes the decree an outdated document that hampers 21st-century police work.

Current Mayor Jim Strickland is even waging a P.R. campaign of sorts, to get public buy-in for the notion that the consent decree is largely ineffective in today's high-tech world.

"Under this decree, MPD's ability to use modern technology to fight crime can be severely restricted," Strickland wrote in his weekly email message last week. "The consent decree was signed long before the Internet, social media and other modern technology became a routine part of our daily lives."

The mayor argues that language in the decree not only restricts the ability of police to fight crime, but also curtails their ability "to coordinate with other law enforcement agencies in providing public safety."

He specifically mentioned Sky Cops, traffic cameras and social media posts that could be off limits to police under the consent decree.

"My legal response to that is b--- s---," said attorney Bruce Kramer, one of the ACLU lawyers who filed the original lawsuit against the city in 1976. "They want to be able to engage in surveillance on a broad scale without being constrained by the principles embodied in the Constitution."

The present-day dispute over public safety vs. heavy-handed policing prompted me to stroll down memory lane and revisit my coverage of this case in the late 1970s.

Memphis police for years had been using undercover officers and paid informants to conduct non-criminal surveillance on a variety of individuals and groups. They included the NAACP, the Ku Klux Klan, the Memphis chapter of Operation PUSH and the Black Student Association at then-Memphis State University.

Once ACLU lawyers filed the lawsuit and asked for a court order to get their hands on secret police surveillance files, then-mayor Wyeth Chandler ordered the documents destroyed. Police hurriedly burned most of the files and disbanded their intelligence unit.

But in a later deposition, police Capt. Pat Ryan basically admitted that the unit – which had a $1 million annual operating budget – spied on citizens and organizations that the police felt could be potential threats to public safety.

For example, he said undercover officers and paid informants conducted surveillance on Operation PUSH for about three years because of the organization's involvement with labor disputes, mass marches and other demonstrations. Documents that were not destroyed also showed that two undercover officers infiltrated the meetings of city sanitation workers during their 1968 strike.

In most instances, the informants were members of the organizations under surveillance, and were paid from a separate $10,000 annual fund.

"If we knew of any demonstrations, it was our duty to let the (police) chief know this so that he could, from an administrative standpoint, allocate the proper manpower on the days that these things were happening," Ryan said in his deposition.

In the consent decree, the city officially denied any wrongdoing, but in effect agreed to stop doing wrong. And to this day, police are prohibited from "engaging in law enforcement activities which interfere with any person's rights protected by the First Amendment ... including, but not limited to, the rights to communicate an idea or belief, to speak and dissent freely, to write and to publish, and to associate privately and publicly for any lawful purpose."

Police also are barred from conducting political intelligence, which simply means "gathering, indexing, filing, maintenance, storage or dissemination of information, or any other investigative activity relating to any person's beliefs, opinions, associations or other exercise of First Amendment rights."

That seems clear to me – even in today's high-tech world. Police are not supposed to be creating fake identities on Facebook solely for the purpose of getting in on the conversations and meeting plans of activists.

And the city is not supposed to create a "blacklist" of suspected demonstrators who cannot enter taxpayer-funded City Hall without being escorted by security.

None of these sensible restrictions have anything to do with Sky Cops in city neighborhoods or cameras on Beale Street and the interstate loop. If someone is posting plans on social media to commit a crime or is using language that could be interpreted as threatening and dangerous, of course police should know about it and act accordingly.

And without question, the protesters who staged the "die-in" on Mayor Strickland's front lawn in 2016 were trespassers and should have been arrested.

But the intent of the consent decree of 1978 is the same as the intent of the U.S. Constitution of 1787 or the First Amendment of 1791 – to safeguard our freedoms.

To borrow from the eloquence of Dr. Martin Luther King Jr. in his famous 1968 "Mountaintop" speech in Memphis, "Somewhere I read of the freedom of assembly. Somewhere I read of the freedom of speech. Somewhere I read of the freedom of press. Somewhere I read that the greatness of America is the right to protest for right."

This week, I reread a 41-year-old federal court consent decree. And it seems fine to me.

—— —— ——

ON COMMUNITY

A Morehouse Man | March 28, 2019

Van Turner Jr. amassed a number of impressive titles within a relatively short time span. But at his core, Turner is a Morehouse Man.

That means, quite simply, that he is a scholarly, well-dressed man of distinction and influence who, according to the internet's Urban Dictionary, "charms everyone he meets."

Turner, now in his second term as a Shelby County commissioner, fully embraces the moniker, just as countless other influentials who attended the prestigious men's college in Atlanta did before him – Julian Bond, Maynard Jackson, federal Judge Odell Horton and, of course, Martin Luther King Jr.

And while Turner, 44, would not compare himself to any of those legends at this point in his life, it's clear he is charting his own leadership path – one that could take him to much higher ground in politics or even the judiciary.

Though he proudly calls himself a Morehouse Man, Turner is far from haughty. Since graduating magna cum laude from Morehouse in 1997 and earning a law degree from the University of Tennessee College of Law in 2002, the Whitehaven High School alumnus has methodically worked to build a career in law, politics and public service.

He is a partner in the law firm of Bruce Turner PLLC and started his political climb in 2009 when he was elected chairman of the Shelby County Democratic Party, a position he held for four years.

In 2010, he actively supported Democrat Mike McWherter's failed campaign for Tennessee governor, and made a cameo appearance in one of McWherter's TV ads.

Then in 2014, Turner won the District 12 seat on the County Commission. But it was on the night of Dec. 20, 2017, that Turner's prominence took a giant leap. That was the night he, Memphis Mayor Jim Strickland and the City Council orchestrated the sale of two city parks to a recently chartered nonprofit group called Memphis Greenspace, of which Turner is director and president.

Hours after the sale, Turner personally oversaw the dismantling of the statues of Confederate Gen. Nathan Bedford Forrest from Health Sciences Park and Confederate President Jefferson Davis from Fourth Bluff Park.

The history-altering transfer of public property to an upstart nonprofit group instantly transformed Turner from a relatively mild-mannered lawyer and county commissioner to a gutsy political and community leader willing to take the heat for removing from the city's landscape two giant symbols of slavery, oppression and racism.

Turner later told Inside Memphis Business that the monuments were put in the parks "to say to the African Americans in the city 'you're still second-class citizens.'"

He added, "If we pulled down the 'whites only' signs in public places, then why did we still have Confederate monuments up, which bolsters segregation? The remnants of segregation and Jim Crow Memphis that still survived in those public parks was a problem. Memphis is a great city and I think it can be even greater. It was just time to move forward and put the past in the past."

Turner now serves as commission chairman and is leading other governmental and public policy changes in a community that has always been his home. Late last year, he started pushing for more transparency and accountability in the awarding of tax incentives that are used to lure businesses to Memphis and stimulate new development.

And this week, he and his commission colleagues voted unanimously to partner with the city to offer universal need-based prekindergarten throughout Memphis and the county. The commission also approved by an 8-5 vote along party lines a resolution supporting a $15 minimum wage for all public sector employees in the county.

The pre-K vote, Turner said, was a no-brainer. "Quite honestly, it had such a broad range of support, that helped us move it forward." He credits corporate executive Kathy Buckman Gibson, a strong advocate of early childhood education, for working with the city and county on pre-K expansion.

As for the minimum-wage resolution, Turner says it was simply a case of the commission using its bully pulpit to send a message to other public-sector employers that a $15 salary is good for the community.

And yet, not one of the five Republicans on the 13-member commission voted in favor of the resolution. Vice chairman Mark Billingsley, a Republican, called it more show than substance.

"I'm not really big on resolutions that don't have teeth," said Billingsley, who also took an opposing stance from Turner last year over the hiring of former commissioner Julian Bolton as the commission's legal adviser. Billingsley said, however, those differences do not diminish his respect for Turner, whom he called "a trusted friend and colleague."

But it's the upcoming city mayor's election that could strain Turner's relationship with another commissioner from his own party. Freshman Tami Sawyer, who founded the TakeEmDown 901 movement to push for removal of the Confederate statues and who was elected to the commission last August, announced earlier this month that she will run for Memphis mayor in the October election.

Turner is supporting Strickland and says he will be actively involved in the campaign if he's asked. "I think Mayor Strickland has done a good job," Turner told me in an interview this week. "When it comes to incumbents, you have to ask, is there a reason to get rid of them." In this case, he says, the answer is no.

Turner is not the only African American elected official supporting Strickland. But with his recent visibility, he just might be the most significant.

He points specifically to Strickland's efforts to hire more police officers and his appointment of Mike Rallings as police director. And while Strickland was wrong when he boasted that city contracts with minority- and women-owned businesses had doubled since he took office, Turner still gives the mayor credit for increasing those percentages from 12% in 2015 to the current 18%.

In stark terms, Turner's support of Strickland means that the African American chairman of the Shelby County Commission is openly favoring a white man for mayor over an African American woman in Sawyer and an African American man in former mayor Willie Herenton.

In Memphis, that can be a tough spot to be in, and Turner acknowledges that he has received some backlash for his decision, "but not the type of backlash you would have seen 20 years ago.

"Of course, there will be people who vote race. But there will also be people who vote on platform or how well (the incumbent) is running the city."

When I asked if he thinks Sawyer is qualified to be mayor, Turner gave a qualified yes. "She has just now become a commissioner. I believe she has the mental acumen in order to learn the job (of mayor) and the initiative to get it done."

But Turner said Sawyer is not as qualified as either Strickland or Herenton, "because one is doing the job and one has done the job before."

Finally, there is the question of Turner's own political ambitions. If Strickland wins reelection, he will be forced through term limits to leave that office in 2023. Turner said without hesitation that he is interested in seeking higher office, but it would be an issue of timing.

Billingsley, however, said he sees another path for Turner. "I envision him one day being a very powerful judge. Either way, I think he's got a bright future in leadership."

And leadership seems to be the operative word to describe Turner. What else would you expect from a Morehouse Man?

— — —

Young Black men in crisis | July 25, 2019

I spent Monday afternoon talking with 17 teenagers – all but two of them African American – inside the detention facility at Shelby County Juvenile Court.

As they filed into the dining area, all of them appeared subdued. But they were respectful and inquisitive, and it wasn't just because they were being closely watched by sheriff's deputies and other Juvenile Court employees.

They seemed genuinely interested in our discussion about setting ambitious goals, imagining their lives beyond just the next day or the next week, and refusing to allow the mistakes that landed them in detention to define who they are and what they can become.

"We believe it is our responsibility to provide our youth the support they need, which will help them thrive as they continue to mature," said Joyce Anderson, programs manager at Juvenile Court. "We need volunteers who can mentor, provide music, art, creative writing instruction or tutor these students."

A few hours earlier and a couple of miles south at the National Civil Rights Museum, Shelby County Schools Superintendent Joris Ray announced an ambitious goal of his own: to reverse the fortunes of the district's African American male students – just like the ones I saw in juvenile detention – and set them on a path to success, rather than a path to prison.

Ray is calling it the "African-American Male Empowerment" initiative. But this is no short-term project. It represents a complete culture change within the school system to no longer stigmatize most young Black male students as troublemakers incapable of achieving at a high level.

Meanwhile, some 200 miles away in Nashville, an East Tennessee lawmaker is calling for a state study to examine why Tennessee's homicide rate among mostly young African American men is more than five times the national average. His aim is to create legislation that will effectively address the disturbing homicide trend.

What's going on here is simple. More people are finally waking up to the fact that societal ills – poverty, crime, little or no education and implicit bias – have the most devastating impact on young Black men. This is not just my opinion. It's backed up by credible research.

For example, studies by the California-based Haywood Burns Institute and other national think tanks show that Black youths are five times more likely to be incarcerated than their white counterparts. And poor educational attainment is one of the root causes of juvenile delinquency.

A 2018 report by The National Association for the Education of Young Children found that the achievement gap between Black and white students not only hurts African American kids long term, it also hurts our economy.

"The achievement gap is a problem not only for African American students and their families and communities; it affects the well-being of the entire country," the report concluded. "Researchers have found that 'the persistence of the educational achievement gap imposes on the United States the economic equivalent of a permanent national recession.'"

At Monday's empowerment rally at the Civil Rights Museum, Superintendent Ray cited his own statistics to highlight the crisis in SCS. Among them:

• Fewer than 16% of Black male students in grades 3 through 8 had proficient TNReady reading scores in 2018.

• Only about 18.5% of Black males tested at or above grade level in math.

• Only 431 of 5,632 Black male students were proficient in English. That equates to a dismal 7.6%.

• Just 152 of 2,859 Black males were proficient in algebra. That amounts to 5.3%.

On paper, these numbers are embarrassing for the district. But they are often the result of the overwhelming outside forces of poverty and family dysfunction that place academic success well below the struggle just to pay bills, put food on the table, maintain a place to live and survive from one day to the next.

"Our African American males have been overwhelmingly identified as the foremost vulnerable and challenged population in our system," Ray said. "In Shelby County Schools, we cannot and will not allow African American males to languish in the midst of antiquated systemic practices that do not take into account the very real challenges that deeply and directly affect them every day."

Among the district's long-term solutions are placing more Black men as teachers in elementary grades, recruiting more Black men to serve as mentors, working to end the so-called school-to-prison pipeline by reducing the number of suspensions and expulsions of Black males, and setting up an equity office to drive the culture changes that will be needed to see positive results.

The school-to-prison pipeline is a systemic issue that has come under increasing criticism, including from groups as disparate as the American Civil Liberties Union and the American Bar Association.

The ACLU, in a recent policy statement, said it is committed to challenging the pipeline, calling it "a disturbing national trend wherein children are funneled out of public schools and into the juvenile and criminal justice systems. Many of these children have learning disabilities or histories of poverty, abuse, or neglect, and would benefit from additional educational and counseling services. Instead, they are isolated, punished and pushed out."

And the bar association, in an August 2017 report, said, "For far too many students, entering the gateway to incarceration begins with a referral from the classroom to the courtroom."

SCS is hoping to turn that around in Memphis, and Ray has enlisted support from Shelby County Sheriff Floyd Bonner Jr., Memphis Police Director Michael Rallings, University of Memphis men's basketball coach Penny Hardaway and a host of community leaders.

But everyone involved should be realistic. The African-American Male Empowerment effort won't produce changes overnight. It could take years to see noticeable results. The superintendent is fine with that. And I completely agree with him. The road to bringing more young black men from delinquency to a diploma starts now.

Maybe in the future when I visit Juvenile Court, there will be fewer detainees in need of an encouraging word.

—— —— ——

I am (still) a man | December 12, 2019

At a recent 70th birthday party for my first cousin, DeWitt Sanford, I was probably the most recognizable person in the room. But I was far from being the most significant.

That honor went to Elmore Nickleberry, who is without a doubt one of the most unassuming heroes Memphians will ever see.

If you don't know that name, you don't know Memphis history. Nickleberry is one of the few surviving sanitation workers who went on strike in 1968 to force city government to treat them with dignity. In other words, to see them as men – not as insignificant and subservient laborers.

At the birthday gathering, Nickleberry sat quietly at a table near the back of the banquet hall. Few people even knew he was there, until the emcee called his name. Then, the gray-haired gentleman started making his way around to nearly every table, shaking hands and posing for selfies with anyone who asked.

At 87, Nickleberry, who retired just this year, is clearly a rock star.

But in late winter and early spring of 1968, he and his co-workers were treated like pawns in a tug-of-war between labor and civil rights leaders on one side and a stubborn – some would say racist – city mayor on the other. We all know how that struggle ended – with the assassination of Dr. Martin Luther King Jr.

Today, the stakes are not nearly as grave. But sanitation workers are again being used as pawns in a political tussle at City Hall. Mayor Jim Strickland, who executed a brilliant election-year move by improving trash collection in the city last May, now says layoffs of sanitation workers and reduced service are likely unavoidable because the City Council refused to fund the improved service going forward.

In his weekly email report to city residents last week, Strickland said he promised nearly 17 months ago "to fix our issues with picking up your trash in a consistent and timely manner. And we did it."

The mayor made Solid Waste a separate division of city government, hired additional workers and bought new equipment to collect outside-the-cart trash two times per month.

But what Strickland did not do, because it was an election year, was ask the council to add a rate increase to this year's budget to pay for the expanded trash service long term. Instead, he used about $15 million from the city's general fund.

"We wanted time to see how our new model would work and exactly what it would cost," the mayor said. That may be true, but no mayor involved in a reelection campaign is going to push for a 30% rate increase on anything.

Now, he says, his team has "crunched the numbers." And he needs a $7.16 increase per month to keep the enhanced trash collection service going.

City residents currently pay $22.80, and the increase would take it to $29.96. But the council last week, in a 6-6 vote, said nothing doing.

Without the rate hike, Strickland said the city will have to lay off 199 full-time Solid Waste employees and 75 temporary workers. Trash for recycling will be picked up just once per month and outside-the-cart items will not be collected.

Essentially, Strickland is saying if that happens, it will be the council's fault, which one council member told me amounted to a blatant scare tactic.

"I'm never a fan of raising rates. But to maintain this new level of service, unfortunately, it's our only option," the mayor said.

In this case, Strickland is correct. It's at least the only viable option. The city could outsource one or more of the collection routes, but that would still require some layoffs. Plus, outsourcing trash collection has had its own problems in recent years with unreliable service. And taking away an improved city service that residents are getting used to is never a good move.

The bigger problem, though, is again treating some of the lowest-paid municipal employees with disrespect. It's not like 1968, but it's still disrespect.

Whether the mayor was being an alarmist or a pragmatist in his email, the council is expected to reconsider the vote at its year-end meeting Dec. 17. Council chairman Kemp Conrad, who voted for the rate increase, told me he expects one or more council members who voted no to move for reconsideration. And the proposal will likely pass with eight or nine votes.

A spokesman for Strickland indicated the same thing.

"We are not going to let this happen," Conrad said, referring to the layoffs and cutbacks in trash collection. To those members who opposed the increase, Conrad asked, "If you're not for it, what are you for?"

Councilman Martavius Jones, who also supported the rate increase, said he too is hopeful the issue will be revisited. "We have not invested enough in Memphis," he said.

Other council members who voted for the increase were Ford Canale, Sherman Greer, Worth Morgan and Patrice Robinson. Voting against it were Berlin Boyd, Joe Brown, Frank Colvett, Gerre Currie, Cheyenne Johnson and Jamita Swearengen. Reid Hedgepeth missed the vote.

No doubt some of the opponents believe the rate hike places a heavy, and perhaps unfair, burden on lower-income Memphians – particularly at a time when Memphis Light, Gas and Water also is seeking a rate increase.

But no one wants to see trash languishing again at the curb for weeks on end. And history tells us we do not want to see sanitation workers treated the way they used to be – as expendable.

So, City Council, do the right thing. Approve the increase, and let's keep cleaning up Memphis.

—— —— ——

No Sunday school | March 26, 2020

I have been going to Sunday school and regular Sunday worship services virtually all my life. I started at a tiny wood-frame country church atop a remote hill on the north side of the dividing line between Panola and Tate counties in North Mississippi.

Appropriately named Hammond Hill Missionary Baptist Church, the building was where I was first introduced to Christian worship, Bible study, fiery preaching and robust gospel singing. In other words, the old-fashioned Black church experience.

My father, a full-time farmer and full-time carpenter, was a deacon and superintendent of the Sunday school. So my attendance really wasn't optional. But honestly, I looked forward to it.

In the mid-1960s, Dad led the construction of a new sanctuary on flatter land across the road where a schoolhouse for African American children once stood.

Three pastors and several remodeling projects later, Hammond Hill still proudly stands on that corner. But I have long since moved on to other churches in cities in which I have lived and worked.

These days, I split my time between two churches, and I teach a weekly Sunday school class at one of them, Greater Middle Baptist Church in the Parkway Village section of Memphis.

But last Sunday, March 22, I was not there because of the coronavirus, even though the church doors were open for regular morning worship service.

I missed my class. I missed the fellowship. But I absolutely have no regrets.

The COVID-19 outbreak has disrupted our lives and that includes our church life. And while most places of worship did the right thing last week by suspending in-person services, others did not.

Hopefully that will change this weekend, despite mixed messages from President Donald Trump, who is eager to get things back to normal for the sake of the economy – and his presidency. He wants to see "packed churches all over the country" for Easter Sunday, April 12. He thinks it will be a beautiful sight, even though it could be life-threatening for many.

But the fact that many Memphis churches, particularly those with predominantly African American congregations, have not suspended in-person worship so far underscores the importance that the church continues to have in African American life.

Yes, attendance at all churches has been declining for years. And traditional Sunday school classes like mine are disappearing because few people are interested in them. That was true long before COVID-19.

But because of the virus, the remaining faithful are being asked by political leaders and health experts to stay away from church as they also stay away from their jobs, schools or any other place that attracts a sizable crowd in a confined space.

Some of those who are wisely complying are opting to conduct worship services through livestreaming on their church websites. Others simply are grabbing a cellphone, laptop or computer and are preaching and praising via Facebook Live. Social media platforms were full of sermons last Sunday from across the country.

You could drop in on a video service in Los Angeles, Houston, Chicago or Detroit. Plus, you can easily contribute to your church's coffers through cash apps such as Givelify.

But for some church leaders, canceling services was a nonstarter, despite the health warnings. For them, the in-person worship experience represents normalcy during a time of chaos, fear and uncertainty. They are relying on God's grace and protection – through prayer and faith – to keep them and their congregants safe from a novel coronavirus.

As New York Times international correspondent Vivian Yee wrote this week, "Religion is the solace of first resort for billions of people grappling with a pandemic for which scientists, presidents and the secular world seem, so far, to have few answers. With both sanitizer and leadership in short supply, dread over the coronavirus has driven the globe's faithful even closer to religion and ritual."

But the ritual of gathering to worship, even in a spotlessly clean building, is now much too risky, not to mention contrary to Mayor Jim Strickland's shelter-in-place order. The mayor's order lists various businesses and services that are deemed essential and can remain open.

Church is not on the list. But that applies to the structure, not the practice.

Rev. Dr. Gina Stewart, senior pastor of Christ Missionary Baptist Church in South Memphis, suspended in-person services two weeks ago. It wasn't an easy call, she said, because Memphis initially was not considered a hot spot for the virus. But it was the right call. "I did not want blood on my hands," she told me.

Stewart was in Indianapolis earlier in March when news accounts first reported that COVID-19 was spreading beyond Washington State and New York City. "I started praying about it," she said. The answer to the prayer was to suspend her services, which she did beginning March 15.

She was keenly aware that had she done differently and announced that church services would continue as usual, some vulnerable members of her congregation would show up, even if they were told to stay home if they were not feeling well.

That's the thing about the Black church, in particular, she said. "(Congregants) respect spiritual authority. And I knew that if I said we would have service, they would get there. But people's lives are more important. I don't want anybody having to go to the hospital because they were trying to make their way to church."

Instead, Stewart is among those streaming her message via the church's website and Facebook Live. She also is working with other faith leaders in Memphis to figure out ways to help smaller churches that may not have the technology to stream services into the homes of members.

Dr. Stewart gets it. She knows full well the significance that the church has in our society, and on African American life in particular among baby boomers, pre-boomers and some Generation Xers. But the old cliché is true. Church is not about a building. The church is inside of us.

My spiritual faith was nurtured at Hammond Hill, and it still helps define who I am today. But although I am a believer, I also believe in medical science. And this coronavirus is no joke. I am in the age group considered most susceptible.

So, I'm willing to live without the church building for a while and get my spiritual fill online. That likely means no Easter service in person. Sorry, POTUS.

But as the old church hymn says, I'm so glad troubles don't last always.

— — —

'No more parlaying' | April 9, 2020

West Memphis Mayor Marco McClendon isn't fooling around. He has seen too many people in his city of about 25,000 residents taking a cavalier attitude toward the novel coronavirus.

He's seen groups of young men gathering on playgrounds for pickup basketball games. He knows about the packed churches for recent funerals and Sunday services. And he's heard about groups congregating at street corners and elsewhere as if this pandemic is somehow off-limits to them.

As one of only two African American mayors – the other being Shelby County Mayor Lee Harris – in charge of running jurisdictions adjacent to Memphis, McClendon is also aware of mostly anecdotal evidence that the COVID-19 outbreak is slamming Black residents disproportionately in many places around the country.

The 2018 U.S. Census estimates that about 60% of West Memphis' population is Black. But McClendon says it's now closer to 70%.

Knowing that, and with many residents in his town struggling financially without adequate access to health care, McClendon took what his mayoral authority gave him. He imposed a curfew in his city that went into effect Tuesday, April 7.

From 9 p.m. to 5 a.m., at least until the end of April, West Memphians are allowed outside their homes only to conduct essential business. And even during the day, residents are urged to stay home, and to practice social distancing whenever they must go out.

"No more parlaying," McClendon told me Tuesday, about an hour before the curfew went into effect. That means, "No more hanging out with your buddies."

And if the new rules are running counter to the wishes of Arkansas Gov. Asa Hutchinson, so be it. State leaders have never really shown much interest in the fate of West Memphis anyway – except for the revenue it generates through Southland Casino Racing.

The Associated Press reported this week that Hutchinson opposes allowing cities to issue their own stay-at-home orders. The governor says those restrictions should be handled on a statewide basis and, so far, he is rejecting them.

But that's not stopping McClendon from moving forward with his curfew. "I'm protecting my people," he said. "He (the governor) might slap my hand, but we're going to do it anyway."

The mayor's reasoning is perfectly logical. "I'm in a very unique position here," he said, referring to his city's proximity to Memphis and several other suburban cities in Shelby and DeSoto counties. How the coronavirus outbreak affects one city, impacts every other city in metro Memphis.

"You can literally walk across the Big River Crossing from Memphis to West Memphis," McClendon said. "We are all part of one metro area and we are doing our part right here in Crittenden (County)."

But aside from a possible dispute with an obstinate Republican Southern governor, the negative effect that the coronavirus is having on Black populations has McClendon equally concerned. And for good reason.

No one really knows the full extent. Because the federal government and most states are not releasing data on the pandemic's impact on African Americans.

In a letter Monday, April 6, the Lawyers' Committee for Civil Rights Under Law urged Alex Azar, secretary of Health and Human Services, to immediately begin reporting racial and ethnic demographic data about the spread of the virus.

"This administration's alarming lack of transparency and data is preventing public health officials from understanding the full impact of this pandemic on Black communities and other communities of color," the letter said.

"We are concerned that Black communities are being disproportionately impacted by the pandemic, and have lower access to COVID-19 testing which may cause delayed care, an increased risk of high mortality rates, and the acceleration of the spread of the disease in our communities."

The issue was finally addressed by President Donald Trump and others on the White House Coronavirus Task Force at Tuesday's briefing. Task force member Dr. Deborah Birx pointed out that African Americans are not more susceptible to the virus than other racial groups.

But because of other adverse factors, including health disparities and a general lack of access to quality health care, Black Americans who contract the virus are more likely to have worse outcomes – including death.

Where more concrete data does exist, it shows troubling signs for African Americans. In Illinois, for example, African Americans make up 14.6% of the population, but 28% of confirmed cases, according to The Atlantic.

In Chicago, Black residents account for nearly 70% of the deaths reported so far and 50% of confirmed cases, according to The Washington Post, citing data from the Chicago Department of Public Health. This despite the fact that Black Chicagoans make up just 30% of the population.

Similar racial disparities are popping up in Louisiana, Michigan and North Carolina. One key to getting more comprehensive and accurate information is improved testing.

In Shelby County, Health Department officials acknowledged Wednesday that a preliminary review shows Black residents are suffering disproportionately from the virus. Of 238 of the confirmed cases in the county, 68% involve African Americans. And 71% of those who have died are African American.

Those percentages are unlikely to change as more of the nearly 900 cases are studied. But even without complete data on race locally and nationally, it's clear that longstanding racial inequities involving access to health care are a key reason Black people are contracting the virus and dying disproportionately.

That and other systemic racial biases won't be solved overnight. So, the best thing now for African Americans – indeed all Americans – is to protect ourselves through social distancing and better hygiene.

A small-town mayor like Marco McClendon in West Memphis understands that better than most. It's why he has adopted a get-tough stance for his city. It's why he has broken up the playground basketball games and is trying to stop crowded church gatherings. It's also why he's willing to buck the governor.

And it's why this week, at least, McClendon deserves a long-distance pat on the back for putting the residents of his majority African American city first.

—— —— ——

Reassuring words | April 30, 2020

People are recovering.

Those three words stood out most as I watched the live streaming of the COVID-19 local update Tuesday, April 28. An update full of vital information to help get us through this unprecedented crisis in which we find ourselves.

Lots of people who call Shelby County home have contracted the coronavirus in ways still being determined through contact tracing. Despite our best efforts, we still know very little about this disease and why it attacks some people worse than others.

That's what makes it so scary. It's what has most of us confined to our homes and distancing ourselves from others, including family.

But people are recovering. And at the moment, that's more important. Because despite what the politicians in Washington and some governors think, people should come first, then the economy.

As of the Tuesday briefing, 2,358 people had tested positive in Shelby County for COVID-19. And sadly, 46 of them had died. It could be worse, and likely would have been had not our local political leaders early on made public health the top priority.

It's as if COVID-19 took a wrecking ball to our daily lives in just seven weeks. But watching Alisa Haushalter, director of the Shelby County Health Department, explain our new reality in a calm, measured and fact-based message, I came away with more optimism than pessimism about our prospects for overcoming this ruthless pandemic.

No elected leaders were present that day. They didn't need to be. They had accomplished one important mission a day earlier when seven of the eight mayors in Shelby County appeared at a briefing together. The missing mayor, Keith McDonald of Bartlett, sent his top assistant.

It was a welcome sight – amid partisan disagreements elsewhere – as they expressed a unified front in fighting the coronavirus outbreak while carefully planning for reopening the county's economy at a time that's still uncertain.

"Our approach will be data-driven not date-driven," said Memphis

Mayor Jim Strickland. Which means the health care experts, not politicians, are taking the lead steering our economic engine back on its tracks.

So on Tuesday, except for brief comments by Doug McGowen, chief operating officer for the City of Memphis, and Dr. Bruce Randolph, the county's health officer, Haushalter carried the day. She painstakingly shared the most up-to-date toll that COVID-19 had taken on people in our community.

Then she pivoted nicely into a litany of steps her department – working with other agencies, private businesses and governments – is taking to increase testing, do effective contact tracing and reach highly vulnerable areas where the virus is especially menacing.

She talked about focusing much needed attention on nursing homes, detention facilities and various neighborhoods that have been under-served by testing. She talked about being more effective in reaching the Latino community with testing, and was quick to stress that undocumented immigrants had no need to fear that their immigration status would be reported to federal authorities if they got tested.

Haushalter took each question from reporters, including the convoluted ones, and framed her answers around the overall message that Shelby County collectively is fighting the COVID-19 battle the right way.

And no, that does not mean our local officials have always done things promptly or perfectly. Testing initially was slow to ramp up, and we did not sound the alarm soon enough that African Americans, especially, were at higher risk of contracting the virus and an even greater one of dying from it.

But when it comes to overall responsiveness, believability and coordination, local officials and policymakers have performed far better than those at the state and federal level. Which means this fight is a local fight.

Yes, we need federal and state help through stimulus money that will go toward helping the Health Department increase contact tracing. Cash-starved local governments need stimulus funds to keep paying first responders and other essential public workers.

Small businesses throughout the county need stimulus help as well to stay afloat. And individuals who qualify for one-time stimulus checks should get them without further delays.

But when the talk turns to reopening the economy, local leaders know best. And we are not there yet. The virus is still a problem for African Americans who make up 54% of Shelby County's population, but account for about 68% of cases and more than 70% of deaths.

Those disparities are not all the result of poor health conditions or unwise life choices. Black residents are more likely to work in industries, such as nursing homes, that are more susceptible to the spread of the coronavirus.

"While people of color make up one-quarter of the total U.S. workforce, they comprise the majority of the nursing (home) assistant workforce," according to New York-based PHInternational, a nursing home and senior care advocacy group. "Over one-third of these workers are Black or African American."

It's one reason why the Tennessee Black Caucus of State Legislators is calling on Gov. Bill Lee's administration to increase the collection and sharing of ethnicity-related data on COVID-19, including by county, ZIP code and census tract.

The state Department of Health previously announced it is creating a statewide health disparities task force aimed at determining the impact of the pandemic on minority communities.

In Memphis and Shelby County, that means more testing of Black and brown residents, more information going to impacted neighborhoods about the need for continued social distancing and other safety measures, and greater protection and incentives for those who work in nursing homes, jails and confined – yet essential – businesses.

Haushalter and her team get that. So do our elected leaders, city and suburban. It's why I have much greater confidence in the messages I'm getting from our local responders than anything I'm hearing from the White House or Nashville.

People are recovering, Haushalter said with assurance Tuesday. I believe her. And in time so will our economy.

—— —— ——

Remembering Fred Davis | May 14, 2020

It was just another routine Tuesday City Council meeting at Memphis City Hall. That is, until Fred Davis pulled out the short, handwritten statement from his pocket and began to read it.

As the words came from his mouth, so did the tears from his eyes. And everyone in the room — fellow council members, reporters, staff and spectators — immediately knew this was no ordinary meeting.

Instead, June 5, 1979, would be remembered as the day Davis announced his retirement from the council. He would finish out his 12th year and not seek a fourth term representing District 4 in that year's October municipal election.

For someone who never seemed to have trouble speaking his mind, Davis found these written words difficult to utter. But he was certain of his decision. His council service was demanding and was exacting a toll on his family and his growing insurance business.

"I don't think I can bear the cost of time and money over the next four years," Davis said. "It has become necessary for me to re-examine the impact of my public commitment on my family and my personal business. I've decided so step aside."

This past Tuesday, May 12, I learned of Davis' death at age 86 the same way most of us get our news these days — via a news feed that popped up on my cellphone. It left me saddened and depressed, but also thankful. Because the truth is that while Davis may have left elected office more than 40 years ago, he never stepped aside.

He and I had become good friends in recent years. We'd meet occasionally for breakfast at CK's Coffee Shop on Poplar in Midtown. And, of course, the topic always included politics. We had regular telephone chats as well.

In 2016, he agreed to a series of interviews with me while I was researching my book, "From Boss Crump to King Willie: How Race Changed Memphis Politics."

And in 2018, he graciously accepted my invitation to speak to students at the University of Memphis about his role on the council during the tumultuous city sanitation strike in 1968, that led to the assassination of Dr. Martin Luther King Jr.

In some ways, I took for granted that I was getting to hang out with a Memphis treasure — a kind and generous soul who played the game of politics by his own rules. But a guy who paved the way for many other elected officials — Black and white — and who helped them understand what pubic service really means.

"Fred Davis was more than a good politician and a good businessman. In the truest sense of the word, he was a good human being, perhaps the best," said political consultant Susan Adler Thorp, who covered Davis as a young city hall reporter for the Memphis Press-Scimitar in the early 1970s.

Davis was just 33 years old when he was elected to the council in 1967, one year after Memphis voters approved a referendum replacing the antiquated, all-white city commission with a mayor-council form of government.

The new council consisted of six members elected citywide, or at-large, and seven elected by district. The district lines were drawn to ensure that at least two African Americans would be elected to a city office for the first time.

Davis, who had a strong hand in setting up the district format, decided to seek the District 4 seat, which at the time was racially diverse. But the odds were against a Black candidate.

Davis got the Press-Scimitar's endorsement, but The Commercial Appeal endorsed Lonnie Briscoe. On election day, Oct. 5, 1967, Davis was tops among nine contenders with 5,559 votes. But he was forced into a runoff with white candidate Elmer B. Vaughn, an administrator at Southern College of Optometry.

Surprisingly, The Commercial Appeal joined the Press-Scimitar in endorsing Davis in the Nov. 2 runoff, and he defeated Vaughn by 1,215 votes out of 18,653 total votes cast. And a 12-year political career was born.

"Fred was a political novice, but he was politically savvy," Thorp told me. "He quickly learned to suffer fools gladly because he understood that to get along he had to go along in order to get things done for his constituents."

That get-along, go-along attitude sometimes put him at odds with Black community leaders and other Black politicians — notably former councilman John Ford, who joined the council in 1972, and his brother, former U.S. Rep. Harold Ford.

Following the beating death of Black teenager Elton Hayes at the hands of police and sheriff's deputies in 1971, Davis criticized both the officers and Black protesters, some of whom he called agitators, for using Hayes' death for political gain.

He once described his political philosophy this way: "It was not necessary to pit whites against Blacks and rich against poor to be elected to public office or reelected to public office."

Davis' moderate views paid off in 1972 when his colleagues elected him council chairman, at the time the highest-ranking government position ever for a Black person in Memphis. Despite a few tiffs from time to time, Davis was well-liked and well-respected by his council colleagues, mostly because of his fairness and his constant push for conciliation.

Later as chairman of the housing and public works committee, Davis oversaw the building of the Mid-America Mall and Mud Island Downtown.

Although he left the council at the end of 1979, Davis remained a strong advocate for Black-owned businesses and political inclusion for African Americans. He also had little tolerance for those whom he believed set a bad example.

Who can forget the billboard message he put up near his insurance agency office on Airways in 2013 showing a young Black man, wearing a cap and gown and holding a diploma, next to another young Black man with his pants sagging? The caption read, "Show your mind. Not your behind."

So much for stepping aside.

In 1991, he also ran afoul of several Black community leaders for his opposition to doing away with at-large council seats. Davis believed that at-large positions were the only way Black voters could influence which white candidates got elected.

"I say what I believe, and I try to pull my own weight," Davis said in a 1991 interview with Commercial Appeal political reporter Terry Keeter. "But anytime Black people put themselves in the position of not having any say about which white people get elected, we've lost our leverage."

He continued, "Because white folks finance the Black campaigns, there's no question of whites having a say on who the Black leadership is. But the only Black impact is by their votes."

At-large council positions were eventually scrapped in favor of six superdistrict seats. The western half of Memphis elects three superdistrict members and the eastern half elects three. Davis was never a fan.

But he was always a fan of good government, equal opportunity and a strong work ethic. Now, all of Memphis has lost an iconic figure who blazed an impressive political and business trail in the Bluff City.

And I will miss our meals at CK's and our occasional phone chats.

"Fred Davis was a man of conviction and courage even in the days when courage was in short supply," Thorp added. "Of the entire 13-member council elected that historic year in 1967, I believe only one now is still living, the Rev. James Netters. Which makes me wonder if God simply saved the best ones for last."

— — — — — —

LeMoyne-Owen's gift | July 9, 2020

Carol Johnson-Dean was sitting in her office at LeMoyne-Owen College late in the afternoon on Tuesday, June 30, with — as usual — several things on her mind and more than that on her plate.

The interim president of the 158-year-old institution of higher learning was working on how to facilitate the college's next weekly COVID-19 task force meeting and fretting just a bit over preparations for the start of fall classes. She had more questions than answers.

What are we doing to sanitize the campus more? What will fall enrollment, and thus tuition income, actually be? And how do we ensure that students, faculty and staff, particularly the older ones, are protected against a pandemic that loves crowds and feeds on close encounters of any kind?

All that was running through her mind when, out of the blue, Bob Fockler, president of the Community Foundation of Greater Memphis, buzzed her cellphone. It was a call that stands to change the trajectory of LeMoyne-Owen's future, and ensure that Memphis' only HBCU (Historical Black Colleges and Universities) will live on in perpetuity.

Without beating around the bush, Fockler told Johnson-Dean that the Community Foundation had approved a $40 million endowment for LeMoyne-Owen to help grow enrollment, currently at 850 students, with virtually no strings attached. It is the largest single gift in the school's history.

Each year on Jan. 15, the school will receive a check amounting to 5% of the endowment's total value, or about $2 million.

"I literally began to cry," Johnson-Dean told me this week. "Because I really couldn't imagine that level of generosity at this moment in time. I had to collect myself. I was overjoyed."

How the endowment came about and what it means for the college and the Memphis community is a story that was several years in the making, starting with the phenomenal growth of the foundation's assets.

Over the last 10 years, those assets have increased from about $300 million to $800 million, Fockler told me. Then last fall, the foundation's board of governors began meeting to develop a new set of community investment principles.

The board approved the final document in April just as the coronavirus was spreading through the community and disproportionately impacting people of color. The finished product is encapsulated in this two-sentence vision statement:

"We will create a just and equitable region where all individuals and groups receive the resources and opportunities they need to reach their full potential, and where identity and geography do not determine their outcomes. We will build a community where everyone is welcome, valued, resourced, and informed, one where people can easily access opportunities to contribute and thrive."

Fockler explained it this way: "We are transforming from being a charitable banker to being more involved in what's going on in our community."

Then came the May 25 killing of George Floyd, a Black man who died face down on the pavement with a white Minneapolis police officer's knee pressing down on his neck for nearly nine minutes.

The video image of Floyd and how he died sparked a reckoning with racism in America. And one by one, organizations, institutions and individuals of all races started to seize the moment to do self-examinations about what they can do to actively promote racial equity in all corners of society.

In other words, this became a moment when large sectors of the nation began to learn what it means to be anti-racist.

Finally, in mid-June, Reed Hastings, chief executive of Netflix, and his wife, Patty Quillin, announced they were pledging $120 million to the United Negro College Fund and two historically Black colleges in Atlanta — Spelman and Morehouse. The money will be split equally, totaling $40 million each.

And that became the Community Foundation executive committee's aha moment. "It kind of made us say, we can do this," Fockler said. "So we said this is the right thing at the right time."

The endowment comes with few stipulations, although the annual payments will likely go toward more scholarships to increase enrollment and to enhance innovation and technology at the school in South Memphis.

Fockler simply told Johnson-Dean in his surprise phone call that the foundation believes in the college's effort to educate more African Americans in Greater Memphis.

"We are not telling you how to spend the money," Fockler said on the call. "Just live up to your mission."

Which is something LeMoyne-Owen has done successfully throughout its existence, despite years of financial struggles, dissension between past administrations and faculty, and intermittent strife on the college's board of trustees.

The school traces its origin to 1862 after the occupation of Memphis by Union troops during the Civil War. Initially named Lincoln Chapel, it was an elementary school for freedmen and runaway slaves.

Renamed LeMoyne, it became a junior college in 1924 and a four-year institution six years later. In 1968, it merged with Owen Junior College to become LeMoyne-Owen.

The college is best known for graduating students who went on to be key political and civil rights leaders in Memphis and nationally. They include former NAACP executive director Ben Hooks, former Memphis Mayor Willie Herenton, Slavehaven founder Elaine Lee Turner, former city councilman and now City Court Clerk Myron Lowery, retired state representative Johnnie Turner, the late longtime state representative and House speaker pro tempore Lois DeBerry and current state legislators Joe Towns and Larry Miller.

In 1960, students from LeMoyne and Owen led the city deeper into the civil rights movement when they staged sit-ins at "whites only" lunch counters Downtown and at public libraries where African Americans were excluded. The protests resulted in nearly 40 students being arrested and hauled before a racist city court judge who made it clear he was "not concerned at all about civil rights."

But the arrests served as a wake-up call for both African American and moderate white Memphis residents. And six months later, most public facilities in the city were desegregated.

It is that history that LeMoyne-Owen is seeking to build on at a time when racial equity has reached the top of the national agenda. "There is renewed interest in HBCU's," LeMoyne's board chairman Dr. Chris Davis told WDIA radio's Bev Johnson earlier this week. "We're seeing it around the country. This is a wonderful time for Memphis to look again at LeMoyne-Owen."

For Johnson-Dean, that look must also include ongoing financial support, despite the $40 million gift from the Community Foundation. Before the pandemic hit, she and the college's gospel choir were attending local church services practically every Sunday spreading the word about the school's academic mission to improve the quality of life for African Americans in Memphis.

"We can't be isolated from the community that we are a part of," Johnson-Dean said. And the churches have been tremendous financial contributors for the college, she said.

The Community Foundation and Fockler hope that the endowment sends a strong and unmistakable message that the best way to tackle this city's nagging issues around poverty, crime, blight and racial disunity is through equity in education.

Because while the college will benefit greatly from a $40 million endowment, Fockler was clear. "We didn't do it for LeMoyne-Owen. We did it for the community."

—— —— ——

Retiring the national anthem | July 30, 2020

The late soul singer Isaac Hayes crooned it. Saxophonist extraordinaire Kirk Whalum soulfully serenaded it. And a host of Mid-South school choirs studiously harmonized it.

Since their arrival in the fall of 2001 – and until COVID-19 brought an abrupt halt to the 2019-2020 season, the Memphis Grizzlies, like every other major sports franchise, began each game with the singing or playing of the "Star-Spangled Banner," which since 1931 has been our country's national anthem.

And the time has finally come to retire the anthem from routine sporting events. Call it heresy if you like. But the performances – with a few exceptions – long ago lost their meaning. They are more ritualistic than patriotic.

Many fans are not even at their seats when the anthem starts. They are purposefully milling around in the concourse waiting for tipoff, while the concessions continue to do brisk business. I don't believe those fans and concession workers are any less patriotic than those standing at attention in the arena with their hands over their hearts.

But unless the performer is a well-known recording artist, like Hayes was and Whalum is, spectators take the anthem for granted. And it's time to end the ritual.

I'll admit that some of what drives my feeling on this issue are the anger and division created by the fact that players – since the murder of George Floyd – have resumed kneeling in protest of racial inequity in America.

When Major League Baseball kicked off its pandemic-shortened 60-game season Thursday, July 23, all of the players for the New York Yankees and Washington Nationals took a knee during a 20-second demonstration of unity in support of the Black Lives Matter movement before a pre-recorded version of the anthem was played to a stadium of empty seats. Social media immediately lit up with praise for, and condemnation of, their gesture.

Later that evening, players and coaches for the San Francisco Giants and Los Angeles Dodgers also knelt during a moment of silence supporting Black Lives Matter. All, that is, except one – Giants pitcher Sam Coonrod, who continued standing. Some Facebook users later posted that Coonrod, someone they obviously never heard of, is now their favorite player.

Since baseball's opening night, some players have continued kneeling during the playing of the anthem. Meanwhile, several NBA players have told news organizations they plan to kneel during the anthem when their season resumes this week in Florida.

And Saturday, July 25, WNBA players for the New York Liberty and Seattle Storm held a moment of observance in memory of Breonna Taylor, who was fatally shot in March by Louisville police. But the players did not take a knee when the anthem was played. Instead, they walked off the court in solidarity with the Black Lives Matter movement.

"Kneeling doesn't even feel like enough to protest," Liberty player Layshia Clarendon told reporters. "I don't want to hear the anthem. I don't want to stand out there. I don't want to be anywhere near it, because it's ridiculous that justice and freedom are just not offered to everybody equally."

When and if the NFL season begins, you can bet that some players will be kneeling during the anthem, despite strong criticism of the move by former Chicago Bears head coach Mike Ditka. Asked recently about players kneeling, Ditka said, "If it was up to me, I'd say no. If you can't respect our national anthem, get the hell out of the country. That's the way I feel. Of course, I'm old-fashioned. So I'm only going to say what I feel."

Old-fashioned, perhaps. Utterly offensive and borderline racist, definitely. Telling Americans to "get the hell out of the country" for exercising their constitutional rights is itself un-American.

But that's beside the point. The "Star-Spangled Banner" may have been a clarion call for patriotism when it was written by Francis Scott Key in 1814 and in the years that followed. But it is largely ineffective in today's America, when we are finally trying to come to a reckoning on systemic racism in our society. Not to mention that the third stanza of Key's poem is an overt nod of support to slavery.

I am not by any stretch the first person to call for doing away with the anthem at sporting events. The sentiment has been around for years and is now resurfacing. USA Today columnist Nancy Armour wrote this in 2019:

"Playing the anthem before our football, baseball, basketball, hockey and soccer games has become a lazy excuse for patriotism. Standing at attention – or a loose approximation of it – for 2 minutes no more proves love of country or gratitude for those who serve than wearing an American flag pin does.

"The truth is, most of us tuned out our national anthem long ago. Or lost sight of its supposed purpose. I've long griped about the singers who treat the anthem as if it's their audition for 'American Idol,' drawing out words for dramatic effect or punctuating their performance with theatrical hand gestures."

Sports columnist Jimmy Traina, writing in June for SI.com, also asked why, "other than tradition," is the anthem a required performance at sporting events.

"What does the national anthem have to do with a Brewers-Padres game or a Vikings-Bears game or a Lakers-Celtics game? Why is the national anthem not played at the movie theaters before the previews begin? Why is the national anthem not played at Broadway shows before the show begins?

"Why is the national anthem not played at restaurants before you get your meal? Why is the national anthem not played before White House briefings?"

Actually, according to a 2018 report by National Public Radio, the song was played during the showing of newsreels at movie houses prior to World War II. Before that, it had been played intermittently at baseball games in the late 19th century.

But the song gained a new and enduring popularity with baseball fans when it was played by the U.S. Navy band during the 7th inning stretch of a 1918 World Series game between the Boston Red Sox and Chicago Cubs. World War I was raging at the time and patriotism was high. From there, the anthem became routine at baseball parks. And eventually it was played at football, hockey and basketball games.

Don't get me wrong. There are sporting moments when the "Star-Spangled Banner" remains appropriate. During the Olympics when an American athlete wins the gold medal, the national anthem absolutely should be played. And at the Super Bowl, a truly All-American event combining sports and entertainment, the anthem has its place. Who can forget Whitney Houston's classic rendition of the song at the 1991 Super Bowl 10 days after the start of the Persian Gulf War?

But the song has clearly lost its luster at every game, including meaningless preseason games. Saying that does not make me unpatriotic. It makes me practical. Love of country does not require going along with tradition for tradition sake.

Our national focus now should be on fighting the deadly spread of COVID-19, addressing systemic racism and tackling a host of other ills. Ongoing divisions over what people should and should not do during the playing of the national anthem is unproductive.

So at our ball games, let's thank the anthem for its service. And wish it well in retirement.

—— —— ——

ROOSTER
SCRATCH
PRESS

Made in the USA
Columbia, SC
06 November 2020